SCIENCING

4th Edition

SANDRA CAIN

Central Michigan University

Merrill
Prentice Hall

Upper Saddle River, New Jersey
Columbus, Ohio

Library of Congress Cataloging-in-Publication Data

Cain, Sandra E.
  Sciencing / by Sandra Cain.—4th ed.
    p. cm.
  Includes bibliographical references and index.
  ISBN 0-13-095627-9
  1. Science—Study and teaching (Elementary) 2. Science—Study and teaching
  (Elementary)—United States. 3. Education, Elementary—Activity programs. I. Title.

  LB1585 .C23 2002
  372.3'5044—dc21

                                                              2001030254

Vice President and Publisher: Jeffrey W. Johnston
Editor: Linda Ashe Montgomery
Production Editor: Mary M. Irvin
Design Coordinator: Diane C. Lorenzo
Project Coordination and Text Design: Carlisle Publishers Services
Cover Designer: Ceri Fitzgerald
Cover Photo: Uniphoto
Production Manager: Pamela D. Bennett
Director of Marketing: Kevin Flanagan
Marketing Manager: Krista Groshong
Marketing Coordinator: Barbara Koontz

This book was set in New Baskerville by Carlisle Communications, Ltd., and was printed and bound by R. R. Donnelley & Sons Company. The cover was printed by Lehigh Press.

Earlier editions ©1990 by Merrill Publishing Company

Photo Credits: Lorraine Berak, p. 80; Dave Burgess, p. 84; Sandra Cain, p. 99; Scott Cunningham/Merrill, p. 43; Laima Druskis/PH College, p. 12; Kevin Fitzsimons/Merrill, p. 2; Harvard College Observatory, p. 34; Terrie Kielborn/SUWG & Carla Pollard/Bremen High School, p. 292; Anthony Magnacca/Merrill, pp. 5, 14, 40, 70, 76, 105, 158, 182, 202, 264, 276, 302; Barbara Schwartz/Merrill, p. 244; U.S. Fish and Wildlife Service, p. 64; U.S. Space Camp/U.S. Space & Rocket Center, p. 132; Anne Vega/Merrill, pp. 18, 165; Tom Wilcox/Merrill, p. 30; Todd Yarrington/Merrill, p. 154

Pearson Education, Ltd. *London*
Pearson Education Australia Pty. Limited, *Sydney*
Pearson Education Singapore Pte. Ltd.
Pearson Education North Asia Ltd., *Hong Kong*
Pearson Education Canada, Ltd., *Toronto*
Pearson Educación de Mexico, S.A de C.V.
Pearson Education–Japan, *Tokyo*
Pearson Education Malaysia Pte. Ltd.
Pearson Education, *Upper Saddle River, New Jersey*

Merrill
Prentice Hall

10 9 8 7 6 5 4 3 2 1
ISBN 0-13-095627-9

Preface

This fourth edition of *Sciencing* contains much new information with continued focus on "science as inquiry." The text offers preservice and inservice teachers a chance to become directly involved in a constructivist approach that is organized around the National Science Education Standards. Students are exposed to science education philosophy, direct and first-hand experience involving science equipment and materials, and science concepts. Students are encouraged to be active participants in the learning process as they acquire the specific skills and knowledge necessary for teaching elementary and middle school science. The text is organized so that students build upon prior knowledge as they gather, organize, analyze and evaluate information from completing the reading and suggested activities portions of each chapter.

TEXT STRUCTURE SUPPORTS COOPERATIVE GROUP LEARNING

Each of the twelve chapters contains an introduction, background reading material and suggested activities. The core of each chapter is a set of suggested activities arranged and designed to guide the students toward meeting the Science Teaching Standards associated with (1) The planning of inquiry-based science experiences (2) The actions needed to guide and facilitate student learning (3) The assessments made of teaching and student learning and (4) The development of environments that enable students to learn science.

Further, the textbook is based on the philosophy of student-instructor involvement. Students are encouraged to work in small cooperative learning groups to complete each activity. The instructor's role is to guide and facilitate the learning process by interacting with each small group, providing additional information and resources such as a copy of the National Science Education Standards, Benchmarks, a variety of science textbooks, selected children's literature books and inquiry-based science materials and activities. Whole class discussion and reflection are built into each chapter. Assessment tasks are included which involve the students in applying what they have learned by developing an activity file, doing mini-workshops with their peers, developing daily lesson plans and creating long term integrative units. Suggestions are made to students to and try out their ideas in actual elementary and middle school classrooms.

TEXT ORGANIZATION

Chapter 1 begins by asking readers to reflect on their own views and attitudes related to science and leads into the information presented on the nature of science and scientific knowledge. A brief overview of the nature of learning and teaching science for understanding based on the principles set forth in Benchmarks for Scientific Literacy and the National Science Education Standards and other related research efforts is also included.

Chapter 2 takes the reader on a brief trip through time to explore past events and philosophies that have shaped and reshaped science education. The questions, "What can we learn from the past?" and "How does the past impact on the future?" are explored. Readers are given the opportunity to use the past to build links to their present teaching ideas. They are also encouraged to form expectations about their future roles in the teaching and learning of science. These reflections will lead them into the next two chapters as they seek information about effective teaching and learning practices.

Chapter 3 discusses planning, organizing and managing inquiry–based science experiences, students, curricular materials, and the science learning environment. The importance of considering students' individual learning characteristics, as well as typical developmental characteristics in planning science experiences is stressed along with selecting science experiences that match with students' cognitive capacity. The reader is also presented with the idea that the science curriculum should be seen as the total experience students have while in school and not be limited to "the textbook." Several different science programs and textbook series are presented and assessment criteria are provided for students to use in determining how well each one supports students' achievement of the learning goals recommended in Benchmarks for Scientific Literacy and The National Science Education Standards. Some important features for teachers to consider when selecting children's books with a science theme are presented as part of an assessment instrument in this chapter. Chapter 3 also provides background reading and activities to help the reader develop ideas about arranging the learning environment to encourage self-directed, responsible student behavior and to support students' efforts as they engage in inquiry–based science learning. Several ways to extend the classroom beyond the four walls are discussed along with some safety issues associated with active science investigations.

A variety of research–based and experience–tested strategies, techniques and methods used to guide and facilitate active science learning are examined in Chapter 4. Chapter 4 also engages students in activities that are designed to expand their pedagogical content knowledge. They learn how learning theory has influenced science instruction. The impact of Piaget and Vygotsky on the strategies, techniques and methods that teachers use to guide and facilitate active science learning are examined. The constructivist approach is looked at as well as Gardner's multiple intelligence theory and brain research. The complex issues of equity, students with disabilities and gifted students are also discussed. Chapter 4 also includes information and guidelines for science integrative unit designs that help meet the goals set forth for science instruction in Benchmarks for Scientific Literacy and the National Science Education Standards.

The benefits of using instructional technology in meeting the needs of students and promoting increased student performance and learning is the focus of Chapter 5.

The readers are given many opportunities through the suggested activities to gain insights into the effective use of instructional technology in the classroom. Through suggested activities they are asked to reflect on the ways instructional technology has redefined the way we teach science and how it is transforming the local classroom into a global classroom. Chapters 6 and 7 examine the multiple roles of assessment in inquiry based classrooms. Authentic assessment is described, explained, and compared to traditional testing methods. Concerns are discussed that teachers must be aware of as they begin to use authentic assessment strategies. A wide variety of assessment tools are presented for readers. Both the benefits and concerns of each are discussed.

Chapters 8-11 focus on content areas identified in the National Science Education Standards. The four content areas examined include physical science, life science, earth/space science, and science and technology. Each area is summarized, concepts identified and activities provided to engage readers in actual construction of content and pedagogical knowledge. By completing the suggested activities in these chapters, readers will have a collection of activities representing each of the four content areas included and have worked with others to present their ideas for using selected activities with elementary and middle school students.

Chapter 12 is designed to involve the readers in a personal assessment. They are encouraged to build upon their present knowledge as they continue to gain further insights, refine their thinking and build a deeper understanding of the content as well as the pedagogical knowledge related to science teaching and learning. The final activity in Chapter 12 involves preparing a personal *Sciencing* action plan in which the readers identify specific actions that will be taken to continue progress toward becoming an effective science teacher.

ACKNOWLEDGMENTS

I wish to thank my students at Central Michigan University who have contributed their time and energy to provide valuable suggestions during the preparation of the fourth edition. I am also indebted to the teachers and students in the Mt. Pleasant Public Schools who made significant contributions to the text. I want to express my admiration and gratitude to my colleagues Dr. Lorraine Berak, Dr. Ray Francis and Dr. Lee Rose, who researched and wrote four of the chapters for this edition. Without their dedication and support, this edition would not have been possible.

I also want to recognize and thank Mary Irvin, the Senior Production Editor at Pearson Education for her watchful eye over the production process. I must offer Linda Ashe Montgomery, my editor at Merrill, my deepest thanks for her encouragement, interest, and helpful suggestions during the entire revision process. Thanks also go to Lea Baranowski at Carlisle Publishers Services for all of the help provided in the long phone calls during the final editing process.

Finally, I want to thank my son, Jeff who graduates from high school this year, for his support and understanding of the many long hours that were necessary to complete this fourth edition.

Discover the Companion Website Accompanying This Book

THE PRENTICE HALL COMPANION WEBSITE: A VIRTUAL LEARNING ENVIRONMENT

Technology is a constantly growing and changing aspect of our field that is creating a need for content and resources. To address this emerging need, Prentice Hall has developed an online learning environment for students and professors alike—Companion Websites—to support our textbooks.

In creating a Companion Website, our goal is to build on and enhance what the textbook already offers. For this reason, the content for each user-friendly website is organized by topic and provides the professor and student with a variety of meaningful resources. Common features of a Companion Website include:

FOR THE PROFESSOR

Every Companion Website integrates **Syllabus Manager**™, an online syllabus creation and management utility.

- **Syllabus Manager**™ provides you, the instructor, with an easy, step-by-step process to create and revise syllabi, with direct links into Companion Website and other online content without having to learn HTML.

- Students may log on to your syllabus during any study session. All they need to know is the web address for the Companion Website and the password you've assigned to your syllabus.

- After you have created a syllabus using **Syllabus Manager**™, students may enter the syllabus for their course section from any point in the Companion Website.

- Clicking on a date, the student is shown the list of activities for the assignment. The activities for each assignment are linked directly to actual content, saving time for students.

- Adding assignments consists of clicking on the desired due date, then filling in the details of the assignment—name of the assignment, instructions, and whether or not it is a one-time or repeating assignment.

- In addition, links to other activities can be created easily. If the activity is online, a URL can be entered in the space provided, and it will be linked automatically in the final syllabus.

- Your completed syllabus is hosted on our servers, allowing convenient updates from any computer on the Internet. Changes you make to your syllabus are immediately available to your students at their next logon.

FOR THE STUDENT

- **Topic overviews**— outline key concepts in topic areas
- **Web Links**— topic-specific lists of links to Websites that feature current information and resources for educators
- **Electronic Bluebook**— send homework or essays directly to your instructor's e-mail with this paperless form
- **Message Board**— serves as a virtual bulletin board to post—or respond to—questions or comments to/from a national audience
- **Chat**— real-time chat with anyone who is using the text anywhere in the country—ideal for discussion and study groups, class projects, etc.

To take advantage of these and other resources, please visit the *Sciencing* Companion Website at

www.prenhall.com/cain

Brief Contents

Table of Contents

Chapter 5   Using Instructional Technology to Enhance Science
Teaching and Learning   132

Science as Inquiry

Are you a scientist? For most readers, the immediate response to this question is no. But think about it for a minute. What is a scientist? What does a scientist do? How would you define or describe science or sciencing? Take a few minutes and reflect on what you know about scientists, science, and sciencing. When young children are asked to draw their idea of a scientist, many of their pictures reveal a rather wild-looking man in a lab coat surrounded by bubbling bottles and connecting tubes. Did you have a similar picture in your mind? What do you remember from your science classes in elementary school? If possible, find someone to share your ideas with and listen to theirs. How do your ideas differ from those of others? Where did your ideas come from? Is there more you would like to find out about what scientists do, how science is described, and what is meant by sciencing? These questions are designed to help you begin to think about the nature of science. It is extremely important that you are aware of and understand the nature of science to successfully involve elementary children in appropriate sciencing experiences.

THE NATURE OF SCIENCE

Many people see science as a body of knowledge, or facts, to be learned, remembered, and repeated later on a test. Did your reflection focus on this description of science? This is science as a *noun*. This limited view of science puts the emphasis on the content or product aspect of science. Just "knowing" the facts, laws, and theories associated with natural and physical phenomena becomes the driving force in science as a *noun*. While such knowledge is an important aspect of "understanding" our world, **how** we learn scientific facts, laws, and principles becomes critical.

Inquiry-Based Science

Sciencing is a verb. It is doing, active, investigative—it is something learners do. It is a way of finding out about our world. Sciencing is constructing knowledge, not just memorizing it. Sciencing involves active hands-on, minds-on experiences in which information is gathered, organized, analyzed, and evaluated. No longer is the learner seen as merely a sponge "soaking up" the information given. The sciencing approach demands the active participation of the student, with the teacher serving as a "guide on the side," facilitator, and resource person. Sciencing puts the emphasis on how we learn scientific facts, concepts, laws, and theories. This approach fosters growth and development in all areas of learning, not just in the memorization of facts. In your reflections about how you see science, did the active, doing, investigative aspects of science stand out? If so, then you are way ahead of the game. You already have prior knowledge and experiences that will help you in planning and facilitating inquiry-based learning experiences for your students.

The current reform efforts in science education focus on science as inquiry. The vision put forth in *Science for All Americans* (SFAA), *Benchmarks for Scientific Literacy* (American Association for the Advancement of Science, 1993), and the *National Science Education Standards* (National Research Council, 1996) identify science as a continuous process of inquiry. Science textbooks must become only one of the resources that teachers use. Direct hands-on experiences that involve the learners in using the process-inquiry skills to gain knowledge by investigating physical, life, and earth/space science concepts must become the norm if we are to experience sustained reform that enables all our students to become scientifically literate. This is the goal of the reform effort.

One of your major responsibilities as a sciencing teacher is to design learning experiences that help students learn about the nature of scientific inquiry. *Benchmarks* suggests that in order for students to understand the nature of scientific inquiry, they must "participate in scientific investigations that progressively approximate good science." This means that we must sharply reduce or eliminate the types of science activities that only require students to follow a step-by-step, recipe-like procedure to see what happens. These types of mechanical-oriented activities do not involve learners in active construction of knowledge. In inquiry-based science, learners construct knowledge by being involved in science experiences in which they frame a question and design and carry out an investigation that will provide data to answer the question. Both the *National Science Education Standards* and *Benchmarks* suggest that by the time students graduate from high school, they should be able to do this. In order for students to reach this level of inquiry—which, according to *Benchmarks,* includes framing the question, designing the approach, estimating the time and costs involved, calibrating the instruments, conducting trial runs, writing a report, and finally responding to criticism—we must begin in the earliest grades to involve young children in exploring phenomena in fun and exciting ways.

Sciencing involves children exploring phenomena in interesting and exciting ways.

Process-Inquiry Skills: The Tools of Inquiry

To be successful with the sciencing or inquiry approach, the learner must develop the ability to use the tools of inquiry—the process-inquiry skills. These skills are as follows:

1. Observing: Using the senses to find out about subjects and events
2. Classifying: Grouping things according to similarities or differences
3. Measuring: Making quantitative observations
4. Using spatial relationships: Identifying shapes and movement
5. Communicating: Using the written and spoken work, graphs, drawings, diagrams, or tables to transmit information and ideas to others
6. Predicting: Making forecasts of future events or conditions on the basis of observations or inferences
7. Inferring: Explaining an observation or set of observations
8. Defining operationally: Creating a definition by describing what is done and observed
9. Formulating hypotheses: Making educated guesses on the basis of evidence that can be tested
10. Interpreting data: Finding among sets of data patterns that lead to the construction of inferences, predictions, or hypotheses
11. Controlling variables: Identifying the variables of a system and selecting from the variables those that are to be held constant and those that are to be manipulated to carry out a proposed investigation
12. Experimenting: Investigating, manipulating variables, and testing to determine a result

The first seven skills listed are considered basic skills. The learner must acquire them to successfully perform skills 8 to 12. These last five skills (8–12) are considered integrated skills. Several of the basic skills are integrated within skills 8 to 12. In grades K to 3, emphasis is given to the first seven basic skills. This does not mean that younger children should not be provided with opportunities to acquire the higher-level integrated skills if they are capable of handling them. It does mean that the teacher will have to take a more active role in guiding younger learners when use of higher-level skills is desired. Active questioning, guided discovery, and constant sharing of information between and among the learners and the teacher will facilitate the use of the higher-level skills for those learners who are developmentally ready for them. In grades 4 to 8, the higher-level integrated skills receive more focus. The basic skills must be reviewed often because they are incorporated within these higher-level skills.

Process-inquiry skills are basic to all later learning. They are not separate from science content; rather, they provide the learners with the means to active investigation. They allow the learner to gather, organize, analyze, and evaluate science information in order to construct meaning and develop science concepts.

A popular activity with teachers and students is one called "pennies in the water." It is a great way to get learners to use the process-inquiry skills in a simple investigation. No background information is needed. The students are involved in building on their prior knowledge and constructing new knowledge on the basis of observations made during the investigation. A modified version of this activity can be found at the end of this chapter.

Developing a Scientific Attitude

Developing a scientific attitude is another aspect of sciencing as well as an integral part of the nature of science. Good teachers capitalize on children's natural curiosity and promote an attitude of discovery. Students are encouraged to "find out for themselves" how and why phenomena occur. Developing objectivity, openness, and tentativeness, as well as basing conclusions on available data, are all a part of the scientific attitude. The concept of intelligent failure should be a part of every sciencing experience. Children should not be afraid to stick their necks out and make intelligent mistakes. Much scientific knowledge has resulted from such mistakes.

Sciencing can be fun and stimulating. It can be structured and yet at times involve learners in "messing about" activities that provide personal learning experiences on which learners can begin to construct new knowledge. In preparing to teach science, one must explore and understand the nature of science in order to make decisions about what and how to teach.

Are you curious? Do you like to find out about things, how they work? Do you like to try new and different things? Do you ask questions, watch for unusual things? Scientists do these things. If you like to be actively involved in solving problems, finding new and different ways of doing things, then you just might be good scientist or good science teacher material. Most children are curious. They like to find out about things. They like to try new and different ways of doing things. They ask lots of questions and tend to be very active. Children are good scientist material. Teachers must provide many opportunities for students to be involved in active hands-on, minds on exploration and investigation of the world around them. They will be able to construct their own knowledge from their own learning experiences with the skillful guidance and resources of a good sciencing teacher.

You have been briefly introduced to some of the main aspects of the nature of inquiry-based science so that you may begin to integrate these ideas with those that you already possess. Think about how they support what you already believe or how they differ from your own prior knowledge. How can you use what you have read to increase your understanding of the nature of science? If you have questions or information to share related to what you have read so far, discuss these with others who are reading this material and bring them up during in-class discussions. This active participation on your part as you read, react and interact, and offer insights and further information is a good example of how knowledge is constructed. It is a process that you will want to involve your students in when you teach.

A two-part interviewing activity is included at the end of this chapter that has been designed to give you firsthand experience in talking with K–8 learners and their teachers related to how they view science.

VIEWING THE WORLD SCIENTIFICALLY

One of the tasks of a sciencing teacher is to help learners develop a scientific worldview. According to *Benchmarks,* scientists see the universe as a "vast single system in which the basic rules are the same everywhere," and these "rules can be discovered by careful, systematic study."

The Concept of Consistency

An understanding of the consistency of nature is an important initial concept for learners to grasp. At the early grade levels, learners should have ample opportunities to be involved in science experiences that support this scientific worldview by making observations or doing an activity; repeating it with a friend, comparing results with others in the class, and then perhaps repeating the activity at home with family members. *Benchmarks* suggests that by the end of grade 2, learners should begin to discover that they can expect to get similar results when a science activity is repeated the way it was done before, even if it is done in a different place.

A learner's understanding of consistency should grow and develop as a result of many encounters with the natural world that support this basic view. When repeated investigations yield different results, learners who understand the concept of consistency will recognize that something has been allowed to differ in the various trials and will want to find out what it might be. Most learners in the middle elementary grades 3 to 5 should begin to recognize that similar investigations will rarely yield exactly the same results. This should lead to a closer examination of the differences and questions about what might have caused the results to differ. These learners are able to retrace their steps to check for accuracy of observations, measurements taken, and basic methods used to conduct the investigation. Was more than one variable allowed to be manipulated at one time? Were the conditions exactly the same? Did the focus of the investigation differ? Was there something else that might have caused the difference in results? As learners are given more and more opportunities to engage in active sciencing, using the "tools" of process-inquiry and reflecting on the design and the results of various investigations, they will begin to develop the ability to evaluate differing results and make decisions as to whether they are significant or trivial. *Benchmarks* suggests that this should occur during grades 6 to 8. In addition, by this age, learners should understand that before scientists accept similar results as correct, they wait for many repeated efforts that support the original findings.

By the end of grade 8, learners should understand that "scientific knowledge is subject to modification as new information challenges prevailing theories and as a new theory leads to looking at old observation in a new way" (*Benchmarks*). At the same time, learners need to understand that just because scientific knowledge is very old does not necessarily mean it is no longer applicable. Some knowledge and theories have been around for a long time but are still relevant today.

Science as One Way of Knowing

Can all matters be looked at by using the processes of science? No. Science is only one way of knowing. Not all matters can be tested and examined using scientific methods. *Benchmarks* identifies two such areas—those things "by their natures that cannot be tested objectively and those that are essentially matters of morality." By the end of eighth grade, learners should be able to grasp this philosophical view of scientific knowledge.

Beliefs That Scientists Share

To summarize, it is important that learners began to view the world from a scientific point of view. They should understand the important beliefs that scientists share that form the foundation of the scientific view. According to *Benchmarks*, there are three basic beliefs that scientists share that are not necessarily held by nonscientists. First, scientists believe that "working together over time, people can in fact figure out how the world works." Great care is taken to explain that this underlying belief does not indicate that scientists *will* figure out everything about the world, only that the world *can* be understood by conducting scientific investigations. It is also believed that scientific investigations raise as many questions as they answer and that there is a limit to the knowledge that can be generated from scientific investigations. Therefore, this belief—that by working together scientists can understand how the world works—carries with it the understanding that the quest for knowledge is a continuous process.

The second belief that scientists share is refered to as the "unity of the universe." This is explained by *Benchmarks* as the belief that "knowledge gained from studying one part of the universe can be applied to other parts." Again, a disclaimer is offered that tempers the belief so that we understand that this application of knowledge from one part of the universe to another part is true only part of the time. *Benchmarks* gives the example of a given organism's behavior being different, in some cases, when observed under laboratory conditions and in its natural environmment.

The third underlying belief is that "knowledge is both stable and subject to change." It is easy to see why this belief could be confusing to students, but it is very important that they understand it. *Benchmarks* points out that it is necessary that students see scientific knowledge as being very stable. It is only changed as new information is gained through repeated investigations. However, it is equally important that they understand that *openness* to new knowledge based on scientific investigation is a key ingredient in the scientific view. That is why, even at the earlier grades, teachers need to help students use the phrase "based on the data gathered" when making a conclusion.

UNDERSTANDINGS RELATED TO SCIENTIFIC INQUIRY

The *National Science Education Standards* presents the following understandings related to scientific inquiry. Box 1.1 contains the understandings emphasized in grades K to 4. Box 1.2 contains the understandings emphisized in grades 5 to 8. In order to understand science as inquiry, you must be familiar with these ideas and plan science experiences that help students incorporate them into their thinking as they are involved in inquiry-based sciencing. These basic understandings provide teachers with helpful guidelines, as they provide opportunities for their students to engage in inquiry-based science experiences that promote the active construction of knowledge in the content areas of physical, life, and earth/space science. An inquiry or sciencing approach necessitates a change in the traditional roles of both the teacher and the student. No longer is the student to be merely a sponge "soaking up" the information given. This approach demands the active participation of the student, with the teacher serving as guide, facilitator, and resource person. Inquiry-based science fosters growth and development in all areas of learning, not just in the memorization of science facts and concepts.

So far in this chapter, you have been introduced to the concept of sciencing, inquiry-based science, the nature of science, and viewing the world scientifically. Basic information related to these areas presented in parts of the Association for the Advancement of Science's reform document *Benchmarks* and the National Research Council's document *National Science Education Standards* was reviewed. We will take a closer look at both of these documents in the next chapter. The information presented in each of these areas should provide you with a basic foundation of knowledge that you can use to continue to construct meaning and understandings related to becoming an effective science teacher. We will now turn our attention to the nature of the learner. What developmental characteristics must teachers be aware of, and how do these characteristics affect a learner's ability to "do science"?

BOX 1.1 Basic Understandings About Scientific Inquiry, Grades K to 4

1. Scientific investigations involve asking and answering a question and comparing the answer with what scientists already know about the world.

2. Scientists use different kinds of investigations, depending on the questions they are trying to answer. Types of investigations include describing objects, events, and organisms; classifying them; and doing a fair test (experimenting).

3. Simple instruments, such as magnifiers, thermometers, and rulers, provide more information than scientists obtain using only their senses.

4. Scientists develop explanations using observations (evidence) and what they already know about the world (scientific knowledge). Good explanations are based on evidence from investigations.

5. Scientists make the results of their investigations public; they describe the investigations in ways that enable others to repeat the investigations.

6. Scientists review and ask questions about the results of other scientists' work.

BOX 1.2   Basic Understandings About Scientific Inquiry, Grades 5 to 8

1. Different kinds of questions suggest different kinds of scientific investigations. Some investigations involve observing and describing objects, organisms, or events; some involve collecting specimens; some involve experiments; some involve seeking more information; some involve discovery of new objects and phenomena; and some involve making models.

2. Current scientific knowledge and understanding guide scientific investigations. Different scientific domains employ different methods, core theories, and standards to advance scientific knowledge and understanding.

3. Mathematics is important in all aspects of scientific inquiry.

4. Technology used to gather data enhances accuracy and allows scientists to analyze and quantify results of investigations.

5. Scientific explanations emphasize evidence, have logically consistent arguments, and use scientific principles, models, and theories. The scientific community accepts and uses such explanations until displaced by better scientific ones. When such displacement occurs, science advances.

6. Science advances through legitimate skepticism. Asking questions and querying other scientists' explanations is part of scientific inquiry. Scientists evaluate the explanations proposed by other scientists by examining evidence, comparing evidence, identifying faulty reasoning, pointing out statements that go beyond the evidence, and suggesting alternative explanations for the some observations.

7. Scientific investigations sometimes result in new ideas and phenomena for study, generate new methods or procedures for an investigation, or develop new technologies to improve the collection of data. All these results can lead to new investigations.

From *National Science Education Standards.*

DEVELOPMENTAL CHARACTERISTICS OF LEARNERS IN GRADES K TO 2

By the time children enter kindergarten, their brains have grown to nearly their adult size, hand preference has become stable, and distance vision is greatly improved, although near vision may remain a problem for some. Motor skills are used as a means to an end now. The typical kindergartner can be expected to use scissors, draw people, copy simple letters and numbers, and build complex structures with blocks. They are beginning to throw and catch with some skill and accuracy.

Cognitively, K–2 students are becoming more and more proficient in the ability to represent experiences symbolically. This growing ability to engage in symbolic thought helps learners organize and process what they know as well as communicate

Young children learn to use all of their senses to make science observations.

it to others. For example, this age child may pantomime the actions involved in dressing without actually putting on clothes. It is this capacity to *think* about actions that allows a learner at this level to become more involved in cognitive tasks in the areas of reading, science, and mathematics. Piaget refers to this stage of cognitive functioning as the *preoperational phase.* According to Piaget and other researchers, children are now able to describe their thoughts and the things around them with increasing accuracy. They base their thinking on their own personal perspectives and experiences, which makes it difficult for them to see things from another's point of view. Their behavior reflects a self-centeredness; however, this should not be interpreted as selfishness. It means that a child's understanding, or knowing, is dependent on personal experience and background. For example, a child who has a hedgehog for a pet has a different understanding of the word *hedgehog* than a child who has only seen pictures of a hedgehog.

The Importance of Active Observation Opportunities

Benchmarks suggests that children in kindergarten through grade 2 should be engaged in active observation—doing something to the things around them and noting what happens. It suggests further that simple tools such as thermometers, magnifiers, rulers, or balances be used to gather more quantifiable information than is possible with simple observation alone. Children at this level should also begin to make accurate descriptions of their observations so that comparisons can be made with those of other classmates. When conflicts arise because children give different descriptions of the same event, a fresh set of observations is called for. In this way, arguments about who is right and who is wrong can be eliminated. Young children are naturally curious, and inquiry-based science offers a way to capitalize on that capacity.

Teachers of young children should offer a variety of sciencing activities that encourage the use of all the senses. Activities can be structured so that all or several senses are used together in making the observations, or only one sense (e.g., touch) can be the focus. It is extremely important to help children grasp the difference between an observation and an inference even at this early level. An observation is information that one takes in directly through one of the five senses—we see it, we hear it, we taste it, we feel it, we smell it. Inferences differ from observations. An inference is a conclusion or judgment based on observations. It is arrived at indirectly rather than directly through one of the senses. For example, you reach your hand in a bag and use your sense of touch to feel an object. It feels hard, smooth in some areas, but it has raised places that run in lines and is somewhat cool to the touch. As you manipulate the unknown object (still concealed in the bag) by holding it in your hand and moving your hand over it, you also observe through your sense of touch that it is spherical. These are observations. You have gained information about the object by using your sense of touch. If you conclude that the object is a baseball, you have made an inference. Based on the observations that you made using your sense of touch and your past experiences, you made a judgment or conclusion that the unknown object concealed in the bag was a baseball. You can test your inference by taking the object out of the bag and looking at it to see if it is a baseball. Early observational experiences give young children the opportunity to learn how to make good observations, and making good observations is a necessary first step of inquiry-based science. In the suggested activities at the end of this chapter, you will be given an opportunity to make observations and inferences as well as to use the other process-inquiry skills as you engage in inquiry-based science activities.

Limited Abilities and Skills

There are other characteristic behaviors of K–2 learners that relate closely to a child's ability and skills related to sciencing. This age child tends to focus on only one property or variable to the exclusion of others, to give contradictory or magical explanations, to depend on trial and error for most actions, and to lack the ability to reverse actions mentally. If given opportunities, children learn from their errors. Caring adults and teachers do not reprimand or show the child "how to do it right." They provide many opportunities that enable children to recognize and correct their errors as they are involved in developmentally appropriate experiences. By the time most children reach second grade, these limitations are beginning to fade, and they are beginning the transition to the next stage of cognitive development, *concrete operations.*

DEVELOPMENTAL CHARACTERISTICS OF LEARNERS IN GRADES 3 TO 4

Fundamental motor skills continue to improve during the school years and gradually become specialized in response to each child's particular interests, physical aptitudes, life experiences, and the expectations of others (Seifert & Hoffnung, 1997). Learners in these grades become much more able to work together, each contributing in his or her own way in completing learning tasks that involve the use of both fine and large motor skills. Coordination improves. Some learners handle measuring tools, microscopes, and other data-gathering devices with care and precision. Others make charts and tables that are neat and that accurately communicate investigation results. Still others draw pictures, construct models, or use their bodies in effective and creative ways to communicate and demonstrate science concepts. Learners at this level are becoming proficient at taking notes and making journal entries as they gather and organize information gained from direct observations and other sources.

The Development of Conservation

Cognitive abilities at this level also continue to expand and become more complex. Learners at this level are able to consistently conserve. Conservation is the realization that if nothing is added or taken away from a thing, then it remains the same

Greater cognitive development in third and fourth graders enables them to conserve number, matter, length, area, weight, and volume.

even though it may *look* different. When given tasks that involve pouring equal amounts of liquid into different-shaped and -sized containers and then asking if the new containers have the same amount or different amounts of the liquid, almost all beginning third graders will be able to not only answer that they contain the same amount as before but also explain why this is so. They have come to understand that when no additional liquid is added or taken away, the amount of liquid has to be the same even though it is poured into a shorter, taller, or different-shaped container. They also develop the ability to conserve number, matter, length, area, weight, and volume (usually in this order) during the middle elementary years.

Suggested Activity
Piagetian Tasks
1.1

If you have had an opportunity in the past to do some of these conservation tasks with children, share your experiences with others in a small-group or whole-class discussion. It is fascinating to see the difference in cognitive functioning on these tasks between children who are not conservers and those who are. If you have never had this experience, ask your instructor or a veteran teacher for more information and consider doing some of these conservation tasks with a variety of children ages 5 to 10. Report your findings in class. *Begin to think about how these developing cognitive abilities affect the way children learn and therefore the way you will teach.*

Skills and Abilities Needed for Inquiry-Based Science

By the time learners reach third grade, they should have had many interesting investigating experiences that involved them in observing and inferring that included classifying, measuring, communicating, using spatial relations, and simple predicting. They should also be encouraged to ask questions about what they observe. They most likely will not be able to give accurate explanations for all they observe, but at this level theory is not the focus. The major emphasis is on helping students engage in active observation, carefully describing what they see, feel, hear, taste, and smell by using simple tools that allow them to gather more information than by just observing. With a firm foundation of simple observational inquiry-based science experiences, the typical third grader is ready to work with small groups in conducting simple investigations of their own.

In grades 3 to 5, students should begin to become more and more careful in making observations. Accuracy of measurements, recording of data, and communication of results improve. Graphs, simple charts, and tables can be effectively used by students at this level in presenting results to classmates. Whole-class discussions related to the investigation can be productive. Students should become more and more aware that they are engaging in the the same sort of processes that scientists engage in.

Third and fourth graders are beginning to think more logically. They are developmentally able to attend to more than one variable at a time and can mentally reverse actions that they have experienced concretely. Because learners at this stage of cognitive development are bound by direct concrete experiences, Piaget labeled this stage the *concrete operational stage*.

The Need for Direct Personal Experiences

The ability to isolate variables and think in steps without relating each step to all the others begins to emerge now. Learners at this stage begin to be aware of contradictions and will try to resolve them. However, most cannot yet go beyond that which is empirically given and are able to deal only with ideas and thoughts that result from direct personal experience. The ability to think about one's own thoughts is not yet present for most. Even so, by fourth grade many students can design and conduct simple science investigations in which a "fair test" is administered to determine a reasonable answer to a question. A good example of this type of investigation might involve students in finding out which brand of paper towel will absorb the most water in a specified time frame. Materials from which they can choose would be provided by the teacher, but not instructions for performing the fair test. The students are divided into small groups, and each is responsible for designing a fair test, collecting and organizing data, and reaching a conclusion on the basis of data collected. The results from the different groups are then compared and discussed. Students are asked to offer explanations for any conflicting results. Opportunities are given for additional "testing" to deal with conflicting findings. This rather simple investigation offers students an opportunity to use their emerging cognitive skills by engaging in developmentally appropriate inquiry-based science experiences in which they construct knowledge that will become part of later, more complex science concepts.

You may wish to try the suggested activity at the end of this chapter that is designed to help you gain some firsthand experience in designing a fair test. Your challenge will be to answer the question, Which brand of paper towels will absorb the most water in 30 seconds? In this way, you will use your prior knowledge to construct new knowledge related to designing and conducting a simple investigation. This experience will also help you construct knowledge related to planning and organizing inquiry-based experiences for your students. (See Suggested Activity 1.5.)

DEVELOPMENTAL CHARACTERISTICS OF LEARNERS IN GRADES 5 TO 8

Typically, one begins to develop the ability to think in abstract terms—beyond personal experiences—around fifth or sixth grade. The thought processes begin to be markedly different from those who have not yet reached this level of abstract or formal thought. At this stage, *mental* experiences as well as actual ones can be carried out. A student who has developed cognitively to this level can deal with the possible and is not satisfied with simply the empirical event given. Deductive reasoning—the ability to consider all possible combinations—and controlled experimentation become possible at this level of cognitive functioning. Cause-and-effect connections can be made and understood, and record keeping becomes more descriptive and precise.

Metacognition

Learners at this level develop the ability to think about their own thoughts and their own learning. Psychologists refer to this kind of knowledge as *metacognition*. Reasoning and problem solving improve as a result of their ability to become more aware of factors that can affect their performance. They are able to develop broad learning strategies that draw on the emerging cognitive skills associated with logical thought. The following techniques are engaged in more often and with less prompting than at younger ages: (1) rehearsal (repeating information to be learned either aloud or silently), (2) elaboration (relating new knowledge to existing knowledge, adding to it, and making connections), and (3) using organizing tactics (looking for patterns in the structure of new information and using it to help them remember and use the information later). According to Siegler (1995), learning strategies such as these are acquired in at least three ways: trial and error, logical construction, and observational learning. Teachers can assist students in becoming aware of and developing these techniques by sharing them with students; demonstrating how they, as teachers, use them in everyday life; asking other students to share their "secret" ways for thinking about, learning, and remembering important information; emphasizing the advantages of using such techniques; and, most important, providing many opportunities for students to engage in inquiry-based problem solving, investigations, and simple experiments.

Recognizing the Need for Logical Thought and Evidence

By the end of fifth grade, *Benchmarks* indicates that students should be aware that there are many different forms of scientific investigations and that these investigations can involve questions related to the physical, biological, and social areas. Students at this level should begin to realize that the results of scientific investigations are seldom exactly the same. At the same time, they should recognize that large differences are a reason for further investigation to determine the cause(s) of the differences. *Benchmarks* also suggests that students at this level understand that scientists sometimes "have different explanations for the same set of observations." This happens because explanations come partly from what is observed and partly from what is thought. When different explanations are offered, what usually happens is that more observations are made to resolve the differences. Another important understanding for students to develop by the end of fifth grade is that scientists

Older children grades 5 to 8 generally are able to participate in more sophisticated inquiry, using logical reasoning and demanding consistent evidence before drawing conclusions or explaining observed phenomena.

demand that in order to accept an explanation, it must be presented in a logical argument with evidence that can be confirmed.

In order for students to begin to master the skills needed to be successful in inquiry-based sciencing at this level, they need lots of hands-on, minds-on experiences in which they pose a question, gather data, analyze the data, and reach conclusions on the basis of the data collected and their past experiences. Good sciencing teachers will provide "starting" activities that capture the students' attention and imagination and that lead to student-formulated questions that can be investigated. They will also be on the alert for and receptive to unexpected opportunities that arise for inquiry and provide time, help, and encouragement for students as they search for answers.

Conducting Scientific Investigations

At grades 6 to 8, *Benchmarks* states that teachers can expect students to become more capable of systematic, sophisticated inquiry. By this level, they should be familiar with the different aspects of a scientific investigation and be able to design and conduct long-term experimental investigations in which one specific variable is manipulated while all other variables are controlled. They should understand that if more than one variable is allowed to change at the same time, the results cannot be attributed to any specific variable and therefore that the investigation is flawed. Students need to be able to use logical reasoning as well as imagination in their investigations. While student investigations constitute a major focus of the sciencing program at this level, there are other important aspects of the total science experience that must be included. Not all science concepts that students need to know and understand can be discovered. Selected readings provide an important backup for laboratory investigations. It is important that students know and understand a wide variety of science concepts from the physical, life, and earth/space science areas. The role of collaboration among investigators is also emphasized at this level.

Maintaining objectivity when involved in inquiry is another important aspect that fifth to eighth graders should come to understand. They may find that what they observe is often affected by what they expected to observe. Sometimes it is very difficult to be open to data that differ from those we are expecting. We have a tendency to ignore such data or just be unaware of them as we focus on the results that we expected. Students come to learn that we, as well as scientists, must take steps to avoid the danger to objectivity. One way, suggested by *Benchmarks*, is to have different investigators conduct independent investigations of the same questions. By the time students complete elementary and middle school, they should be ready to tackle the abstractions and hypothetical nature of secondary science. They will have engaged in many firsthand inquiry experiences that resulted in concrete understanding of important science concepts. This important foundation of science knowledge, skills, attitudes, and understandings will enable students to continue to grow and develop in their ability to explore new phenomena, compare different theories, engage in making scientific predictions, and make sense out of the unfinished and tentative nature of science.

SPECIAL NEEDS LEARNERS

We have been looking at typical learner characteristics (K to 8) that you can expect to see in the students you will teach and how those developmental characteristics relate to the abilities and skills needed for inquiry-based science. You will also need to be familiar with the characteristics of learners who have special needs. Some learners will not follow the typical cognitive age–stage development format. Others will have physical or emotional needs that must be met in order to be successful in school. These learners may need modification of objectives, content, methods, actual activities, and assessment in order to be helped to succeed in science. There most likely will be other learners in your classroom who have not been identified as special needs learners but who might have similar educational needs. As a teacher, you will find that the more you learn about the different needs of the children in your class, the better able you will be to make effective decisions about how best to facilitate their learning. Chapter 4 will provide you with more information related to special needs learners as well as with multiple strategies, techniques, and methods that will help each learner make the most of his or her talents, intelligences, past experiences, and present opportunities to construct meaning and understanding about the nature of our physical world.

Suggested Activity 1.2

Active Decision Making Related to Students' Individual Needs

1. Get into a small group and discuss the following:

   a. Why is it important that teachers be knowledgeable about students' developmental characteristics?

   b. How have the science reform efforts provided for these typical developmental patterns?

   c. How do students' developmental characteristics affect their learning and your teaching?

   d. What questions or concerns do you have at this point about your role as an active decision maker related to growth and development patterns and their impact on science teaching and learning?

   e. How will you deal with the questions and concerns raised?

We will explore some specific suggestions for guiding and facilitating student learning in inquiry-based science in Chapter 6. You may wish to jot down the thoughts, concerns, and questions that were shared in this discussion and save them for reference when you read that chapter.

Suggested Activity 1.3

Interviewing

1. Interview some young children (ages 5–7). Ask them (1) "What is science?" (2) "What does a scientist do?" (3) "What would you do if you were studying science?" and (4) "Are you a scientist?" Video or tape record the conversation and play it for others in the class. How do young children see science? How do you see science? What did you learn from this interview?

2. Interview several elementary teachers. Ask them to define their "philosophy of science." Ask them how much time they spend teaching science and what they generally do in science. Ask them what resources they use in making decisions about what to teach in science and when to teach it. Share your findings with others in the class. What did you learn from this experience?

Suggested Activity 1.4

Using the Process-Inquiry Skills to Investigate the World

This activity is designed to be used with the entire class working in groups of five or six.

1. Each small group should obtain an identical small beaker or plastic cup and a pie pan. Set the container in a pie pan to catch spills. Using another larger container, carefully fill the first container full of water. (The water level should be level with the top of the container.) Have several paper towels on hand to help with cleanup. Observe the container of water carefully.

2. Estimate the number of pennies (paper clips can also be used) that can be added to the full cup of water before the water spills. Write your estimate on a "post-it" note and place it on a chart (that has been prepared by your instructor) within the range that includes your prediction. The chart should look like this:

TABLE 1.1 Number of pennies that can be placed in the container before the water spills out

0–5	6–10	11–15	16–20	21–25	26–30	30+
	8					

Post-it notes are placed, starting at the bottom in the column under the appropriate number range. For example, if a student predicts that it takes 8 pennies before the water spills, she or he will place the post-it note with the number 8 written on it in the 6–10 column. When all the post-it notes have been placed, each column will form a bar graph to show the class prediction.

3. Discuss your predictions with your small group. Give reasons for your predictions. Look at the chart on which you placed your original prediction and answer the following questions:

   a. What was the range of the most common prediction?

   b. Were the predictions generally above or below 25?

   c. What range, if any, was not picked?

   d. How does the graph help to organize information about the group's predictions?

4. Gently place the pennies (or paper clips) sideways into the water, counting them until the water spills. Have someone in your group record the number.

5. Discuss the following with your group:
   a. How close was your prediction to the actual number?

   b. Were most people surprised by the results? Why or why not?

   c. Were there any differences in the results obtained by different groups? If so, why do you think the results may have been different?

   d. How do *you* explain the results of this activity? How do you think a K–4 learner would respond to this question? How about a 5–8 learner?

   e. How does the concept of surface tension relate to this investigation? Ask your instructor to provide you with additional information so that you could help learners understand how surface tension works and apply that understanding to this investigation.

6. Join in a class discussion with your instructor and other classmates that focuses on how the process-inquiry skills were used to gather, organize, analyze, and evaluate information in this investigation. Discuss how the data gathered are used to explain science content and concepts.

7. Discuss the following extention ideas related to this investigation. How could these ideas be used to help learners use the "tools" of inquiry in active investigations involving science concepts?
   a. If a taller container were used, could more pennies be added? How about a wider container?

b. Estimate how many drops of water could be placed on a penny. Would it make any difference which side of the penny were used? What other factors might affect the outcome?

c. If something were added to the water, such as soap or salt, would that affect the number of drops that would fit on a penny? Why or why not?

Suggested Activity 1.5
Designing a Fair Test: Paper Towel Testing

Question: Which brand of paper towel will absorb the most water in 30 seconds?

1. Form a small group with three or four others in your class and design and conduct a "fair test" to gather data that can be used to answer the previous question.

2. Discuss the question with your group. Share any prior knowledge and experiences with your group that you think might be relevant to the design of the fair test. Think about factors that should be considered in designing a fair test. Do any other preliminary research (read, review resources, think, or brainstorm) that you think would be helpful in providing additional information and ideas related to the investigation.

3. Select a hypothesis—a tentative answer to the previous question. What do you think would be the most promising answer?

4. Develop a plan for carrying out the fair test you have designed. Decide on the materials and equipment you will need. Outline a step-by-step procedure. Explain what will be measured and how and when the measurements will be taken.

5. Carry out the plan/procedures. Consider running a pilot test and using the information to improve the design. Perform the procedure. Repeat the procedure three times to be sure that you have accurate results.

6. Record the information gathered thus far in your investigation.

7. Look over your data and find a way to organize the results so that they can be presented to others. Can a graph, chart, or other visual be used to organize and present your data to others?

8. Analyze your results. What conclusions can you reach? Was your hypothesis supported? Should other tests be made? Do you need more data? What other investigations might be done to learn more?

9. Share your results with others.

10. As a total class, discuss the following:
    a. Were the results the same for all the groups?

    b. What caused any differences in results?

    c. Did any group experience problems? What were they, and how were they resolved?

    d. What would you do differently if you were to do this investigation again?

    e. What did you learn about the properties of paper towels?

    f. What other investigations might be done to learn more?

    g. What did you learn about designing and conducting a simple investigation? Review the process or steps that you followed in completing this investigation. These "steps" provide guidelines that are a part of good inquiry-based science. Learners must become aware of the process of inquiry and be able to design and conduct investigations and experiments that incorporate this process. In this way, they approximate good science.

    h. Read over the lists in Boxes 1.1 and 1.2 and discuss with your small group how this activity relates to those understandings.

    i. What have you learned about planning and organizing inquiry-based science experiences for students?

This investigation can be kept simple so that children at the concrete operational level can conduct it effectively, or it can be designed for the formal thinker so that higher-level thinking is required and true experimenting can take place. In inquiry-based science experiences such as this one, students are able to "participate in scientific investigations that progressively approximate good science," which is one of the benchmarks given in *Benchmarks*.

SUMMARY

Are you curious? Do you like to find out about things, how they work? Do you like to try new and different things? Do you ask questions, watch for unusual things? Scientists do these things. If you like to be actively involved in solving problems and finding new and different ways of doing things, then you just might be good scientist material or good science teacher material. Most children are curious. They like to find out about things. They like to try new and different ways of doing things. They ask lots of questions and tend to be very active. Children are good scientist material. Teachers must provide many opportunities for students to be involved in active hands-on, minds-on exploration and investigation of the world around them. They will be able to construct their own knowledge from their own learning experiences with the skillful guidance and resources of a good sciencing teacher.

The first five chapters of this text are designed to provide you with information and experiences that will add to your prior knowledge and help you construct a solid core of understanding related to your role as a sciencing teacher. This first chapter has asked you to reflect on your knowledge and attitudes related to science and to share these with others. It has provided you the opportunity to review basic information about the sciencing concept, inquiry-based science, the nature of science, scientific knowledge, and the nature of learners. You were presented with information adapted from *Benchmarks* and the *National Science Education Standards,* which provide guidelines and insight into the concept of scientific inquiry. You were reminded that the process-inquiry skills are the tools of scientific inquiry. The ideas and information presented should help you understand the rationale for the inquiry-based approach, which is the focus of the present reform effort in science education. You have also been given several opportunities to engage in firsthand, inquiry-based science activities. These activities involved you directly in using the process-inquiry skills to gather, organize, analyze, and evaluate data related to understanding how the world works. These activities gave you an opportunity to combine theory with practice and provided you with concrete experiences that will help you plan and facilitate learning opportunities for your students related to inquiry-based science.

Chapter 2 will take you on a brief trip through time as we explore the past events and philosophies that have shaped and reshaped science education. You will be given an opportunity to use the past to build links to your present teaching ideas and to use these links to go forward into the future. Chapter 3 looks closely at what an effective sciencing teacher does to "set the stage" for learning to take place. An inquiry-based science approach must be led by an active decision-making teacher who is able to use acquired information, ideas, and skills effectively in the planning, organizing, and managing of the teaching/learning environment. The components of the teaching/learning environment—students, curricular materials, the physical setting, and the teacher—are discussed and activities provided that give you opportunities to examine teaching resources, classroom arrangements, safety issues, management techniques, and your own teaching philosophy. The role of the sciencing teacher as a guide and facilitator is the focus of Chapter 4. A variety of research-based and experience-tested strategies, techniques, and methods that can be used to guide and facilitate active science learning are examined. You will be involved in designing and developing both short- and long-range inquiry-based science lesson plans. You will also be encouraged to try out your planned learning experiences with actual elementary or middle school students and to reflect on how you might improve them on the basis of the results that come from "real world" use. Chapter 5 explores the use of instructional technology in the science classroom. Teachers are well aware that instructional technology has become a very important part of the educational system and that we must be able to take advantage of this outstanding tool. Using the Internet for science activities, such as taking a virtual field trip, doing historical and content research, exploring current science events, and communicating with scientists, are just a few of the areas included in this chapter. You are also given many opportunities to experience firsthand how you can impact student learning in science by using instructional technology to transform the local classroom into a global classroom.

The current movement in science assessment is away from the traditional single paper-and-pencil test to using multiple authentic assessments in assessing what students have learned. Chapters 6 and 7 examine the concept of continuous (before, during, and after instruction) multiple authentic assessment and provide you with a wide array of assessment tools from which to select to use in assessing students' science learning.

Chapters 8 through 11 focus on four of the specific areas of content—physical science, life science, earth and space science, and science and technology—identified by the *National Science Education Standards*. These chapters provide a review of the content standards in each of the identified areas as well as activities that are designed to give you an opportunity to experience firsthand involvement with objects and materials similar to those you will provide for your own students. This active hands-on, minds-on involvement on your part will give you an opportunity to experience the process of constructing and understanding knowledge related to each of the identified areas and prepare you to provide students with inquiry-based learning experiences related to these same areas.

Chapter 12 is designed to involve you in reflecting on the learning and understanding that has taken place as you progress through the text and activities, sharing ideas with others, listening, and trying things out. You will be asked to do a personal assessment of where you are at that point and what your plans are for continuing to learn and grow as you prepare yourself to be an effective elementary or middle school science teacher. An action plan in which you are asked to set both short- and long-term goals will be the final activity. Learning is a lifelong process, and setting personal learning goals for the future will help you continue that process.

Suggested Activity

Identifying Personal Learning Goals

1.6

Think about what your goals are for this class. What do you hope to accomplish in this class by reading this text, participating in the suggested activities, sharing your ideas with others, examining other resources, actively participating in class discussions, and seeking out others' ideas? Jot down your personal learning goals and keep them until you complete the course work in this class. When you reach Chapter 11, retrieve these goals and use them as you reflect on your past progress and comtemplate your future learning goals.

REFERENCES

American Association for the Advancement of Science. (1993). *Benchmarks for scientific literacy.* New York: Oxford University Press.

Association for Supervision and Curriculum Development. (1996). *Science standards: Making them work for you, grades 3 and 4.* Alexandria, VA: Author.

Association for Supervision and Curriculum Development. (1996). *Science standards: Making them work for you, primary grades.* Alexandria, VA: Author.

Brooks, M. G., & Brooks, J. G. (1999). The courage to be constructivist. *Educational Leadership, 57*(3).

Erikson, E. H. (1963). *Childhood and society.* New York: W. W. Norton.

Furth, H. G. (1970). *Piaget for teachers.* Englewood Cliffs, NJ: Prentice Hall.

Havighurst, R. J. (1972). *Developmental tasks and education* (3rd ed.). New York: David McKay Co.

Inhelder, B., & Piaget J. (1964). *The early growth of logic in the child.* New York: Harper & Row.

Kroll, L. R., & LaBoskey, V. K. (1996). Practicing what we preach: Constuctivism in a teacher education program. *Action in Teacher Education, 18*(2), 63–72.

Lowery, L. F. (Ed.). (1997). *NSTA pathways to the science standards: Guidelines for moving the vision into practice* (Elementary School Edition). Arlington, VA: National Science Teachers Association.

National Research Council. (1996). *National Science Education Standards.* Washington, DC: National Academy Press.

Rutherford, F. J., & Ahlgren, A. (1990). *Science for all Americans.* New York: Oxford University Press.

Schulte, P. L. (1996, November/December). A definition of constructivism. *Science Scope,* 25–27.

Seifert, K. L., & Hoffnung, R. J. (1997). *Child and adolescent development* (4th ed.). Boston: Houghton Mifflin.

Siegler, R. (1995, March). Nothing is; everything becomes; recent advances in understanding cognitive developmental change. Paper presented at the biennial meeting of the Society for Research on Child Development, Indianapolis, IN.

CHAPTER 2

A Brief History of Science Education:

Where Have We Been, and Where Are We Going?

HISTORY OF SCIENCE EDUCATION: WHAT CAN THE PAST TELL US?

Since the late 1950s, a number of major task forces, committees, and commissions have focused their attention on guiding and facilitating science education reform efforts. Let's examine some of the past major events that have contributed to our current efforts of reform.

Prior to the late 1950s, science generally was not taught in the elementary school. Science, if taught at all, was usually some form of nature study. The textbooks that did exist were usually science readers that described Bob and Brenda's visit to the zoo and what they saw or that described a particular experiment and its result. Clearly, not much student involvement took place in the science programs of this era.

In 1957, an event destined to change American education occurred: the Soviet Union launched *Sputnik,* the world's first artificial satellite. The immediate reaction of the United States was to question the quality of our science programs from kindergarten to college. We found that most science programs, especially elementary programs, were inadequate; that most teachers did not have much science background; and that textbooks were obsolete.

The National Science Foundation (NSF) was established by the federal government to provide financial help for science projects, and a crash program to reform science education was under way. What came to be known as "alphabet soup" science curriculum materials were developed and widely adopted during the early 1960s reform effort: Elementary Science Study (ESS), Science A Process Approach (SAPA), and Science Curriculum Improvement Study (SCIS). These materials were developed by teams of scientists, educators, teachers, and psychologists for use with elementary children. They were designed to involve children in hands-on science that emphasized the process-inquiry skills of science—observing, classifying, measuring, using spatial relationships, communicating, predicting, inferring, defining operationally, formulating hypotheses, interpreting data, controlling variables, and experimenting—rather than the memorization of facts. Student activities were designed to be experimental rather than just for verification.

About the same time, Jean Piaget and, soon after, Jerome Bruner, Celia Stendler, Robert Gagne, and other psychologists published work indicating that children in elementary school learn best by manipulating concrete objects. This became the basis for the hands-on laboratory approach method that we still advocate today. Even though most teachers today have never used ESS, SCIS, or SAPA , they **do** use the concepts and teaching strategies found in these programs.

The reform efforts of the 1960s seem to have been successful. The United States landed a man on the moon, and hands-on science curriculum materials were being made available to elementary schools throughout the United States. However, by the mid-1970s, monies from the NSF that were used in support of curriculum materials development were cut off. The public seemed no longer interested in the reform effort, and science education in the schools began to take a different path from the goals that were established in the 1960s.

Several studies were undertaken in the late 1970s and early 1980s that revealed that most teachers had dropped the direct-experience laboratory approach and were using textbooks, lectures, and/or question-and-answer techniques based on information existing in the textbook. Clearly, a second crisis was in the making. The reform efforts begun in the 1960s had failed to have a sustained impact on the science education curriculum. By the 1980s, active hands-on investigations had been replaced by almost total reliance on textbook knowledge. Yet studies done in the early 1980s comparing the performance of students in traditional textbook courses with students using the NSF hands-on laboratory curriculum materials revealed that the students using the NSF materials outperformed the students using the traditional textbook approach.

Science reform efforts that had been initially embraced in the schools were hard to locate by the mid-1980s. It was painfully apparent that reform was to be a long-term and even continuing effort and would perhaps need to be approached in a different way. In the 1960s reform effort, the focus was on developing curricular materials. Within only a few years, these innovative programs were found gathering dust in the back of our elementary classrooms. Monies were no longer available to replace the consumable materials needed for the hands-on experiences or for the lost or damaged parts. New teachers were hired, and no money was available for in-services. Therefore, these innovative programs were abandoned.

A Nation at Risk, an educational reform wake-up call published in 1983 by the National Commission on Excellence in Education, is considered by many to be the most important reform piece of the 20th century. Numerous assessment studies followed this publication that supplied additional data to support the original assertion that our students were not adequately prepared in mathematics and science. Results from these various studies painted a very bleak and worrisome picture of science achievement in our schools, especially when U.S. student achievement was compared to achievement of students from other nations. We ranked near the bottom. It was the consensus of science educators, scientists, and others involved in the reform efforts that our citizens were functionally illiterate in science and technology and that, unless we began a broad-based reform effort to improve science and mathematics, our nation would become a second-rate power. New interest was generated, numerous reports were compiled, and a new reform effort was under way.

THE CURRENT REFORM EFFORT

The current reform effort can be traced to Project 2061, initiated by the American Association for the Advancement of Science (AAAS) in 1985. The name, Project 2061, is significant because it was chosen by the scientists and educators who began work on this long-term reform effort to remind us of the new approach and ultimate goal of the project: scientific literacy for all.

This new reform effort began in 1985, which was the year Halley's comet was last visible from earth. The comet will return in the year 2061, 75 years later—a human

Written in 1985 when Halley's comet was last visible on earth, Project 2061 is a science reform document reminding us of the need for a long-term effort to promote scientific literacy for all. Perhaps this goal will be reached before Halley's comet is visible once again, in the year 2061.

life span. What changes will have taken place in our world by the year 2061? Will the children we teach today be prepared to act responsibly as adults and influence in a positive way what life will be like for the next generation when Halley's comet returns in 2061? These were the questions that helped focus attention on the long-term approach taken by Project 2061.

A Look at Our Past

Think about what the world was like in 1682, when Edmund Halley first observed the great comet, which was later named for him. What did things look like in the New World? What kinds of transportation were available? What about the style of dress? What were houses like? How did people make a living? What did we know about diseases and medicine? Just 75 years earlier, in 1607, John Smith founded the first English colony at Jamestown in Virginia, and the Pilgrims arrived at Cape Cod and founded the Plymouth Colony 13 years later in 1620. By 1665, Robert Hooke had published his microscope observations. Marquette and Jolliet were exploring the Great Lakes region and the Mississippi River in 1673. It was not until 1690, eight years after the first sighting of the great comet, that Benjamin Harris published the first American newspaper in Boston. Witchcraft trials were held at Salem in New England in 1692, and Yale University was founded in New Haven, Connecticut, in

1701. These selected happenings, as well as others you may recall, should help give you a feeling for the world as it was then. Now let's jump ahead 75 years to the year 1758, when Halley's comet returned. What kinds of life-altering changes had taken place in the 75-year span between 1682 and 1758?

The American colonies were beginning to rebel against the various taxes imposed by England. In 1765, Samuel Adams helped found the Sons of Liberty to oppose the Stamp Act, a tax on all publications in the American colonies. The act was repealed in 1766. In 1776, the Continental Congress adopted the Declaration of Independence, and the revolution was under way. Life had changed quite a bit for the colonists, and this was only the beginning. What would the next 75 years bring?

By 1835, the next sighting of Halley's comet, we had formed a new nation and were continuing to explore the western territories and add new states. The American Anti-Slavery Society was inaugurated in Philadelphia in 1833, American educator William Holmes McGuffey began editing his readers, and Texans under Sam Houston defeated Santa Anna at the San Jacinto River in 1836. Michigan became the 26th state of the Union in 1837, and Samuel Morse developed the Morse code for electric telegraph systems in 1838. In 1842, explorer John C. Fremont began his survey of the Oregon Trail. These changes called for new skills and knowledge in order to survive and thrive in this new independent nation. New challenges awaited the next generation.

In 1910, Halley's comet was highly visible in the United States and caused quite a stir. Newspapers carried pictures of it streaking across the sky. How had life changed since its last visit? The Wright brothers had invented the airplane and tested it at Kitty Hawk, North Carolina, in 1903. The Ford Motor Company had produced the first Model T automobile in 1908. Transportation would be forever changed. The country gained two new states in 1812: New Mexico and Arizona. This made a total of 48 united states. In 1913, the federal income tax was introduced, and Samuel Goldwyn founded his first movie company with Jesse Lasky and Cecil B. De Mille. The Panama Canal was completed in 1914, and Albert Einstein formulated his General Theory of Relativity in 1915. For the first time, in 1916, we had a female member of the U.S. House of Representatives, Jeannette Rankin, and Margaret Sanger was arrested for opening a birth control clinic in Brooklyn. By 1917, we had declared war on Germany and entered World War I. Airmail service began among New York, Philadelphia, and Washington, DC, in 1918, and the 19th Amendment to the U.S. Constitution gave women the right to vote in 1920. In just one human life span, 75 years, so many life-altering changes had taken place. So many challenges still were ahead.

Many scientists, educators, and others eagerly awaited the return of Halley's comet in 1985. It would be the first chance and most likely the last that many would have to see this once-in-a-lifetime phenomenon. Unfortunately, it did not pass directly over the United States and was not visible to many because of city lights and cloudy skies. Those fortunate enough to book passage on boats and cruise lines and travel south did get to see the comet streak across the sky, but it was not as spectacular as the 1910 sighting. However, think about all the changes that had taken place between 1910 and 1985—another life span. The world was very different now. The

United States had landed a man on the moon, air travel was commonplace, and we had our first woman vice-presidential candidate, Geraldine Ferraro, in 1984. In that same year, astronauts tested the manned maneuvering unit and moved freely in space, and President Ronald Reagan and President Mikhail Gorbachev of the Soviet Union held their first summit meeting. The following year, in 1986, a hole in the ozone layer was detected over Antarctica, and a major nuclear reactor disaster took place at Chernobyl in the Soviet Union. The *Voyager 2* spacecraft transmitted pictures to the United States of the planet Neptune in 1989, and basketball star Magic Johnson announced that he had HIV, the virus that causes AIDS, in 1991. Amid these happenings, Project 2061 was initiated and developed. A crisis in science education existed, and Project 2061 hoped to provide a vision for the reform effort that would transform the nation's school system and provide the kind of education for our students that would enable them to thrive as adults in tomorrow's world of change.

What Does the Future Look Like?

Think about all the changes that have taken place since Edmund Halley first sighted the great comet in 1682. With each return visit, 75 years had passed—a human life span, 75 years of changes and technological advances. What will life be like in 2061? What major changes will have taken place? We can expect that it will be radically different from life as we know it today and that science, mathematics, and technology will be the driving forces that will help shape our world of tomorrow. The challenge facing the Project 2061 reform effort was to develop a vision that would clarify the goals and purposes of K–12 science education and provide a long-term, multiphase plan that would make specific recommendations for achieving scientific literacy for all.

Project 2061

Project 2061 was organized into three phases. Each phase is briefly summarized here.

> Phase I: Define scientific literacy by identifying exit outcomes for students—what students should acquire—in the areas of knowledge, skills, and attitudes as a result of their total K–12 school experience.

The major outcome of phase I was the book *Science for All Americans* (*SFAA;* American Association for the Advancement of Science, 1989), which is a slightly altered version of the national report of the same name. *SFAA* drew heavily on the conclusions reached by the three-year collaboration of five separate panels made up of many scientists, mathematicians, engineers, physicians, philosophers, historians, and educators. Each panel prepared a separate report that addressed questions related to knowledge, skills, and attitudes in their specific areas that students should possess. This book did not provide any specific answers to the problems facing the educational community. It did serve as a starting point for the long-term, multiphase reform process by providing the conceptual basis for the recommended changes involving all parts of our educational system. In addition, it provided incentive and direction for those who wanted to be a part of and contribute to the reform effort to reappraise, redirect, and recommit.

> Phase II: Develop several alternative curriculum models and draw up blueprints for reform in teacher education, teaching materials and technologies, testing, the organization of schooling, educational policies, and educational research.

Benchmarks for Scientific Literacy, a document that breaks down the exit outcomes by grade levels and specifies the skills, knowledge, and attitudes to be attained at each of the identified levels, was developed and published as a result of phase II (American Association for the Advancement of Science, 1993). There were many elementary, middle, and high school teachers who participated in the development and critique of *Benchmarks,* along with school administrators, scientists, mathematicians, engineers, historians, and learning specialists. *Benchmarks* is meant to serve not as a standard curriculum but as a tool and resource for local schools as they develop their own curricula. It is seen as a companion report to *SFAA.* It clearly defines "what *all* students should know or be able to do in science, mathematics and technology by the end of grades 2, 5, 8, and 12." We will take a closer look at the implications that this publication has for you as a future teacher in later chapters.

> Phase III: Use the tools and resources that result from phases I and II to facilitate necessary and lasting changes in our educational system to produce citizens who are scientifically literate.

We are now experiencing phase III. The two products of Project 2061, *SFAA* and *Benchmarks,* have already been mentioned as tools to be used in the reform effort, but there is a third publication that also merits our attention: the *National Science Education Standards* (National Research Council, 1996).

National Science Education Standards

In the summer of 1992, a group of representatives from the major science and science education associations were convened by the National Research Council (NRC) to help identify and recruit staff and volunteers who would develop national science education standards in three areas: content, teaching, and assessment. The need for such a group to set national standards for what students should know and be able to do became apparent as the result of an education summit of the nation's governors convened by President George Bush. The governors agreed that national goals for education were needed, and they set about developing them. In his 1990 state of the union address, President Bush unveiled the *National Education Goals,* which were developed as a result of the education summit. Goal 4 states, "By the year 2000, U.S. students will be first in the world in science and mathematics achievement." Progress toward these goals would be monitored by the National Education Goals Panel. In order for students to meet this ambitious goal, specific national science standards had to be identified. President Bill Clinton continued the support for the standards after his election in 1992. In December 1995, the *National Science Education Standards* were published after critique and review of predraft and draft releases by selected groups. These standards, like *SFAA* and *Benchmarks,* provide teachers, curriculum developers, public school administrators, science educators, and scientists, along with parents and local communities, with a set of principles, tools, and resources to use in developing local curricula that will enable our students to meet the national goal of becoming first in the world in science achievement. These standards and benchmarks should be studied, deliberated, adapted, elaborated on, and adopted so that school programs and practices in science education will undergo permanent reform that results in a scientifically literate citizenry.

Suggested Activity
Reviewing Current Reform Documents 2.1

1. Obtain a copy of *Benchmarks* and the *Standards*. Look through these resources and discuss their value in providing guidance to teachers in reforming science education.

2. Many state and local school systems have developed their own science standards and exit outcomes on the basis of work done at the national level. Find out what your state and local school system has developed. Get copies of them and compare them to the national standards. How closely do your state and local programs align with the national standards?

3. Talk to local teachers about the local science curriculum. Ask them to tell you how it was developed. Find out what they know about *Benchmarks* and the *Standards*. How closely do they follow the vision set forth in these national documents in their day-to-day science teaching?

   1. National Science Education Standards

      (http://books.nap.edu/catalog/4962.html)

   2. Benchmarks

      (http://www.project2061.org/tools/benchol/bolframe.html)

WHAT'S MY ROLE?

Putting the vision of the science education reform effort into actual practice is your challenge. It must begin early in kindergarten and continue throughout the elementary and middle school years, where the foundation is laid for later science understanding. Elementary teachers as well as middle and high school teachers must have a solid knowledge base from which to draw, coupled with an understanding of and support for the need for active involvement on the part of their students. Science activities that promote exploration, critical thinking, and doing—a sciencing approach—are necessary for achieving the challenge set forth in the reform effort.

Teaching is both an art and a skill, both affective and cognitive. A sciencing teacher is an active decision maker, a manager, and a coordinator. A sciencing teacher develops, modifies, adapts, and implements. A sciencing teacher is never simply a recipe follower. You should begin to form some expectations about your role in the teaching and learning of science. As you continue to read and discuss the materials in this text and engage in selected activities, reflect on past events and philosophies that have shaped and reshaped science education. What can we learn from the past? How does the past impact on the future? How can the vision, information, and guidelines found in *Benchmarks* and the *Standards* help us as we seek to become more knowledgeable about effective teaching and learning practices? As a future teacher of science, you will be expected to know and be able to do specific things in order to help elementary and middle school students become involved in sciencing. It is important that you are able to use the past to build links to your present knowledge and teaching ideas and to use these links to go forward into the future.

REFERENCES

American Association for the Advancement of Science. (1989). *Project 2061: Science for all Americans*. Washington, DC: Author.

American Association for the Advancement of Science. (1993). *Benchmarks for scientific literacy*. New York: Oxford University Press.

Deboer, G. E. (1991). *A history of ideas in science education: Implications for practice*. New York: Teachers College Press.

Grolier's Encyclopedia. CD-ROM.

National Commission on Excellence in Education. (1983). *A nation at risk: The imperative for educational reform*. Washington, DC: U.S. Government Printing Office.

National Governor's Association Task Force on School Leadership. (1986). *Time for results: The Governors' 1991 report on education*. Washington, DC: Author.

National Research Council. (1996). *National Science Education Standards*. Washington, DC: National Academy Press.

Shymansky, J. A., Kyle, W. C., & Alport, J. M. (1982, November–December). How effective were the hands-on science programs of yesterday? *Science and Children*, 14–15.

Yager, R. E. (1993). The need for reform in science teacher education. *Journal of Science Teacher Education, 4(4)*, 144–148.

CHAPTER 3

Planning, Organizing, and Managing Inquiry-Based Science Experiences

The most effective and successful learning experiences result from systematic, creative planning. This chapter will focus on guidelines and information related to "setting the stage" for inquiry-based science to take place. The kinds of decisions that must be made, as well as the resources available to help in the decision-making process, in planning for, organizing, and managing the classroom for inquiry-based science will be reviewed. Curricular resources will be identified and guidelines and criteria provided for use in reviewing selected science programs and textbook series. We will take a close look at the learning environment, including management strategies, to see how effective organizing and planning can enhance science learning and teaching. This chapter provides you with an opportunity to continue to build on and expand your knowledge base by becoming actively involved in using the information provided in planning and organizing inquiry-based science experiences.

 An inquiry-based science approach must be led by an active decision-making teacher who is able to use acquired information, ideas, and skills effectively in the planning, organizing, and managing of the teaching/learning environment. The following areas are discussed as they relate to planning, organizing, and managing inquiry-based science experiences.

- The students
- Curricular materials
- The learning environment
- You, the teacher

THE STUDENTS

As you plan and organize for active inquiry experiences, you must consider your students; their individual learning characteristics; typical developmental characteristics that they share with others related to physical, cognitive, and psychosocial growth; and other specific needs that might affect their ability to fully participate in and learn from the science experiences that you provide.

Although most primary, elementary, and middle school students have a natural curiosity about the world in which they live, we know that learning does not occur in the same way for each learner. As teachers, we must provide alternate avenues for students to use in reaching the same science objective. In some cases, we must even provide alternate objectives. Your students will differ in many ways. Gender, race, ethnic background, intelligence, cognitive style, and social, physical, and affective characteristics are some of the major areas of individual differences. You must take these individual differences into consideration in planning appropriate science experiences for learners at any level. We will look closely at these difference factors in Chapter 4 as we discuss guiding and facilitating active science learning. In addition, your planning must take into account developmental changes that take place in learners' physical, cognitive, and psychosocial growth and how these developmental

Individual differences—background knowledge, cognitive development—can affect how students understand science concepts.

changes affect learning. These developmental changes were reviewed in Chapter 1. See if you can recall the developmental characteristics of K–2 learners, 3–4 learners, and 5–8 learners that were discussed in that chapter. Can you describe what physical expectations would be appropriate for each developmental level? Cognitive expectations? Psychosocial expectations? What do you remember about specific characteristic behaviors of learners at each of the levels that relate closely to ability and skills needed for inquiry-based science learning? You may wish to look at this material again to refresh your memory.

Teachers are beginning to become more aware of the need to select science concepts and skills that match the cognitive capacity of students. Findings from research studies support the notion that students experience many problems related to mismatching science content with cognitive capacity. When this mismatch occurs, scientific misconceptions and a decreased interest in science are two of the unfortunate results (*Benchmarks for Scientific Literacy*, American Association for the Advancement of Science, 1993). Teachers can find the guidance needed to correctly match science content and cognitive capacity by using both the *Benchmarks* and the *National Science Education Standards* (National Research Council, 1996). These documents provide guidelines for local schools as they develop their own science curricula and match it up with the appropriate cognitive level of the students. Both of these documents were discussed in Chapter 2, and you were involved in examining them as part of the planned activities.

CURRICULAR MATERIALS

The fixed program of studies, classes, or subjects offered by a school, in total and by grade level, is considered its curriculum. *Benchmarks* refers to the school curriculum as "planned by the teachers and administrators, delivered by the teachers, and experienced by the students." It is also described by this same publication as both "an overview of the scope and sequence of student experiences" and "a detailed delineation of learning experiences." Recent reforms and state mandates to develop a core curriculum (essential studies for all students) have assisted many schools as they attempt to write curricula in specific content areas. These core curricula have been based on national, regional, and state standards and provide "benchmarks," or reference points, that are used to determine the level of work that students are expected to attain while in school. In order to reach these benchmarks, objectives are developed for each grade level.

The focus here is on the part of the curriculum that concerns itself with the teaching and learning of science concepts, skills, and attitudes. Specifically, this section will focus on curricular resources that are available to help teachers plan, organize, and manage inquiry-based science.

The decisions teachers make regarding curricular materials is reflective of how they define *curriculum*. Some teachers define curriculum as "the textbook," and others view curriculum as the total experience students have while in school. As teachers come together to select curricular materials, there is usually an attempt made to clarify this definition. How do you view science curriculum? Do you see it as defined by the textbook that is being used in a classroom, or do you tend to include the total school experience in your definition? You will be making many important curricular decisions when you teach. This section will provide you with information and direction as you develop and refine your thinking related to curricular materials. The activities at the end of this section will provide you with opportunities to examine and explore firsthand the various curricular resources that are introduced and discussed here.

Inquiry Approach Curricular Materials

The curricular materials you use and how you use them will affect the learning outcome of your students. Many schools will already have a science program of some type. If you are fortunate enough to teach in a school that provides inquiry approach curricular materials such as the following, you will have a firm foundation on which to build an exciting science program for all your students.

Full Options Science System (FOSS), K–6

Insights—the Senses Module (EDC), K–2

Science for Life and Living (BSCS), K–6

Great Exploration in Math and Sciences (GEMS), 3–6

Science and Technology for Children (STC), 3–6

Science Curriculum Improvement Study 3 (SCIS3), K–6 or

Life Lab Science Program, K–6

These programs provide teachers with activities that can be used to involve learners in a variety of active science inquiry experiences. Content is drawn from the physical, life, and earth/space areas. FOSS and BSCS also provide materials that focus on science and technology topics.

Textbook Series

Many schools still adopt a textbook series, such as Merrill, Addison-Wesley/Scott, Foresman, Macmillan/McGraw-Hill, Prentice Hall, and Hartcourt Brace. Most of the recently published textbooks have integrated the strengths of the inquiry approach into their programs. Thought-provoking questions and hands-on, minds-on activities that use process-inquiry skills to involve learners in constructing science knowledge are included; however, they are not always **required** for completion of each unit of work. They do, however, provide an active decision maker/teacher with ample factual material, activities, demonstrations, illustrations, references, and suggestions for teaching.

Kits with both consumable and reusable materials to be used with the activities are available for purchase with many of these textbook programs. An instructor's manual and other teaching aids, such as transparencies, bulletin board ideas, computerized test bank, videos, and various kinds of software are often available as part of the total package when a textbook series is purchased by a school district. For newer teachers, particularly those with little science background, a textbook program can provide needed organized resource materials that build on the science concepts students were introduced to in a previous grade. Most textbooks are organized into units of work. These unit topics are usually clearly defined, which can help the teacher decide what to teach without infringing on material taught in other grade levels.

The major problems with textbooks in the past is that they tended to substitute words for hands-on experiences. In addition, while many programs are hands on, they do not promote inquiry learning. As the classroom teacher, you will have to provide the strategies that demand problem solving and the use of process skills, along with required manipulation of objects, to understand the underlying science concepts. There is a difference between just having the students sink and float various items in a water tub and having them also make cognitive connections to past experiences and knowledge, explain why they think some things float and others do not, and test to see if their explanation will extend to other items. Once again, it is through active inquiry that teachers can learn about any scientific misconceptions that students are formulating and plan for more learning experiences that confront the misconceptions and help the students construct new knowledge to replace the misconception. This type of planning is difficult to put into a textbook because of the variety of avenues that may be opened up by the discussions and inquiry held with the children.

Another common dilemma faced with the use of textbooks is that many times in the past, they were used by teachers as the **only** source of information. This seems to be changing. In a survey, reported in the May 1998 issue of *Science and Children,* it was found that 28% of teachers responding reported that they use a textbook only as reference material, while 33% said they rarely or never use textbooks. Only 28% said that they use a single textbook. With the explosion of knowledge, new brain research, and our rapidly changing world, the use of only one source of information is no longer adequate to meet the needs of students in the 21st century.

What if you are one of the unfortunate new teachers who finds that the textbook series or science materials used by the school in which you are hired are old and out of date or perhaps uses a very poor, non-inquiry-based approach? Several options are open to you. As a beginning teacher, you should talk to other teachers or the principal to find out how you are expected to use the materials provided. They can tell you whether you are supposed to follow these materials closely, whether you can digress somewhat, or whether you are free to develop your own program. This is important because you do have to meet the expectations of the school system that employs you. Remember, though, that you can **exceed** the expectations by supplementing the minimum requirements. Even out-of-date textbooks and/or materials can be used as **one** of your resources. These can provide you with an idea of the content that is commonly taught at that particular grade level. A quick look at the table of contents can provide a beginning point for planning the various science topics to include during the year. The actual material in the text can help you decide how thoroughly or how superficially each topic could be treated. In short, use the textbook as a *resource.* Even the poorest textbook can serve in that capacity. It can provide you with teaching suggestions, experiments, activities, demonstrations, suggested reading lists, teaching aids, and background information. Be selective. You do not have to use every suggestion or activity, but they just might get your own creative juices flowing. Do not ignore this source just because it is old.

Children's Literature

In addition to textbooks, selected children's literature can be a valuable curricular resource to use in helping children learn science concepts. Children's literature tends to have a more familiar story structure and more interest appeal than content texts. The beautiful illustrations in picture books enhance the print, catch the attention of the reader, and provide additional motivation for using children's literature as a science curricular resource. Numerous research studies have shown that using children's literature to enhance science instruction benefits children because it fosters personal connections and builds on prior knowledge related to the targeted science concepts (Eanes, 1997; Lapp & Flood, 1993; Reutzel & Cooter, 1996). Because the narrative story structure in children's literature is familiar to children, they are able to understand and retain science concepts being presented much easier than when those same concepts are presented in an expository text that may contain a variety of text styles (Jacobson, 1998; Maria & Junge, 1993; Wepner & Feeley, 1993).

Teachers can find many effective ways to use children's literature as a curricular resource. Hands-on activities can be developed in connection with the story that involve the students in developing and testing hypotheses; manipulating, collecting, and analyzing data; and drawing conclusions. Questions can be raised to guide science instruction. Clearly, good literature resources can be used to teach and reinforce science concepts. They offer the teacher an avenue for presenting scientific information in a format that is easy for students to identify with personally. However, there are some cautions that must be observed by teachers as they consider using children's literature as a curricular resource.

Deborah Mayer (1995) found that children acquired misconceptions and developed negative attitudes about other issues related to the storyline after listening to a piece of children's literature titled "Dear Mr. Blueberry." She concluded that "certain books may unintentionally foster misconceptions and influence attitudes . . . in a negative way" (p. 17). Wiley and Royce (1999) found in their study that the fictional parts of the story can actually confuse children and interfere with a child's understanding of important science concepts. Several studies have also revealed that no significant increase in the amount of new scientific information was learned by the student when children's literature was used as an instructional strategy (Butzow, 1991; Lamartino, 1995; Mayer, 1995).

What does this conflicting information mean? Should teachers use children's literature as a curricular resource for science instruction? Certainly, some guidelines are needed to assist teachers in the selection of high-quality children's literature that adds to students' understanding of the science concept being taught and that does not create misconceptions or negative attitudes. As McGowan and Guzzetti (1991) note, the well-planned use of children's literature requires teachers to engage in decision making while using their ingenuity, resourcefulness, and knowledge of content. Cain and Rose (1999) have developed the *Assessment Inventory: Selecting Children's Picture Books to Teach Science Concepts*. A checklist developed by Mayer (1995) to measure a piece of literature's appropriateness for teaching science concepts was used as a resource in the development of the *Assessment Inventory*. Mayer's original checklist does not include items related to selecting good literature, nor does it involve the teacher in determining the science content area or identifying the specific science concept that would be learned. The *Assessment Inventory* can assist teachers in examining both the quality of the literature and the science concepts present in the text. A copy of the instrument as well as a description and explanation of the eight categories can be found in appendix Figure 3.1. You may wish to turn to this section now to look over the instrument and discuss its use with others. Activity 3.2 at the end of this section will give you an opportunity to use the instrument to collect information about a specific children's book you select and then use that information in making a decision about how effective that book would be for teaching targeted science concepts.

Each year, the "Outstanding Science Trade Books for Children" list is published in the March issue of *Science and Children*, a professional journal devoted to preschool through middle-level science teaching. Copies of this list, which includes a brief review and appropriate grade-level notation, are available free from the National Science

Teachers Association (NSTA) headquarters, if you send a self-addressed, stamped envelope. This list contains books that are suitable for grades K to 8. These books are selected by a special book review subcommittee appointed by the NSTA in cooperation with the Children's Book Council (CBC). The committee considers both content and presentation. Criteria used include clarity, accuracy, and up-to-dateness of science content. Theories and facts are clearly distinguished, facts are not oversimplified, generalizations are supported by facts, and significant facts are not omitted. Selected books must also be free of gender, ethnic, and socioeconomic bias. Presentation must be logical and sequence of ideas clear. Content level must be appropriate for the intended audience, and text and illustrations must be compatible. Illustrations should enhance the presentation and be accurate in size, color, and scale.

This list offers teachers another excellent resource to help in selecting curricular materials to use for science instruction. You may visit NSTA's and CBC's Web sites at, respectively, http://www.nsta.org and http://www.cbcbooks.org. The school library should have a good selection of these kinds of books available. If not, you can provide the school librarian with the latest list from *Science and Children*.

An Integrated Science Literacy Approach

Some publishing companies are beginning to capitalize on this approach of using children's books to teach science concepts. Scholastic has introduced The Science Literacy Center, which features Emergent Readers, books for young children that "introduce important science vocabulary in repetitive sentence structure or phrases." These books are described as being "specifically designed to support young learners in the earliest stages of literacy while delivering authentic science content." The books are organized around science themes such as animal life cycles, desert, weather, energy and force, and machines and tools. In addition, there are learning center activities that are connected to a specific book. The Wright Group and Rigby are two other companies that publish books for children with science themes that incorporate hands-on experiences. SUNSHINE Science, published by The Wright Group, is a K–2 reading program that incorporates simple group science activities that correlate with the reading. Science themes include space, spiders, seeds, bones, and floating and sinking. Rigby's Science Alive is a K–5 reading program that includes hands-on activities that integrate science and language arts. Both of these programs feature Big Books to be used by the teacher with the whole class and accompanying small books to be used by individual students. These types of integrated programs seem to be very popular with elementary teachers.

A slightly different approach is used by Steck-Vaughn, which offers a program called Pair-It Books, in which a fiction book with a science theme is paired with a nonfiction science book. The teacher can use the fictional story to spark the interest of the children, raise questions, and make personal connections. Then the paired nonfiction book can be used to teach and broaden the science concepts that were introduced in the fictional story. Hands-on activities are also a part of this program.

These are just a few of the major companies that have begun to offer an integrated approach by designing children's books with a science theme and including activities that involve children in constructing knowledge related to that theme. The same cautions mentioned earlier in this section related to textbooks apply equally well with this type of approach. In the activities that follow, you will get the opportunity to examine some of these materials using criteria based on the *National Science Education Standards.* This active involvement on your part will allow you to begin to make some decisions about which materials you find helpful in planning, organizing, and managing an inquiry-based science program.

Other "Curricular" Resources

Professional science journals such as *Science and Children,* which targets preschool through middle-level science instruction, and *Science Scope,* aimed at middle-level and junior high science teachers, are other excellent science curricular resources for the teacher. Both are published monthly and feature articles by practicing teachers, university professors, and other educators who describe effective practices and provide teachers with valuable information and ideas for classroom science instruction. Other education-oriented journals, such as *Educational Leadership, Childhood Education,* and the *Kappan,* also provide teachers with many thought-provoking articles that are useful in planning, organizing, and managing inquiry-based science experiences. Subject area–based journals such as *Teaching Children Mathematics* and the *Reading Teacher* can also provide many useful ideas that teachers can use to help students make effective connections between science concepts and other subject areas. An activity at the end of this section provides you with an opportunity to review several professional journals to see firsthand what kinds of information these resources can provide for you in planning, organizing, and managing inquiry-based science.

The Web is fast becoming a major resource for teachers. Integrated and thematic units, individual lesson plans, activities, ideas, materials to reproduce, and background information are just a few of the things that are available at the numerous sites. Most of the sites offer various links to other sites as well. Science sites specific to physical, life, or earth/space concepts are readily accessible. Other sites provide up-to-date information on current scientific happenings as well as information on past scientific events. At the end of this section, you will be given some Web addresses to explore as possible curricular resources. We will explore in more detail the many and varied uses of the Web in Chapter 5.

There are other "curricular" resources available to you that do not fall into the printed materials category and are sometimes overlooked by the teacher. These resources include other teachers, students, parents, and local residents as well as professional meetings and in-services.

Your fellow teachers can be an excellent curricular resource. Experienced teachers can offer information and helpful suggestions. Teachers who have been in the school system for a few years can help you find equipment, suggest what units might be taught, and offer teaching suggestions. If consultants or resource people are available, do not hesitate to use their services. Too often, beginning and even experienced teachers are reluctant to ask for help because they are afraid it will be construed as a sign of weakness or an inability to do the job they were hired to do. This is nonsense. Good teachers use every tool, idea, or resource available to help improve their teaching.

The students in your classroom are many times the very best resource of all. Find out what their interests are and what problem-solving skills they have. Look for hidden talents that might be useful. Above all, do not underestimate the contributions that your students can make or what they can teach you. Good teachers learn as they teach.

Parents and local residents can provide a rich source of information related to the science technology and society theme. This is an excellent way for students to make real-world connections. What science-related careers and jobs can you think of that could be helpful in fostering students' understanding of an important science concept and its connection to the real world? Did you think of the various jobs in the health and medical fields? Conservation officer? Recycling business? Nurseries? Agriculture? Television weather person? You likely can identify many other areas that relate to the science concepts your students will learn. When you teach, make a point to find out what science-related careers and jobs your students' parents have and plug these into your science program. Consult local residents and look for local businesses that could add depth and real-life experiences to classroom activities. Expand the walls of your classroom to include meaningful real-world learning opportunities.

Attending professional meetings and in-services is an excellent way to add to your knowledge base of content, process, and teaching strategies. Many local school districts offer science-oriented in-services throughout the school year. Nearby universities and colleges offer classes and theme courses as well as specific in-service opportunities for teachers related to science teaching and learning. The National Science Teachers' Association (NSTA) as well as state and regional branches of the organization hold annual professional conferences that offer a wide variety of sessions focusing on practical information and ideas that teachers can take back to the classroom and use to plan, organize, and manage their science instruction. You can find out about the NSTA and the various services offered by accessing the Web at http://www.nsta.org.

Criteria for Curricular Decision Making

The classroom teacher has many resources available to help with curricular decision making. The current reform effort has produced numerous reports, publications, and research results that provide the database necessary for good curricular decision making. *Benchmarks* and *Standards,* which were discussed in Chapter 2, are two such publications. Another excellent resource for teachers is the *NSTA Pathways to the Science Standards: Guidelines for Moving the Vision into Practice, Elementary School Edition,* K–4 (NSTA, 1997), *Middle School Edition,* 5–8 (NSTA, 1998). This practical guidebook for teachers provides concrete ideas and activities for taking the vision of the reform effort into the classroom. Ask your instructor if copies of these are available for you to examine. These publications can be purchased from NSTA's Science Store.

Project 2061, with funding from the Carnegie Corporation of New York, has created an on-line database available to educators that will be regularly updated to provide detailed, evidence-based reviews of science and mathematics curriculum materials. The first report, released in January 1999, contained an analysis of 13 middle school mathematics textbooks. The evaluation of middle school science textbooks is scheduled for release in the summer of 1999. These on-line reviews identify curricular materials that actually help students learn the concepts in specific learning goals from *Benchmarks* or *Standards*. Teachers should find this information extremely helpful in determining which materials best meet their particular students' needs. You can access this on-line database at http://www.project2061.org. Additional up-to-date information related to the evaluation of science curricular materials can be found at this site. Developing science programs that foster active teacher and student interaction and that involve the students directly in inquiry-based science is a worthy goal.

Examining Curricular Materials

The following activities involve you in examining different curricular materials that are available to use in planning, organizing, and managing K–6 inquiry-based science experiences for students. By being actively involved with these materials, you will have an opportunity to find out for yourself what actually is included in them. Guidelines for assessing the materials for effective use in an inquiry-based science program are provided. When you have completed the science curricular materials review, a group discussion of the materials reviewed will allow you and your classmates to interact with one another as you share your observations and conclusions. Your instructor will probably want to take part in the discussion too. You may choose to complete part of these activities on your own or wait to do them in class as part of an in-class activity. Check with your instructor for directions.

As you continue to familiarize yourself with a variety of curricular resources, you will become more knowledgeable about which curricular materials will best help your students meet the standards and benchmarks identified in the current reform efforts. You will also become more skilled at helping to select a new science program for your school, or in modifying, adapting, and supplementing existing programs; or in developing your own program.

Suggested Activity 3.1
Assessing Science Curricular Materials

1. Work with a small group to examine as many of the following science curricular materials (teacher's editions and resource materials as well as student materials) as are available:

Full Options Science System (FOSS), K–6

Insights—the Senses Module (EDC), K–2

Science for Life and Living (BSCS), K–6

Great Explorations in Math and Science (GEMS), K–6

Science and Technology for Children (STS), 3–6

Science Curriculum Improvement Study (SCIS3), K–6

Life Lab Science Program, K–6

Merrill Science, K–6

Addison-Wesley/Scott, Foresman, K–6

Macmillan/McGraw-Hill, K–6

Prentice Hall, K–6

Harcourt Brace, K–6

2. If these materials are not available, examine whatever science curricular material that your instructor can provide or that you can locate.

3. Use the following guidelines to assess how well each program or textbook series supports students' achievement of the learning goals recommended in *Benchmarks* and *Standards.*

Program being reviewed: _____

Reviewers' names: _____

a. What are the explicit goals and expectations for students that guide the design, implementation, and assessment of this program ? Are they clear? Do they support the goals and philosophy of the active inquiry-based science approach of *Benchmarks* and *Standards?*

b. Cite examples that can support the claim that the material is developmentally appropriate for all students. Identify information and activities that are interesting and relevant to students' lives. Is science as inquiry the major focus? Is there a noticeable effort made to connect and integrate the understanding of science concepts with other subject areas?

c. How does the program make connections throughout to mathematics?

d. Does the program encourage students/teachers to access a wide variety of other resources? Are adequate time, materials, supplies, and space needed to conduct scientific inquiry encouraged? Is access to community resources and the world beyond the classroom supported and built into the program? Give examples.

e. How does the program provide for special needs learners?

f. How does the material identify and suggest that teachers deal with the common misconceptions held by students that can cause problems in understanding many science concepts? Give some examples.

g. Do the materials provide well-developed scientific concepts that are void of unnecessary vocabulary?

h. What information does Project 2061's on-line database review have to offer regarding this particular program? (http://www.project2061.org)

i. Identify other areas you think should be evaluated. How well does this program meet your identified concerns?

j. Do you consider this program to support the science teaching and learning goals of *Benchmarks* and *Standards?* Would you choose to use this program as a major part of the science curriculum when you teach? Why or why not?

4. Discuss your group's findings with your instructor. Think about how you might present your group's findings to others in your class. Compare and contrast your findings with those of others who examined different programs . Detetermine which programs and textbooks examined seem to best meet the goals and philosophy of inquiry-based science. Cite evidence in your choices.

Suggested Activity 3.2

Assessing Children's Picture Books for Use in Teaching Science Concepts

1. Work with a small group and select a favorite children's book that has a science theme. Have someone in the group read the selected book to the group.

2. Turn to Figure 3.1. Read the description and closely examine the *Assessment Inventory: Selecting Children's Picture Books to Teach Science Concepts.*

3. Follow the directions given for using the *Assessment Inventory* and evaluate the selected children's book.

4. Discuss your results with other groups and your instructor. Include in your discussion your thoughts on effective ways to use children's literature as *one* resource in planning, organizing, and managing inquiry-based science experiences for students.

Suggested Activity 3.3

Assessing Integrated Science/Literature Programs

1. Examine several of the programs that provide children's books with science themes and related activities to use in an integrated approach such as Science Alive, published by *Rigby;* SUNSHINE Science, published by *The Wright Group;* Scholastic's Science Literacy Center and *Steck-Vaughn's* Pair-It Books. Your instructor may provide you with others of this type, or you may locate them yourself.

2. How well do these programs meet the goals of *Benchmarks* and *Standards* for science teaching and learning? Use the guidelines given in Suggested Activity 3.1 to help you decide. Use the *Assessment Inventory* to evaluate the books that are provided with these programs.

3. Based on the data gathered using the guidelines and the *Assessment Inventory,* would you use the materials examined as a major resource for building your science program? Would you use them as *one* of the resources if they were available? Discuss how you would use such materials most effectively in your classroom.

Suggested Activity 3.4
Assessing Other Science Curricular Resources

1. Choose at least two of the following "curricular resources" to investigate: professional journals, the Web, other teachers, students, parents and local residents, professional conferences, and in-services.

2. Design your investigation so that you collect information about your selected areas related to using them as a resource as you teach. Formulate questions that will help you gather, organize, analyze, and evaluate relevant information. Use what you have learned so far about inquiry-based science experiences to help you reach conclusions.

3. Design a forum for sharing the information you gathered and conclusions you reached with your instructor and others in your class. Allow for feedback and discussion.

Suggested Activity 3.5
Assessing Web Sites as Science Curricular Resources

1. Examine the following Web sites and evaluate them as to their usefulness to elementary and middle school teachers who are searching for good science resources to use in planning and designing inquiry-based science experiences. Look for other good Web sites and add them to your list.

   http://www.nsta.org
   http://www.tryscience.com
   http://ericir.syr.edu/virtual/lessons/science/
   http://sln.fi.edu/tfi/activity/act-summ.html
   http://omsi.edu/sln/ww/background/inquiry/

FIGURE 3.1

Assessment Inventory
Selecting Children's Picture Books to Teach Science Concepts

Dr. Sandra Cain and Dr. Leonie Rose

Title of Book: _____   Author _____

1. **THEME**
   a. What is the author's message, lesson, or moral about life for the reader?

   b. What is the science concept that children would learn?

   c. In which science content area does the science concept belong?
      __physical   __life   __earth/space science   __science and technology

2. **STORYLINE**
   a. Which plot structure does the story use?
      circular _____   repetitive _____   step by step _____   turnabout _____   other _____
   b. Is the story mostly _____fantasy   _____realistic fiction   _____nonfiction?
   c. Are accurate facts present in the book?   yes   no
   d. Does the story allow children to easily distingush fact from fiction?   yes   no

3. **CHARACTERS**
   a. Are animals in the story depicted naturally?   yes   no
   b. Are characters believable?   yes   no

4. **SETTING**
   a. Does the story take place in a realistic setting?   yes   no
   b. Are time relationships appropriate?   yes   no

5. **ILLUSTRATIONS**
   a. Do the illustrations portray accurate scientific representations?   yes   no
   b. Do the illustrations match the story or print?   yes   no

6. **AESTHETIC QUALITIES**
   a. Does the story promote a positive attitude toward inquiry-based science?   yes   no
   b. Will the children at my grade level find this book interesting and enjoyable?   yes   no

7. **STEREOTYPING**
   a. Are any stereotypes present?   gender__ cultural__ other__none__
   b. If so, how will you deal with them?

8. **MISREPRESENTATIONS—MISCONCEPTIONS**
   a. Are there misrepresentations that could lead to science misconceptions?
      __none __some __many
   b. If so, how will you deal with them?

CIRCLE YOUR RECOMMENDATION

Excellent science resource   Needs modifications   Needs many modifications

Adapted from Deborah A. Mayer, *Checklist for choosing children's literature to teach science, Science and Children*, March 1995, 18.

Description of the Instrument

The *Assessment Inventory for Selecting Children's Picture Books to Teach Science Concepts* has eight categories with two to three questions related to each category. The questions are designed to elicit information about a specific book that can be used in making a decision about whether to use that book to teach targeted science concepts. The categories are (1) theme, (2) storyline, (3) characters, (4) setting, (5) illustrations, (6) aesthetic qualities, (7) stereotyping, and (8) misrepresentations or misconceptions. Information about the questions for each category is discussed briefly here.

1. The first category, **theme,** helps establish the book's purpose from a literary as well as a science point of view. Good children's literature will have a message, lesson, or moral about life that permeates the story (Lukens, 1995). Generally, the successful writer communicates the themes through the events and characters rather than through an overt statement, as in a fable. It is important for teachers to identify the literary purpose and use it to teach story grammar to young readers. The science concept that would be learned must also be identified along with the content area(s) to which it belongs.

   The *National Science Education Standards* (1996) identifies the following content standards for K to 4. In the area of physical science, "all students should develop an understanding of properties of objects and materials, position and motion of objects and light, heat, electricity and magnetism" (p. 123). In the area of life science, the understandings focus on "the characteristics of organisms, life cycles of organisms and organisms and environments" (p. 127). Earth and space science concepts center on "properties of earth materials, objects in the sky and changes in earth and sky" (p. 130). There are many children's books that focus on one or more concepts from one of these three traditional science content areas—physical, life, and earth/space.

   The *Standards* also includes a category for science and technology. Students in grades K to 4 are expected to engage in activities that help them understand "that some objects occur in nature; others have been designed and made by people to solve human problems and enhance the quality of life" (p. 138). Teachers should purposefully select books that fall into the science-and-technology area. These books can be used to help children connect to the designed world and foster an understanding of how technological objects and systems work. Stories in which the characters tackle tasks with a technological purpose and solve them can serve as an introduction to firsthand experience with classroom projects in which children design ways to use technology to solve real-world problems.

   It is important that teachers be aware of the intended purpose of the book from both a literature and a scientific viewpoint. Teachers also need to determine whether this intended purpose matches the instructional purpose for which it will be used.

2. The second category, **storyline,** asks the teacher to identify the plot structure and type of story. In picture storybooks, the plot is usually relatively simple. There tends to be one main sequence of events, with few or no subplots to take attention from the main character, and one central problem that needs to be solved. Usually, each action flows from earlier ones to enable the reader to predict what will occur and what the final outcome will be (Hennings, 1996).

   Dorothy Grant Hennings (1996) has identified four types of plot patterns in picture books that are most often used in primary grades. In the step-by-step plot pattern, events flow logically from one to the next, leading the reader to a predictable ending. In a turnabout pattern, the events still flow logically from one to the next, but the ending is an unexpected surprise. In a story with a circular plot structure, the events also flow logically from one to the next, but the story ends with the main character returning to the same place or actions as in the beginning of the story. The final plot pattern is repetitive, where events are repeated, with each repetition varying slightly, but the events are still very predictable. These four plot patterns are reflected in good children's picture books, unless the book is a piece of nonfiction, which would not have a narrative plot structure.

   Most children's picture books can be categorized into one of the following categories: fantasy, realistic fiction, and nonfiction. In a fantasy, the setting, events, and/or characters are usually make-believe. Portions of the story could not really take place. In realistic fiction, the characters, setting, and events could actually occur in the real world. A piece that is nonfiction does not have the elements of a narrative text, such as characters, setting, theme, events, problems, and solutions. These trade books are factual, with details and various text patterns, such as description, listing, sequence, comparison/contrast, cause/effect, or problem/solution (Jacobson, 1998; Reutzel & Cooter, 1996).

From a scientific point of view, it is important to carefully examine the information presented to be sure that it is factual. A fictional story can be based on factual information and represent what is real. Children must be able to easily distinguish the factual parts from the fictional parts, and the teacher must be able to determine if these fictional parts will lead to misunderstandings or misconceptions related to the science concept that is being targeted (Mayer, 1995).

3. The third category addresses the ***characters*** in the story. It is important from a science view that animals are depicted naturally. Animals that talk, wear clothes, and take on other human characteristics are generally not the best way to help children learn and understand the true nature of animals (Cain & Evans, 1990). This can be especially confusing for younger children. In a high-quality piece of children's literature, authors develop characters though description and actions. Characters must be believable, behave consistently, and have a range of feelings so that readers can easily identify with them (Hennings, 1996; Norton, 1995).

4. In narrative text, the ***setting*** is the portion of the story that sets the stage by establishing a time frame and a place where the action takes place. The setting can have little influence on the story or be an integral part of the story that moves the plot forward and heightens feelings (Hennings, 1996; Lukens, 1995). Literature that is suited for teaching science concepts should be realistic in order to promote the believability of the storyline and characters. The passage of time should be clear to children. Check to see that the book makes it clear how much time passes during the story—a few minutes, a day, a week, a year, and so on.

5. ***Illustrations*** in literature that is suitable for teaching science concepts should accurately portray scientific representations. Animals, plants, and other objects, such as the moon, stars, clouds, raindrops, and rocks, should closely resemble the "real thing" and not be drawn as cartoon-like or given features that are inaccurate or misleading. Books for young children tend to be picture stories in which meaning is communicated through words and pictures. At times the pictures dominate. Successful storybooks illustrate the verbal storyline with pictures that harmonize with the words. Authors can harmonize illustrations and words through use of color, detail, and variations in size (Hennings, 1996). Children learn a great deal from the pictures and illustrations that accompany a story. Make sure that they are not getting mixed messages from inaccurate illustrations.

6. The first question under the sixth category, ***aesthetic qualities,*** calls attention to the effects of the book related to promoting a positive attitude toward inquiry-based science. The *Standards* emphasizes the importance of an inquiry-based science approach for grades K to 4. Books that have an active, investigative, process-oriented focus encourage children to take an active hands-on, minds-on role in constructing science knowledge, and that in turn fosters the development of a positive attitude toward inquiry-based science. The second question focuses on enjoyment rather than on learning new information. Cox and Zarillo (1993) note that it is just as important that readers enjoy a story as it is to identify important concepts, facts, or vocabulary embedded in the book. Both of these questions are extremely important, and teachers should be able to answer **yes** to both. If either is answered with a no, then that particular book would not be recommended for teaching science concepts.

7. ***Stereotyping*** deals with issues of negative stereotyping in any of the story elements. Stereotypes can involve gender, culture, religion, ethnicity, or any other way of looking at a group that does not respect individuals or that creates a negative view of those individuals (Hennings, 1996; Norton, 1995). Teachers need to be aware of negative stereotypes that are part of a character's makeup or that are reinforced through behaviors, attitudes, illustrations, or settings. A book that resorts to using stereotypes is neither good literature nor a good science source.

8. The last category, ***misrepresentations—misconceptions,*** is designed to involve teachers in identifying specific parts of the story that might lead children to form science misconceptions. On this portion of the *Assessment Inventory,* the teacher examines the story for misleading information and illustrations that are contrary to scientific findings. Will this story enhance students' understanding of the science concept that was identified in the first category? If there are some questionable or misleading portions of the story, how will the teacher deal with these? Can these inaccurate parts be used to help students learn and remember the science concept that is being taught? Are there so many problems with misrepresentations that this particular book is **not** the best one to use in teaching a science concept? Carefully consider whether the book can be used to increase science understandings and foster deeper meanings related to science content and processes or whether it is more likely to cause serious misconceptions that will interfere with important science understandings.

THE LEARNING ENVIRONMENT

Effective, proactive teachers provide a learning environment that encourages self-directed, responsible student behavior and supports students and their efforts. This can be achieved by making the learning environment inviting, interesting, challenging, and safe. The inquiry-based approach to science teaching and learning demands that teachers be skillful managers. Many of the constructivist-oriented science activities involve children in designing and implementing their own investigations to answer their own questions. Teachers need to ensure that the learning experiences achieve quality results with minimum disorder. The learning environment has both a direct and an indirect influence on the kind of learning that takes place. As a teacher, you must become increasingly sensitive to the learning environment and be able to design, modify, and adapt it so that learning is enhanced. If students are encouraged to construct meaning and pursue their investigations in ways that are meaningful to them, they must be in an environment that fosters and supports this type of effort. Many an otherwise well-planned learning experience has failed because of a nonsupportive learning environment. Three areas of concern that will be discussed in this section are the following:

- Physical learning environment
- Safety factors/legal guidelines
- Managing time and grouping patterns

While reading and discussing the information included here, think of your own experiences in elementary and middle school science. What types of learning environments enhanced or inhibited your learning experiences? Just as you will be learning to teach in a constructivist mode, realize that you are also constructing knowledge out of your own experiences as you read this text and engage in the suggested activities and discussions. During your mini-teaching experiences or various types of actual field experiences, it might be helpful to keep a reflective journal and analyze, question, and reflect on what you are observing and experiencing related to the learning environment. If you have already had some field experience, recall what you remember about the learning environments you observed. Talk to others about what they remember about their experiences in classrooms and working with students related to the learning environment.

Physical Learning Environment

The physical learning environment is by no means limited to the classroom, especially not in science. In reality, however, that is where a major portion of science learning experiences take place for most students. Therefore, we will first look at some of the important factors to consider in the typical classroom as you plan and organize for inquiry-based science. We will also look beyond the classroom walls at other learning environments that offer a variety of science-related learning experiences for students.

The Classroom

The **lighting** in a classroom is one of the factors that can inhibit or enhance the learning process. Both natural and artificial lighting need to be surveyed to determine possible problems. Be aware of light that is reflected on screens, boards, charts, and other visual materials, including computers and other technological tools used for instructional purposes. Try to arrange movable items so that a clear view results and/or allow students to move in order to get the best view. Also remember that light reflects differently at various times of the day. Therefore, make your checks at various times of the day and in various weather patterns. While we all like sunshine, bright sunlight in a classroom can be very distracting. Once you have identified problem areas, possible solutions should be generated and put into effect. These solutions may result in structural changes in the classroom itself, changes in the type and/or arrangement of the lighting fixtures, or additions to and/or changes in the arrangement of other furnishings in the classroom. Many times these solutions can occur only during remodeling and can be long range and expensive. However, it is still important to let the appropriate people know about the problem areas. In the meantime, less expensive and short-term solutions can be utilized. Shades, blinds, curtains, cardboard, or other opaque and translucent objects and materials can be used effectively to control the amount and direction of both inside and outside light. Work areas that need less light should be set up in the darker areas of the room. Bookcases or cardboard walls can be used to block out unwanted light in these areas.

Room temperature is another important factor to consider as you plan and organize for effective science teaching. When classrooms are too warm, children (and teachers) become drowsy and listless. On the other hand, cold classrooms can cause the learners to become preoccupied with their need for physical comfort. Thus, physical discomfort from either extreme can cause a lack of attention to the task at hand and result in a poor learning experience. If the classroom temperature cannot be directly controlled by adjusting the thermostat, other measures must be taken. If the room is too warm, fresh air can be circulated by opening a window or door. A fan can also be used to help circulate the air. If the room temperature fluctuates, the children can be instructed to wear layered clothing that can be added to or taken off as the need arises. Can you think of other practical solutions that might be effective? Stop now and observe the temperature around you. Is it too warm? Too cold? Or comfortable? How is it affecting your ability to read, think about, and understand the information in this text? Is there a practical solution that is available to you if you wanted to make changes in your physical environment that would enhance your ability to accommodate the information you have been reading? You may wish to make those changes and see if your learning experience is positively affected. Sometimes teachers and children become accustomed to the stale air and warm classroom after being there for an extended time period. Make a habit of constantly being aware of how the room temperature is affecting the learning experiences of your students and have ready solutions available.

Distracting background noises and sights are other factors in the physical learning environment that can cause children's attention to be drawn away from the planned learning experience. Minimize these by having children face away from the possible distractions. For example, do not let a caged animal or a window with a view of the playground be the backdrop when you want the students to attend to a specific task at hand or listen as you give instructions, share information, or lead discussions. Sometimes quiet background music helps minimize other distracting sounds. As students mature and become more adept at engaging in inquiry-based science and using cooperative learning strategies, most will be better able to tune out distracting noises and sights and tune in to the task at hand on their own. Thoughtful, effective teachers try to limit distractions so that students get the most out of the planned learning experience.

The arrangement of classroom furnishings can also affect the learning process. Your classroom will contain both permanently placed and movable furnishings. Permanently placed furnishing—such as the sink, electrical outlets, windows, chalk or dry erase board, lighting fixtures, and perhaps storage areas—must become the core of your classroom arrangement. Movable furnishings—such as desks, tables, bookcases, plants, an aquarium, and perhaps the computers—can be used to modify and enhance the core arrangement. No one room arrangement will be appropriate for every science experience. In fact, **flexibility** is the key. Inquiry-based science calls for a variety of room arrangements. Ideally, furnishings are easily changed to accommodate the ever changing needs of your students as they actively engage in a variety of science experiences. There are, however, some factors to consider as you make decisions about the arrangement of the classroom furnishings and the impact it will have, positive or negative, on an inquiry-based science program.

Inquiry-based science programs call for students to have freedom of movement, easy access to materials, and a safe work space that provides the needed physical requirements, such as electrical outlets, sink and water, heating equipment, and appropriate floor covering. Consideration must also be given to creating space that accommodates several small groups working on different aspects of an activity at the same time. The need for teacher supervision and interaction with individuals and groups must also be a consideration as you make decisions about classroom arrangements. Traffic flow becomes important. A poorly designed classroom arrangement can impede and disrupt students' work and cause conflicts to occur between groups that take away from valuable time on task. Your classroom arrangement should seek to minimize these unnecessary conflicts by creating a traffic flow pattern that allows adequate work space away from the main paths. Along this same line, you must consider any special needs that students in your class have related to movement in the room. A student with a vision impairment or one who uses a wheelchair, is on crutches, or has a neurological impairment that would make it difficult to recognize the pattern of traffic flow must be accommodated in your room arrangement.

Think about the classroom that your science methods class meets in. How are the furnishings arranged? Are they easily moved to accommodate the various small-group activities that involve you in using science equipment and materials? Are needed non-movable items, such as the sink or electrical outlets, easily accessible to individuals and groups that need them? Is the normal flow of traffic a constant problem for the various groups as they engage in active inquiry? What changes in the arrangement of classroom furnishings might be made to enhance the learning process in your science methods class? Is it possible to put your ideas into effect? Find out.

Some classrooms have **designated areas** that serve a specific purpose. For example, **a work area** might be arranged to accommodate the manipulative aspect of sciencing. In this area, materials, equipment, and facilities necessary for firsthand data gathering could be located. Measurement instruments (such as balances, scales, thermometers, meter sticks, stopwatches, graduated cylinders, and other nonbreakable containers of all sorts and sizes), graph and chart paper, water source, electrical outlets, heating equipment, and a variety of utensils are a few of the items that will be used often and so need to be accessible daily. Other materials such as magnets, ramps, batteries and bulbs, and rock samples can be stored elsewhere and moved to this work area when needed.

Another area of the classroom could be used as a **resource center.** Here, books, magazines, newspapers, cassette tapes, records, discs, videos, filmstrips, pictures, models, as well as computers and computer software could be available for daily student use in completing inquiry-based activities.

A conference area located away from the center of activity is useful for meeting with individuals or small groups. A certain amount of privacy is needed from time to time for students to speak freely with the teacher or with one another. This area is also useful for testing, tutorial sessions, and quiet study time.

Storage areas are a very important part of the overall room arrangement. Some space for storing materials and equipment in frequent use must be maintained in the work area set aside for the hands-on manipulation aspect of inquiry-based science discussed earlier. Other areas must also be found to store supplies, equipment, and materials not in immediate use. Facilities must accommodate both large and small items. Living things such as small animals, fish, plants, and insects require special attention. There may be a few items that should be kept under lock and key and are accessible only by permission of the teacher. These may include matches, electrical appliances, iron filings, glycerin, iodine, and other chemicals. These sorts of items should be kept at a minimum in most elementary (K–6) classrooms. Most science activities and investigations can and should be done without the use of any potential harmful substances.

A **master list** of on-hand materials and equipment is invaluable. The list can be alphabetized, or items can be grouped according to identified headings. The exact location of each item should be included. This list can be organized to correlate with specific lessons or broad topic areas. Cabinets, drawers, shelves, boxes, and other storage facilities being used should have a materials list posted to identify the items that can be found there. All items should be labeled to facilitate easy identification. Harmful chemicals and other hazardous materials must be so labeled. As discussed earlier, a secure area should be used to house these "off-limits" materials and equipment. More detailed suggestions regarding safety in the classroom are provided in the next section of this chapter. Teachers have used many **techniques for organizing** needed materials and equipment. Shoe boxes are just the right size for storing materials and small equipment for one or two persons. They stack well and can be acquired easily. Plastic dishpans and baskets serve well for holding materials for small groups. They can easily be carried from a storage shelf to a work area where several students could share the materials. You can probably think of other ways to make materials easily accessible to elementary students.

Frequent inventories will help keep the materials and equipment organized for ready use. Consumable items must be replaced as they are used, and equipment must be kept in good repair. A teacher will want to make sure that sufficient amounts of needed materials are always available.

An integral part of most planned science experiences is the **distribution and collection of materials.** If a group of students is working with the same materials within approximately the same time period, a simple routine can be established using student helpers who pass out the equipment or place it in the appropriate work areas. Using boxes, buckets, plastic bags, or dishpans containing only the needed items make this task simple. Students should be directed to clean all items after using them and return them to the appropriate storage container. Consumable materials must be replaced, and student helpers can then return all containers to the appropriate storage area. Effective physical learning environments do not just happen. They are the result of much hard work and planning. In addition to the information and suggestions discussed so far, there are several other things that you can do related to the physical learning environment that will **increase** the chances of effective learning.

The effective **use of color** in the physical learning environment can help draw attention to important information; convey an inviting, warm, accepting atmosphere; stimulate interest; and serve to motivate students in a variety of ways. **Posters, displays, and signs** that are student oriented should be visible around the room. The use of **plants and animals** can create a warm atmosphere and can be integrated into many science activities. Of course, you must consider that some students may have allergies and cannot tolerate certain plants and animals in the room on a continuing basis. If this is the case, you must be flexible. Work with the student and the parents to identify exactly what can and cannot be tolerated, seek workable solutions, and adjust your classroom environment accordingly.

Extending the Classroom Beyond the Four Walls

In addition to finding ways to make the normal physical classroom structure more effective, interesting, and inviting, think of ways to extend the classroom to the world outside the four walls. The physical learning environment can include the area directly outside the classroom windows, the area surrounding the school, the neighborhood, and the community at large. Many schools have vegetable gardens as well as flower gardens that students tend, harvest, and enjoy. Many communities have outdoor learning facilities that include such things as nature trails, amphitheaters, a variety of flower gardens, trees and plants, and even overnight camping facilities. Water sources such as lakes, rivers, streams, and ponds also offer many possibilities. There are numerous other places that are available to many students and teachers

Careful planning for safety and distraction-free environments are important considerations when organizing for inquiry activities outside the classroom.

that can be used to extend the walls of the classroom, such as museums, planetariums, observatories, water treatment plants, and zoos, to name just a few. What other areas available to students and teachers outside the classroom walls can you think of that would make effective science learning environments? Do not inhibit your students' learning possibilities by limiting the physical learning environment to the four walls of the classroom.

As a teacher, you will need to be alert to the many factors in the physical learning environment that could interfere with or enhance your students' science experiences. The key is to be proactive and arrange the physical environment of the classroom so that the students are able to concentrate on the learning at hand and not be distracted by problems that are within the teacher's ability to eliminate or at least limit. Even when teachers organize and plan well for effective use of the physical learning environment of the classroom, problems can still arise. When this happens, involve your students in generating and selecting solutions to remedy the situation. Having students assist in the problem-solving process is what inquiry-based science is all about. Activity 3.6 has been designed to involve you in gathering more information related to the impact of the physical environment on student learning. Select one or more of these or adapt, modify, and/or combine them to meet your particular needs. Perhaps you can design other activities that will provide you with more information related to the impact of the physical environment on the teaching and learning of science.

Suggested Activity 3.6

Researching How the Physical Learning Environment Affects Learning

1. Do some research on the latest findings on the effect of color in the learning process. Present your results and conclusions to others. How will you use this information to enhance science teaching and learning?

2. Identify science activities that might involve students in using the area immediately outside the classroom windows or within the school grounds.

3. Observe several early elementary, elementary, and middle school classroom arrangements. Talk with the teachers to find out why that particular arrangement was chosen. Does the arrangement encourage inquiry-based science experiences? Is the traffic flow a problem for active involvement by small groups? Are science materials and equipment accessible to students, and is adequate work space provided? Is the present arrangement flexible so that different needs can be met successfully? Explain your findings. Use what you have read so far in this chapter to assess the effectiveness of the room arrangements that you observed. Share your conclusions with others and with your instructor.

Safety Factors/Legal Guidelines

Elementary teachers have long been responsible for the safety and well-being of students entrusted to their care. Perhaps because this concept has become so much a part of a teacher's daily responsibilities, it is sometimes taken for granted. Consequently, care and *conscientious attention to detail* are more and more frequently omitted.

Teachers must plan for students' safety. Such planning requires foresight and insight. Teachers must be aware of the potential hazards in any given activity or situation. Moreover, care must be exercised in planning learning experiences to anticipate or, even better, eliminate situations in which an injury might occur. *NSTA Pathways to the Science Standards, Elementary School Edition,* suggests that the following be a part of the safe science classroom:

Splash-proof personal safety goggles

Physician-approved first-aid kit

Centrally located dual eyewash

ABC fire extinguisher at each exit

Smoke/heat detectors

Sink with soap dispenser

Lip edge on any open shelves used for storing bottles or chemicals

If these items are not available in your classroom, request them. If you are unable to obtain them, consider effective alternatives. For example, several plastic dishpans with water in jugs and inexpensive soap dispensers could be used instead of the sink. What other workable alternatives can you think of? If suitable alternatives cannot be provided, then activities and materials must be altered, modified, or eliminated. Safety must be of utmost concern as you plan and organize for science teaching and learning.

Teachers are not born with skill in foreseeing hazards, just as they are not born with skill in planning effective science learning experiences. By attempting to identify hazardous situations, teachers become more aware of such situations. Certainly every teacher would caution students who are boiling water on the stove; perhaps students would not even be allowed to do it at all. Some things are fairly obvious; we are all aware that boiling water poses a potential hazard—The student might be burned.

Not all hazards are so obvious, however. Would we all recognize the potential hazards in other simple activities such as the following? A kindergarten class has been developing observation and simple classification skills. The teacher has provided beans, peas, marbles, buttons, and other small items for the students to use in sorting and grouping the various items according to some identified criteria. The students are to put the objects into different baby food jars to demonstrate their skills in observing and classifying. Can you identify at least *five* potential hazards in this situation?

Did you think of these?

- Having an allergic reaction to handling the objects
- Throwing the objects and perhaps injuring another student
- Putting the objects into ears, nose, or mouth and having them become lodged there
- Breaking the jars and sustaining a cut
- Spilling the objects and perhaps injuring someone who might step on the spilled items and fall

Did you think of something not listed here? If so, please share it with your instructor and the class.

In an inquiry-based science program, students are expected to be self-directed and to engage in active exploration with easy access to materials and equipment. Consequently, potential hazards abound. To decrease the likelihood of injury, teachers must be proactive and identify potential hazards in advance. Alternative methods to accomplish the same goal without the hazard could be substituted. If that were impossible, at least the students could be warned and techniques demonstrated for using extreme caution. Students should be taught proper techniques in handling and caring for materials and equipment. This step is more likely to occur when expensive equipment or materials are being used (e.g., the expensive microscope, rare book, or new computer attachment). However, the cost of an item does not indicate its relative potential as a hazard. Even collectibles can be handled in such a way as to result in injury. Proper techniques can and should be taught.

At the beginning of each year, most teachers involve students in establishing rules of conduct in the classroom and designate specific procedures to be followed in certain situations. Likewise, safety rules should be made concerning the use and handling of science materials and equipment. Students should be involved in generating these rules and posting visual and verbal reminders in the form of charts or cartoon-like posters. The danger of spilling something, stepping on something, and falling might be reduced somewhat by limiting the area in which the activity is to be conducted. Perhaps a carpeted area will reduce injury from a fall and the use of non-breakable containers eliminate the possibility of sustaining a cut.

Safety guides have been developed at the national level and in most states and local school districts. Ask your instructor if the latest edition of *Safety in the Elementary Science Classroom* (NSTA, 1993) is available for you to examine. In addition, locate a copy of the classroom safety guidelines developed in your state or local area and read it carefully; then save it for future reference. The hints and suggestions in such guides can save a lot of time and perhaps even save a child from injury. It is well worth your time and energy to include appropriate safety precautions as an integral part of your planning and organizing for science teaching and learning.

A technique of utmost importance in avoiding injury to students is to *give clear, complete directions* each and every time students are engaging in a planned science learning experience. Do not assume that your students will remember even general directions or safety rules from one day to the next or from one manipulation to the next. Ask them to tell you what safety precautions might be in order. Make "Think Safety" a part of each and every science learning experience. Put the basic safety rules on a chart and refer to it each day.

Make sure that students are able to safely operate any equipment to be used in a science learning experience. Frequently, this may mean spending one or more days just learning how to manipulate the equipment before actually beginning the planned learning experience. Written directions and/or procedures for using the equipment should be provided for each student. These should be given orally as well. Generally, short steps are more easily followed than long, detailed directions. For young children, simple visual illustrations showing safe operating procedure and the sequence (if appropriate) in which it must be performed can be posted for easy reference.

With the growing practice in our society of people entering a lawsuit against someone for minor or maybe even imagined injuries or slights, teachers need to develop an awareness of such action and protect themselves against it. Students can and do bring lawsuits against teachers for injury. The best defense is to make sure that no students sustain injury in your class. However, no one can absolutely ensure against injury. A student will occasionally become injured even with the most careful planning. In that case, a teacher's best legal defense is *careful planning*. Without careful planning, a teacher could be found negligent and perhaps legally liable for the student's injury. Teachers must guard against injury and against negligence.

A standard technique for determining possible negligence is to ask, "Did the teacher do everything any reasonable person would do in a similar situation?" Teachers should keep this question in mind and ask it of themselves. At this phase of your professional development, it would be a good idea to establish the habit of asking this question as a self-check each time you develop a plan for engaging students in science learning experiences.

It is not the purpose of this section to scare prospective teachers, only to build awareness. Prevention is so much better than regret. Therefore, plan carefully, think about safety needs, caution students, and keep hazards to a minimum. Ask yourself, "Have I done everything any reasonable teacher would do in a similar situation?" Do not become careless or be lulled into a sense of false security.

Some teachers believe that the school board or the state would be legally liable for a student's injury. True, teachers do work for the state. However, many states adhere to the doctrine of *sovereign immunity,* which means that one cannot sue the state in cases of injury resulting from the negligence of an employee. In such states, the individual teacher would face possible conviction in a *tort liability suit,* or civil suit brought to establish liability for an injury to an individual. (Of course, in all states the individual teacher is responsible for criminal acts or wrongs committed against society.) The topic of tort liability is far too complex to be covered completely here. The intention here is to build an awareness to help you avoid situations that would leave your students exposed to possible injury and you vulnerable to a claim of negligence. Careful planning is the best prevention. Try at all times to keep your students safe from injury. Many safeguards are simple, commonsense precautions:

1. Make and enforce rules.
2. Label dangerous substances and store them out of the reach of children.
3. Avoid hazardous situations.
4. Remind students regularly of safety rules.
5. Supervise students at all times.

Planning and organizing for safe science learning experiences is a must. Constant supervision of active students is equally important. Students need a **safe learning environment** that fosters self-directed, active exploration of their world and that leads to improved skills and a deeper understanding of science concepts.

Managing Time and Grouping Patterns

Managing and structuring the science program so that students have **blocks of time** to immerse themselves in the inquiry process—gathering data, organizing it, analyzing it, and evaluating it—as well as providing for ample sharing and reflection time within and among groups is an extremely important element in a successful inquiry-based science program. Constructing, reflecting on, and using scientific knowledge takes time. Students need to have the experience of working, sharing, and communicating with their peers. Science learning is enhanced when time is provided for interaction among students. Time must be provided for both short- and long-term investigations. Making connections to the "real world" and with other subject areas can be time consuming, but it is time well spent. As you plan and organize science learning experiences for your students, you must build in the time needed on a daily as well as long-term basis.

Inquiry-based science requires that a teacher use **various types of grouping patterns.** Three basic types of grouping patterns are discussed here:

1. Independent grouping
2. Small groups (two to five people)
3. Large groups (six or more people)

Some parts of a planned science experience may be best accomplished when each student works **independently.** Upper elementary students can be expected to work alone on parts of projects much more successfully than can younger students. Highly motivated students may prefer working alone much of the time. Each specific science experience, the specific needs of the students, as well as what is known about effective learning strategies should be considered in order to determine the appropriate type of grouping. Some parts of a science experience can be done successfully alone; then the individual can join with others in the sharing-and-reflection phase. For example, during data gathering, some students can effectively work alone. They work with the needed materials and equipment to gather data firsthand; they use other sources, such as the Internet, reference books, or the textbook, to help them organize and understand the data, and then they interact with others, compare notes, and evaluate their work. At other times, the interaction with others may take place before the actual data gathering phase. Students may need time to interact, sharing questions and ideas related to past experiences and knowledge before beginning the actual investigation. Students may take on different roles as a result of the preliminary discussion and work alone for a period of time gathering more data or performing some preliminary investigation. The results are shared with the group, and further investigation plans are made. Some science learning experiences require constant interaction among the students, and some students do best when allowed to work with others throughout.

Most inquiry-based science experiences do call for students to work in **small groups** to complete most of the investigation. Good teachers recognize that learning is increased when students are encouraged to interact with their peers—asking questions, sharing ideas, and working together to investigate meaningful science questions. **How groups are formed** is another management issue for the teacher. There are times when the teacher may decide to allow students to determine with whom they would like to work. Students may form their small group on the basis of friendship, common interest, or some other factor of their choosing. Other times, the grouping may be done by the teacher. For example, students could be grouped to minimize behavioral problems, to take advantage of students' special skills, or to encourage participation and leadership.

Random assignment can also be used effectively in grouping students. Occasionally, students enjoy being placed in a group on the basis of luck. For example, names could be drawn from a hat to form the groupings, or students could number themselves, all the 1s forming a group, all the 2s forming a group, and so on. Groupings could also be made on the basis of some selected criteria, such as all students whose birthdays fall in January, February, or March in one group; April, May, and June in a second group; and so on. Often, this kind of random grouping allows relationships to develop between students who otherwise might never have worked together.

Large-group instruction is most successfully used by the teacher for giving information and directions, demonstrations, films, and short lectures that apply to the entire group. It is also used for student presentations, summarizing, and sharing and reflection among the various small groups. During large-group instruction, students are generally put in a somewhat passive role. Interaction necessarily becomes limited. However, a skilled teacher will provide opportunities during large-group in-

Research indicates that learning is increased when students have an opportunity to interact with one another asking and answering questions while engaged in science inquiry.

struction for active listening, questioning, and reflection and sharing. More detailed information on how to keep students mentally active will be discussed in Chapter 4.

Providing blocks of time and determining grouping patterns are two important facets of managing the learning environment. Both should be done purposely to facilitate learning. Teachers must manage science experiences so that the time allotted and student grouping pattern(s) chosen are appropriate to the specific experience. Whether students work independently, in small groups, in a large group, or in different grouping patterns during a science experience, make sure that you are aware of the **purpose** of the grouping and that you have determined that it is the most appropriate for that particular science experience.

YOU, THE TEACHER

The last element, and by far the most important, that you must consider as part of the decision-making process related to planning, organizing, and managing inquiry-based science is you, the teacher. Your own strengths, weaknesses, skills, personality, background, and philosophy will have a profound effect, positive or negative, on those you teach. You must be aware of who you are.

Examining Your Teaching Philosophy

In an interview published in the spring 1999 issue of *Thought and Action,* Ronda Beaman, the winner of the first National Education Association Excellence in the Academy award for an article on the art of teaching, comments that effective teachers find "ways to connect with a student's desire to learn." In another part of the interview, Beaman reminds us that "education should be a process of drawing out rather than putting in." This concept sometimes runs counter to many teachers' ideas of what teaching is all about. What is your reaction to Beaman's comments? How do you see teaching? Think about what it means to connect with a student's desire to learn and to draw out rather than put in. Do you embrace these ideas? How do they fit in with what you are learning about inquiry-based science teaching and learning? Talk to other preservice teachers as well as in-service teachers and get their reactions to Beaman's comments. How does this translate in the "real world"? Are you teaching if no one is learning?

Important Characteristics, Skills, and Abilities of Effective Teachers

What are some of the important characteristics, skills, and abilities that effective teachers possess? The literature identifies the following:

- Enthusiastic, flexible, innovative, and creative
- Caring and accepting
- Skilled in preparation, organization, and management
- Ability to motivate and stimulate thought and interest
- Ability to communicate clearly

- Knowledge and love of subject matter
- Ability to reflect on the teaching/learning process
- Ability to use insights and knowledge to improve teaching and enhance student learning

How do you rate yourself in these important areas? What can you do to continue to develop your skills in these areas? Can you think of other important characteristics, skills, and abilities that you believe make a teacher effective? Think about a teacher who has made a difference in your life. What characteristics, skills, and abilities did this person possess that enabled him or her to be effective? Do you possess these? What are your strengths? How can you use these to effectively connect to your students?

The *National Science Education Standards* call for teachers who have "a firm belief that all students can learn science." This belief supports the notion discussed previously that we must find ways to connect to our students; we must facilitate learning by drawing out rather than putting in. This means that teachers must see themselves as cultivators, not weeders. You must be prepared to help students succeed. Your job will involve creating opportunities for learning to occur. Teachers who provide a safe, warm, open, caring, stimulating environment for students; encourage self-directed learning experiences; and challenge them to do their best do make a difference. How do you see yourself? Will you make a difference?

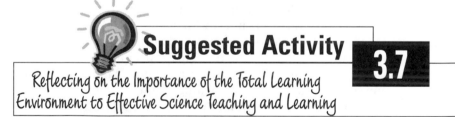

Suggested Activity 3.7

Reflecting on the Importance of the Total Learning Environment to Effective Science Teaching and Learning

1. Review the material presented in this chapter on the learning environment. How would you describe an effective learning environment? Form a small group and discuss your ideas with several others in your class. Discuss what strengths each person in your small group brings into teaching. What areas can each identify as needing the most improvement? How will you continue to develop your skills and abilities related to the learning environment?

2. Get a copy of Science Teaching Standard D contained in the *National Science Education Standards*. Read over this standard and the accompanying information. Reflect on the information presented and discuss it with a small group of your classmates. How important do you think the learning environment is to effective science teaching and learning? Explain and support your reasoning.

REFERENCES

American Association for the Advancement of Science. (1989). *Project 2061: Science for all Americans.* Washington, DC: Author.

American Association for the Advancement of Science. (1993). *Benchmarks for scientific literacy.* New York: Oxford University Press.

Butzow, Carol M. (1991). A comparison of a storyline based method of instruction and a textbook method of instruction on the acquisition of science concepts in the elementary school. Unpublished doctoral dissertation, Indiana University of Pennsylvania, Indiana, PA.

Butzow, Carol M., & Butzow, John W. (1989). *Science through children's literature: An integrated approach.* Englewood, CO: Teacher Ideas Press.

Cain, S. E., & Evans, J. M. (1990). *Sciencing* (3rd ed.).: Columbus, OH. Merrill Publishing Company.

Cain, Sandra E., & Rose, Leonie. (1999). Assessing children's picture books: Assisting teachers in integrating science and literature. *Michigan Reading Journal, 32*(3), 31–44.

Casteel, C. P., & Isom, B. A. (1994). Reciprocal processes in science and literacy learning. *The Reading Teacher, 47*(7), 538–545.

Cox, C., & Zarillo, J. (1993). Teaching reading with children's literature. Englewood Cliffs, NJ: Merrill/Prentice Hall.

Eanes, R. (1997). *Content area literacy: Teaching for today and tomorrow.* Albany, NY: Delmar Publishers.

Eaton, Janet F., et al. (1983, April). When students don't know they don't know. *Science and Children,*

Hennings, D. G. (1996). *Communication in action: Teaching literature-based language arts* (6th ed.). Boston, MA: Houghton Mifflin Company.

Jacobson, J. M. (1998). *Content area reading: Integration with the language arts.* Albany, NY: Delmar Publishers.

Lamartino, A. (1995). *Science and reading.* (ERIC Document Reproduction No. ED 380 770).

Lapp, Diane, & Flood, James. (1993). Literature in the science program. In Bernice Callinan (Ed.), *Fact and fiction: Literature across the curriculum* (pp. 68-77). Newark, DE: International Reading Association).

Lukens, R. J. (1995). *A critical handbook of children's literature* (5th ed.). New York: Harper-Collins.

Maria, K., & Junge, K. (1993). *A comparison of fifth graders' comprehension and retention of scientific information using a science textbook and an informational storybook.* (ERIC Document Reproduction No. ED 364 864).

Mayer, Deborah. (1995, March). How can we best use children's literature in teaching science? *Science and Children,* 16–19, 43.

McGowen, T., & Guzzetti, B. (1991). Promoting social studies understanding through literature-based instruction. *The Social Studies, 82,*16–21.

Metz, Kathleen E. (1995). Reassessment of developmental constraints on children's science instruction. *Review of Educational Research, 65*(2), 93–127.

National Research Council. (1996). *National Science Education Standards.* Washington, DC: National Academy Press.

National Science Teachers Association. (1993). *Safety in the elementary science classroom* (rev. ed.). Arlington, VA: Author.

National Science Teachers Association. (1997). *NSTA pathways to the science standards: Guidelines for moving the vision into practice: Elementary school edition.* Arlington, VA: Author.

National Science Teachers Association. (1998). *NSTA pathways to the science standards: Guidelines for moving the vision into practice: Middle school edition.* Arlington, VA: Author.

Norton, D. (1995). *Through the eyes of a child: An introduction to children's literature* (4th ed.). Englewood Cliffs, NJ: Merrill/Prentice Hall.

Reutzel, D. R., & Cooter, R. B., Jr. (1996). *Teaching children to read: From basals to books* (2nd ed.). Englewood Cliffs, NJ: Merrill.

Thought and Action: The NEA Higher Education Journal. (1999, spring). (interview of Ronda Beaman).

Tolman, M. N., Hardy, G. R., & Sudweeks, R. R. (1998, May). Current science textbook use in the United States. *Science and Children*, 22–25.

Watson, Bruce, & Konicek, Richard (1990, May). Teaching for conceptual change: Confronting children's experiences. *Phi Delta Kappan*

Wepner, S. B., & Feeley, J. T. (1993). *Moving forward with literature: Basals, books, and beyond.* Englewood Cliffs, NJ: Merrill/Prentice Hall.

Wiley, David A., & Royce, Christine A. (1999). *What research tells us about children's literature in the elementary science curriculum.* Presentation and handout for National Science Teachers Association, Boston, MA.

CHAPTER 4

Guiding and Facilitating Inquiry-Based Science Learning

Dr. Lorraine S. Berak

TEACHING FOR UNDERSTANDING AND COGNITIVE DEVELOPMENT

The teacher plays a very important role in guiding and facilitating inquiry-based science. That role centers on helping each student make the most of his or her talents, intelligences, past experiences, and present opportunities to construct meaning and understanding about the nature of our physical world. To do this, teachers need multiple strategies, techniques, and methods. In this chapter we will examine a variety of research-based and experienced tested strategies, techniques, and methods that can be used to guide and facilitate active science learning. We will also explore a template to assist in designing a unit to meet the needs of your learners.

The *National Science Education Standards* (National Research Council, 1996) identify a body of knowledge that skilled teachers of science exhibit. This special knowledge is comprised of understandings and abilities that integrate their knowledge of science content, curriculum, learning, teaching, and students. Such knowledge allows teachers to construct learning situations that meet the needs of individual students as well as groups. This knowledge is referred to as "pedagogical content knowledge" and is described as the "one element that defines a professional teacher of science." In Chapter 3, the ideas of the teacher as decision maker were introduced. Four elements of the learning environment were identified as they related to planning, organizing, and managing inquiry-based science: (1) the students, (2) the curricular materials, (3) the physical learning environment, and (4) you, the teacher. The last three elements were discussed in detail, but in the area of students you were introduced only to some of the individual difference factors such as sex, race, ethnic background, intelligence, cognitive style, and social, physical, and affective characteristics that must be factored into the decision-making process as you organize and plan for effective science experiences. These same individual difference factors come into play as decisions are made about how best to guide and facilitate active inquiry-based science. Let's look at these individual difference factors in more detail now and begin to develop a deeper understanding of how they relate to learning and understanding of science concepts, skills, and attitudes.

Principles of Effective Learning

If given the assignment to teach a third-grade class a science lesson tomorrow, what would you teach? What would your students do during the lesson? How would you present the information? Where would you go to find an appropriate topic? These questions should help you begin to think about the nature of science as well as the ability of your students to learn what you teach.

To effectively plan so that students learn science and become scientifically literate, science content and science experiences must be appropriately chosen to match the cognitive functions of students at various levels of development. Many scientific experts feel that mismatching content and developmental levels leads to many student misconceptions and teacher frustration. For example, expecting kindergarten or first-grade students to understand the motions of planets, moons, and comets in the solar system will undoubtedly cause many anxious moments during science class. Covington and Berry (1976) reported that not understanding cognitive capacities of students can result in a student's inability to extend, apply, or interpret deeper meanings of the content and interest and positive attitudes toward science declining or being exterminated. Therefore, it is imperative that the content to be learned match the student's ability to comprehend it. Achieving this match is essential to learning.

The *National Science Education Standards,* the American Association for the Advancement of Science, and many states (e.g., Michigan Essential Goals and Objectives for Science Education [K–12]) have thought the appropriate match to be so relevant that they have provided suggestions for appropriate grade-level content. These documents can assist you as you begin to plan for your science classes.

Effective Learning

How does learning occur? What are the stages of cognitive development? What does recent brain research tell us about learning? How does learning theory influence science instruction?

Learning does not occur by transmitting information from the teacher or the textbook (or video or computer screen) to the child's brain. Instead, each child constructs his or her own meaning by combining prior information with new information such that the new knowledge provides personal meaning to the child. Educators who accept this theory see their role as that of providing learning experiences to help children develop their mental capacity. In order to provide those appropriate learning experiences, teachers need to understand developmental needs. Development, in this context, means the changes that take place affectively, cognitively, physically, emotionally, and socially. Some of these changes are due to normal growth patterns, while others are a result of various experiences. These changes usually follow a pattern that is unique to each child. Children usually follow the same sequence, but the amount of time from one milestone to the next differs from child to child. Teaching and learning are successful when the developmental needs of each child are understood and appropriate methods employed to foster the next developmental level.

Stages of Development

Science teaching strategies have been influenced by the research of many noted child development theorists. We will explore the findings of Jean Piaget and Lev Vygotsky, two of the noted cognitive development theorists.

Jean Piaget, a Swiss psychologist, has been a major influence in promoting the theory that the ability to think and learn is itself a growing thing. Educators who accept this theory see their role as that of providing learning experiences to help children develop their mental capacity. Teachers need to think of learning as a process rather than a state; knowledge changes as cognitive systems develop. As we grow, our experiences are filtered through increasingly mature ways of thinking and ways of constructing representations of knowledge.

Piaget's research suggests four stages of identified mental development, beginning with birth: the sensorimotor stage, the preoperational stage, the concrete operational stage, and the formal operational stage. Piaget believed that all people passed through the same four stages, but not necessarily at the same rate. The attainment of formal, or abstract, thought (the highest level of development) is not achieved by most children until around the age of 11 or 12. However, to reach this final stage, children must be provided with opportunities to develop the prerequisite skills of the preceding stages. You can begin to see how important teachers' decisions—what to teach, and how to teach—are affected by a child's particular stage of development.

Inquiry-based science experiences are a vital and important part of an elementary/middle school program. It can offer students many experiences that are essential for attaining formal thought. Let's look briefly at some characteristics and scientific thinking associated with each stage of development.

Sensorimotor Stage

The first period identified by Piaget usually occurs from birth to about age 2. It is the time when children begin to learn about the world. Their intellectual activity consists of the senses interacting with the child's environment. Children in this stage are explorers and need experiences to use their sensory and motor abilities to learn

Sensorimotor-stage children need lots of opportunities to explore and manipulate objects. Children explore by using many of their senses.

basic skills and concepts. Children need lots of opportunities to explore (safely) the house and the yard. By interacting with the environment around them and with the passage of time, the young child begins to develop control of motor and sensory skills. Through these activities, they assimilate (take into the mind and comprehend) a great deal of information.

As children progress through the sensorimotor stage, they develop the ability to (1) focus on an object, (2) move toward an object in a coordinated manner, (3) manipulate an object, and (4) repeat an action. These actions reflect the development of what Piaget calls "sensorimotor schemes." Such schemes are not present at birth but are the product of time and children's interactions with their environments. Early science experiences can provide opportunities for developing the schema for further scientific thinking.

By the end of the sensorimotor stage, children have developed the concept of object permanence (something exists even when it is not there). They also learn to identify objects using the information they have acquired using such characteristics as color, shape, size, texture, and weight. It is also during this stage that children acquire the practical knowledge that such objects continue to exist even when they are out of view (object permanence).

Children in the sensorimotor stage are easily distracted by new stimuli and quickly forget original intentions. When children begin to exhibit behavior that indicates greater attention and more goal-oriented activity, and when they can initiate some action of their own, they are beginning to move out of the sensorimotor stage.

Preoperational Stage

This stage occurs approximately between the ages of 2 and 7. Children develop their language capabilities and begin to use speech to express concept knowledge. Children begin to use scientific words, such as "big" and "small," "light" and "heavy," and "long" and "short." They also portray symbolic behavior. For example, they may pantomime the actions involved in eating without actually eating. Play becomes extremely important at this stage, as it is through this symbolic play that children will form the conceptual understandings needed for symbolic letters, numerals, and science symbols.

Preoperational children are egocentric. Everything is based on what they see. They base their thinking on their own personal perspectives and experiences. They cannot see things from another's point of view; their behavior reflects a self-centeredness. This should not be interpreted as selfishness. It means that a child's understanding, or knowing, is dependent on personal experience and background. When engaging in inquiry-based science experiences, always remember to ask young children what they themselves see, not what they think someone else sees. Avoid questions like "What do you think the teacher sees?" or "Why do you think Kristy grouped her leaves the way she did?"

Preoperational children lack the ability to reverse actions mentally. For example, if water in a jar is shown to children at this stage and then frozen and thawed again while in the same container, students will not recognize it as the same substance.

During science lessons, children at this stage can experience one-to-one correspondence in shape and color by comparing. They can work on classification skills, such as putting things in logical groups according to some criteria that they establish, and can verbalize. They can also work on seriation skills, that is, putting things in a logical sequence, such as thick to thin objects or dark to light colors.

Concrete Operational Stage

This stage occurs between the ages of 7 and 12. During this stage, children typically acquire the ability to perform elementary logical operations, but only through concrete means. They are unable to engage in hypothetical reasoning but can perform mentally what has been performed physically. Because of this newly acquired ability, the concrete operational child, unlike the preoperational child, can reverse actions mentally.

During this stage, a child can be given two identical containers of juice with exactly the same amount of liquid in each. Then the juice in one of the containers can be poured into a much shorter but wider container. Ask the child, "Is there more, less, or the same amount of juice in the two containers?" A concrete operational child who has physically experienced the reverse action should be able to mentally reverse the action and reply that there is the same amount in both. If the child has not concretely experienced the reversal, she will probably reply differently. When the child is given the opportunity to experience physically the reverse action—pouring the juice from the shorter, wider container back into the original container—she can see that the amount is the same as before and equal to the other. With many experiences of this kind, children begin to develop the concept of conservation, usually in the order, number, matter, length, area, weight, and volume.

Children during this stage are busy doing. They must see, hear, feel, touch, smell, taste, or in some way utilize their senses to learn. They like to learn things firsthand, and they like to do the manipulation. Many middle-level students (grades 5 through 8) are in this stage. They are constantly in motion and represent a tremendous range of ability. Some of them will have mastered the concept of conservation and will be abstract thinkers, while others will still be concrete thinkers. For these middle-level students, as well as elementary students, science concepts at the concrete operational level should result from direct personal experience. When students can go beyond that which is empirically given, they have reached the formal or abstract thought level.

Formal or Abstract Thought

The final stage of development is called formal operations. This stage usually occurs around age 12 to adulthood. Some may reach this stage as early as 11, and others may never develop formal or abstract thought. Also, arriving at this stage does not necessarily mean that a person will automatically be able to use strategies such as proportional reasoning, isolation and control of variables, and probability thinking.

At the formal stage of development, students are capable of generating questions, designing investigations, carrying them out, and reaching conclusions independently.

Learners at this stage solve problems in a logical and systematic way. They can predict outcomes without actually trying them out.

Another noted psychologist, **Lev Vygotsky,** was developing his theory around the same time as Piaget. He proposed that the origin of our concepts of the world must be found in the early learning of such things as language, culture, and religion. Vygotsky felt that learning could not happen without the help of such people as parents, caretakers, and siblings. His theory of development places emphasis on the role of the adult or the more mature peer as an influence on children's mental development.

While Vygotsky agreed that learning was developmental, he recognized environmental forces. He proposed that just as people developed tools to help them cope with their surroundings, they also developed mental tools to help them master their behavior. He called these mental tools "signs." He viewed speech as the most important sign, followed by writing and numbering.

Vygotsky developed the concept of the *zone of proximal development (ZPD)*. This zone is the area between where the child is now in cognitive development and where he or she might go with the assistance of an adult or a person more mature than the child. He believed, like Piaget, that prior to the age of 2, development came mostly from within the child, from his or her inner maturation, and from spontaneous discoveries. After the age of 2, he felt that scaffolding of knowledge, provided by more mature learners, promoted development. He felt that good teachers presented material that was slightly challenging or ahead of the child's development. He or she might not understand it at first, but with appropriate intervention he or she would begin to construct and develop meaning. For example, a teacher might have her class on a walk and see a bird's nest in the tree. Instead of just pointing out the tree, bird, and nest and letting students construct their own knowledge, she might direct the students' attention to specific features. She would encourage them to ask questions and search for causal relationships dealing with the location of the nest, the size of the nest, and the materials used in the nest. She would eventually lead them to formulate concepts about the bird and the nest. The teacher's intervention did not put pressure on the child's development; instead, instruction supported it as it moved ahead. Concepts constructed independently and spontaneously by the children lay the foundation for the targeted scientific concepts. Teachers must be knowledgeable about each child's ZPD and provide the developmentally appropriate instruction and intervention to facilitate understanding of targeted science concepts. When children receive the appropriate intervention, they are excited and enthusiastic and participate in the learning process.

In effect, both Piaget and Vygotsky believed that children need to construct their knowledge. The major point of difference is that Piaget's followers are concerned about pressuring children, and not allowing them freedom to construct their own knowledge independently. Vygotsky's followers are worried about children being challenged and reaching their full potential. Many teachers, therefore, find that a combination of both theories provides a good developmental foundation that encourages children's interest and enthusiasm while providing mental challenge for intellectual development. Having a thorough understanding of a constructive approach to learning is of utmost importance. With a constructivist framework, many

Learners need to build their own knowledge from their own experiences.

ideas and theories can be interwoven into planning and instruction. Let's take a closer look at what the constructivist approach entails.

Definition of Constructivism

The idea that learners build their own knowledge and their own representations of knowledge from their own experience and thoughts is called *constructivism*. As the *National Science Education Standards* state, students have to construct, or build, their *own* knowledge in a "process that is individual and social." This implies that students need to play an active role in their individual learning process.

Understanding the basics of how learners (ourselves included) construct knowledge is essential to help students build accurate concepts, use process skills, and reject incorrect ideas. We know that learners build cognitive schemata, or organized patterns of behavior, as they develop cognitively, emotionally, and socially. These patterns are enlarged, connected, and multiplied through our daily routines and experiences. We record new experiences into already-existing schemata. When we take in this new information and expand patterns, we are participating in a cognitive process called *assimilation*.

Eventually, we take in new information that does not fit existing schemata or there is no more room to add new information. At this point, we need to open new schemata. When we open new schemata or split existing schemata into new ones, we are using the cognitive process called *accommodation*.

When learners accommodate, they actively seek out additional information to create the new cognitive structure. When encouraged, they ask very exacting questions, observe closely, and examine and manipulate available materials. For teachers, this is the point at which they need to learn how each child is constructing information and help him or her to have new experiences. The child can then come to his or her own conclusions as to what is happening. As stated earlier, the teacher's role is to facilitate student learning. The teacher does this by asking questions to see what schema a student currently has about a topic. In addition, the teacher looks for concepts that are not congruent with currently accepted scientific understanding. With this knowledge in hand, the teacher can provide activities that enable the students to investigate on their own and come up with their conclusions. The teacher interacts with the learner to see how they are constructing the new information and assists with the formation of sound conclusions based on the student's new experiences. Constructivists value the process of accommodation. As students work through experiences, they change their existing ideas in response to new information. By weighing new information against previous understandings and thinking about and working through discrepancies either alone or with others, they come to new understandings.

Inquiry-based science programs need to be rich in experiences. Planned science experiences need to be relevant to the learner. They need to build on past experiences and foster investigation. Teachers need to know what preconceptions and knowledge students have about a topic. Without this information, it would be difficult to build new ideas or create new schemata. With this information, different strategies and methods can be used that will continue to help students in their learning process. The next section on learners' differences presents some strategies and methods that support a constructivist approach to an inquiry-based science program.

Suggested Activity **4.1**

Observing Theorist Influence on Science Learning

1. Observe and interview some elementary teachers. Ask them to describe their theory of how children learn. Analyze their responses. Do they view children through the theories of Piaget, Vygotsky, or both? What did you learn from having this conversation?

2. Observe a science lesson. What evidence do you see of the influence of one or more theorists (e.g., Piaget, Vygotsky, or others)? What did you learn by observing this science lesson?

3. What was your earliest science experience in school? How does it compare to the type of program you see for students today? What do you attribute to the differences you noted? If the two experiences are similar, what do you attribute to the similarities? You might want to compare science teaching with a relative or friend who was in school in an earlier era. Compare and contrast his or her experience with today's classroom.

4. Observe science lessons at different age levels. Can you identify the stages of mental development as the children work on the lesson? What did you learn from this experience?

LEARNER DIFFERENCES

Multiple Intelligences

How would you define intelligence? What makes a person intelligent? Do you consider Bill Gates intelligent? How about Madonna or Jacques Cousteau? If Jacques Cousteau switched roles with Bill Gates, do you think they would still be as successful? How do you think each of these people performed when they were in school, particularly in science classes?

Intelligence testing, commonly referred to as IQ testing, produces a numeric rating based on the standard deviation of the norm group. The rating of 100 is used as the mean or average score for average intelligence. Over the past 20 years, this testing and numeric labeling has come under attack. Many people feel that intelligence is more than just a number derived from one type of test. Looking at all the ways children learn has prompted educators to look at new ways of measuring intelligence. Although the IQ test is still widely used in schools and can provide some useful data, it needs to be combined with other measures of information in order to be of help to teachers in determining how best to facilitate student learning.

Brain research over the last two decades has led to a variety of alternative ways to look at the concept of intelligence. Robert Sternberg's (1990, 1996) research indicates that intelligence is the ability to know your own strengths and weaknesses so that you can react intuitively, creatively, and constructively when faced with new experiences. Therefore, being "street smart" and "book smart" may be equally important.

Howard Gardner (1983b), of Harvard University, defines the nature of intelligence as the ability to (1) use a skill, (2) fashion an artifact, or (3) solve a problem in a way that is valued by the particular culture. Gardner's theory is developed around two fundamental propositions: first, intelligence is not fixed. We all have the capacity to change or influence the intelligence level of each other. Second, there is just not one way to be smart but rather multiple ways. Every person has a unique pattern of multiple intelligences.

Gardner has identified eight specific intelligences: verbal/linguistic, bodily/kinesthetic, logical/mathematical, naturalist, visual/spatial, interpersonal, musical/rhythmic, and intrapersonal (see Figure 4.1).

FIGURE 4.1

Musical/Rythmic

Verbal/Linguistic:
Talking

Bodily/Kinesthetic:
Movement, Coordinated

Intrapersonal:
Reflective, Thinking

**MULTIPLE
INTELLIGENCES**

Logical/Mathematical:
Reasoning, Problem Solving

Interpersonal:
Communicative, Cooperative

Spacial:
Imaginative, Drawing, Spatial

Naturalist:
Sensitive to flora & fauna,
Classifies Species

Assessing students using the eight multiple intelligences should be done for only specific learning purposes. The information gained can be used to assist teachers in determining how to approach a student. Just as identifying a single IQ number for a child does not help the learning process, identifying one strong intelligence in one assessment does not help the learning process. There is no fixed score to achieve when assessing a student's intelligences; rather, a profile should be developed that will indicate areas that are strong as well as areas to be strengthened. The eight intelligences are not meant to be related to one another. Also, a profile can change over time, with an especially dramatic change from ages 10 to 20. In determining areas that are stronger than others, it is helpful to develop a rubric that will help determine exactly which areas are stronger than others. Take a moment and assess your own profile using the rubric in Figure 4.2. You will find that you place yourself high in certain areas and lower in others. This determination will not tell you *how **smart you are;*** rather, it will show *how **you are smart.*** Your profile will be unique and different from others, showing your personal abilities and talents. Having knowledge of your own profile of intelligences can make you aware of techniques you may be using that may accommodate some of your students while possibly alienating others who do not have those areas of strength. It is important to know your own preferences. By knowing your areas of strength, you can begin a conscious effort to expand your profile to respond to student diversity.

FIGURE 4.2

Informal Personal Profile

Verbal/Linguistic

High - Low
(5)   (1)

- Usually think in words
- Learn best through reading, writing, and discussing
- Communicate effectively
- Spell easily
- Have a good vocabulary

Interpersonal

High - Low
(5)   (1)

- Make and maintain friends easily
- Sensitive to others' moods
- Leader and organizer
- Resolve conflict
- Learn best when interacting with others

Musical/Rhythmic

High - Low
(5)   (1)

- Good sense of rhythm and melody
- Enjoy singing, humming, and rap
- Listen to music even when working
- Read and write music
- Play instrument or sing

Logical/Mathematical

High - Low
(5)   (1)

- Good with numbers, patterns, and algorithms
- Learn by appeal to logic
- Like numbers and math
- Enjoy solving logic problems

Bodily/Kinesthetic

High - Low
(5)   (1)

- Unite body and mind for physical performance
- Coordinated
- Use gestures and body language
- Like "hands-on" activities
- Enjoy acting and role playing
- Like dancing and athletics
- Take things apart and fix them

Visual/Spatial

High - Low
(5)   (1)

- Think in pictures and images
- Good with spatial relations
- Enjoy painting, drawing, and sculpting
- Learn through visuals
- Eye for detail and color

Naturalist

High - Low
(5)   (1)

- Keen awareness of the natural world
- Discriminate natural and nonnatural items
- Good at sorting and classifying content
- Good observational skills
- Garden or care for pets or animals

Intrapersonal

High - Low
(5)   (1)

- Aware of own feelings
- Need time to process
- Formulate own ideas and reflect on learning
- Strong opinions and beliefs
- Like quiet time alone
- Introspective

For each area in Figure 4.2, read the description and then rank yourself, with a 5 being most like you and a 1 representing something you might find difficult or usually avoid.

Compare your profile with others around you. Do you see areas of similarity or differences? What does this profile say about your teaching style? How can you build on your strong intelligences while working on the weaker areas?

Many science programs and textbooks rely heavily on the linguistic and logical mathematical intelligences, making science difficult for students who do not have strengths in these areas. In planning science experiences, it is important to plan activities that match each child's strength as well as activities that will develop areas that are not very strong. For example, a learner who is high in visual/spatial but average in logical/mathematical and low in intrapersonal areas may have a difficult time writing up a science experiment or reflecting in a science journal. However, with a visual/spatial strength, that same student may be able to make a graphic interpretation of the science experiment, thereby developing the concepts and the necessary skills of reflecting.

The use of multiple intelligences is another tool that teachers can use with other strategies and techniques. Clearly, understanding how students' minds are different from one another can enhance the teacher's role in helping students use their minds well. The more variety of activities you teach with and offer to your students, the greater chance they have of succeeding. Making a conscious effort to present information and to introduce concepts to students in a variety of intelligences can increase student learning and motivation.

In addition to looking at ways we can teach and learn using multiple intelligences, there are other factors that account for learner differences that we will look at in the next section.

Learning Styles

Just as everyone has his or her unique combination of intelligences, everyone has his or her unique combination of learning styles. As early as 1927, Carl Jung documented different ways that people perceived (sensation vs. intuition), the way people made decisions (logical vs. imaginative), and how active people were while interacting (extrovert vs. introvert).

Since 1927, there have been a growing number of different learning style theorists who have developed numerous learning style profiles that assess many different areas. Some models emphasize personality dimensions and look at the way that information is acquired and integrated on the basis of basic personalities. These models include Witkin's (1954) construct of field dependence/field independences, the Myers-Briggs Type Indicator (Myers, 1962), measuring extroversion versus introversion, sensing versus intuition, thinking versus feeling, and judging versus perceptions and 4-MAT (McCarthy, 1996), which focuses on four learning preferences that each student performs during the course of several days. Other theorists have focused on preferences for different types of learning environments. The learning style model of Dunn and Dunn (1978) focuses on 55 different elements to consider in the student's environment that will facilitate learning. Factors such as the degree of lighting, the temperature in the room, and the type of seating arrangements all contribute to individual differences in the learning process. The learning style inventories mentioned previously are models with reliable, valid instrumentation and have a strong research base. Teachers should be aware that not all learning style models have been researched, so they need to be cautious when using them with students. As a beginning teacher, it is advisable that you use models that have been validated by research.

As a teacher, you will encounter many different students with many different learning styles. When dealing with students one to one, it is advantageous to use a student's preferred learning style. When dealing with students in a science classroom setting, it is virtually impossible to use every single learning style with every student. What you can do is offer variety and choice and maintain diversity in your teaching style. Accommodating styles of learning can result in improved attitudes toward learning and an increase in productivity, achievement, and creativity.

Brain Research and Brain-Based Learning

Knowing that we are intelligent in many different ways and that we have unique styles of learning emphasizes the need to adjust our classroom strategies and techniques that work with the brain, not against it. Medical and cognitive research is presenting new information about how the brain works almost on a daily basis. Understanding the complexity of the brain and how all its layers of organization work together to handle memory, learning, emotion, and consciousness is encouraging many educators to shift their paradigms about teaching and learning. The challenge for those of us in the classroom is to use this information to enhance learning for our students.

Today's research promotes the concept that the brain has a virtually inexhaustible capacity to learn and that it comes equipped with a set of exceptional features. For science educators, these features can be extremely helpful as we look to build a constructivist inquiry-based science classroom. For example, Caine and Caine's book *Making Connections: Teaching and the Human Brain* (1994) summarizes brain-based learning as the brain having the following features:

- Ability to detect patterns and to make approximations
- Ability to self-correct and learn from experience by way of analysis of external data and self-reflection
- Phenomenal capacity for various types of memory
- Capacity to process many inputs at once
- Endless capacity to create

These concepts are extremely compatible to a constructivist approach. As students are learning by doing, they are weighing new information against their previous understanding to construct new meaning. They are detecting the patterns they see and coming to new understandings. They can see, touch, feel, and discuss their observations, creating many types of memory related to the scientific concept being explored. This model of teaching suggests that learning is open ended, connected, and influenced by context and the cognitive schema of the learner. Working with students in the old "factory-like, assembly-line school," where one lesson and one way was supposed to work for all students, can no longer serve today's needs. Instead, we need to provide teachers with the information and tools to see learning as facilitating a diverse group of students to construct and experience meaning that is relational and ongoing.

Curriculum and instruction that are responsive to individual learning need to be developed. Classrooms need to become differentiated; that is, classrooms need to be places where teachers are responsive to students' varying levels of readiness, interests, and learning styles. Brain research suggests three principles that support this need: **Learning environments must feel emotionally safe for learning to occur, appropriate levels of challenge encourage learning, and each brain needs to make its own meaning of ideas and skills.** A classroom following these three principles might have some of the following characteristics:

- Students and teachers who appreciate all their differences and work to accept and integrate these differences respectfully
- Students using essential skills to work on open-ended problems that clarify key concepts and principles
- Teachers and students using stress-reducing techniques in the classroom
- Teachers and students engaging in ongoing assessment and adjustment
- Teachers and students using a range of instructional and management strategies
- Teachers encouraging a variety of choices to use in problem solving
- Students and teachers working collaboratively so that everyone grows
- Teachers allowing students options about what and how to study
- Teachers balancing group and individual norms

Eric Jensen, noted author on brain research, tells us (1995, 1998) that the discoveries about the brain are exciting and full of pitfalls. While there is a small percentage that can be applied to education, a majority of the research is disease oriented. He also warns that the research does not "prove" anything. It suggests activities and strategies we can try to increase the probability of success. In order to effectively use what information is available, Jensen's three-step approach is helpful. First, become "consumer literate" in the field of brain research. Learn the vocabulary, terms, and noted researchers. Second, use some of the ideas and conduct some action research. Teachers have a working laboratory every day that they are with their students; start small, take notes, and look at your results. Finally, share this information with students, parents, and other staff members and incorporate changes that make a difference.

Equity

Imagine that you have just been given an assignment in a science class to write an essay about a scientist you admire. It can be an astronaut, a famous medical researcher, an inventor, a biologist—your choice. Who will you pick? Share with a neighbor. Most likely, your choice was male and probably a white male.

In the field of science, minority and gender gaps are quite pronounced. The National Science Foundation Data Brief in 1999 reported that science and engineering doctorates earned proportionately to their representation in the U.S. population: 36% earned by women, 7% by blacks, 3% by Hispanics, and 0.4% by American Indians. Equity is an issue. Recent school reform mandates emphasize that all our children need to be successful and need to be offered the same opportunities for success.

What is "equity"? Webster (1983) defines equity as a freedom from bias or favoritism. The Council for Educational Development and Research suggests that there are at least four concepts to consider when speaking about equity in education:

- Equity as access to schooling
- Equity as equal distribution of resources
- Equity as access to learning
- Equity as a vision

The National Committee on Science Education Standards and Assessment defines equity as inclusion in its goal of "science for all" and adds that "various styles of learning and differing sources of motivation" must also be part of the equity considerations. Perhaps the definition itself is not as important as striving to reach the concept. Using instructional strategies that embrace all learners and promote equity is a way to meet this need. Science topics such as weather, electricity, or genetics, in themselves, do not promote or detract the issue of equity. Rather, it is the planning and the implementation of each activity that can promote a learning environment that builds on diverse populations and encourages active participation from traditionally silenced groups. These strategies must engage students' thoughts, acknowledge their culture, and provide support for future generations. For example, a lesson focusing on predicting weather could include discussion on the variety of methods used by different ethnic/cultural groups prior to modern weather instruments and technology. Many elders in the early African, Asian, Native American, and Hispanic cultures were known for their ability to predict the weather. Infusing science content with information that would add relevance or information about a particular ethnic or gender group is also a good strategy. For example, the following women and their accomplishments could easily be integrated into many science classes:

Mae Jemison (1956–), physician, astronaut
Chien-Shiumg Wu (1915–), physicist, first woman physics professor

Jane Goodall (1931–), researcher on chimpanzees

Liz Rodriquez (1953–), mathematician

Margaret Lemone (1946–), atmospheric scientist (thunderstorms)

You will be learning many specific instructional strategies throughout this book. Embedded in each of these, you should remember to include (1) avoiding stereotypes in spoken and written materials; (2) maintaining high expectations for all students, (3) giving specific, corrective feedback to all students; (4) using strategies that promote active participation of all students; and (5) making your science curriculum culturally relevant.

Students With Special Needs

As we have been addressing learner differences, it is clear to see that all students are indeed special. However, there are many children that have needs beyond the average child. To meet the needs of "special" children, the federal government has enacted laws that require individual states to legislate laws that provide direction for education of handicapped students. Originally titled Public Law 94-142 (PL 94-142) and 99-457, provisions were provided that eliminated the exclusion of children with disabilities from education. This law outlined in great detail the rights and role of parents in determining the kinds of educational and therapeutic services their children can receive in programs in which public funding is provided.

In 1997, Congress reauthorized the law, and school districts today are obligated to comply with the statutory requirements of the Individuals with Disabilities Education Act Amendments of 1997 (IDEA). The amendments, which were effective on May 11, 1999, total 266 pages in the Federal Resister. You can pursue the entire document by accessing the following Web sites: http://gcs.ed.gov/fedreg.htm or http://www.ed.gov/news.html.

In effect, the law stipulates that a "free public education" exists for all children with a disability aged birth through 21. According to sections 300.530 to 300.536, a disability can be mental retardation; a hearing impairment, including deafness; a speech or language impairment; a visual impairment, including blindness; serious emotional disturbance; an orthopedic impairment; autism; traumatic brain injury; another health impairment; a specific learning disability; deaf-blindness; or multiple disabilities. Special needs students are also those who, by reason thereof, need special education and related services.

Good teachers have always been responsive to the individual needs of the children they teach. However, with mainstreaming and inclusion programs being instituted in many schools, teachers need to modify the environment, materials, methods, concepts, and assessment for the broad spectrum of special needs students that will be in their classrooms. Mainstreaming and inclusion programs place special needs students in regular education classrooms. Often, disabled students are provided additional assistance by having a special education teacher or aide accompany them to class. When this occurs, the classroom teacher maintains the major responsibility for the learning environment and instruction in the class. The special teacher's responsibility is to provide support for the disabled student.

As many regular classroom teachers are not prepared or have not been trained extensively to work with special needs students, it is important to be aware of the following mandates and terminology:

- Parents must be informed about the possible evaluation of a child. This must be done in writing and in the parents' native language. The parent must give permission at every step of the process. All tests, files, and notes are open to the parent for review.

- Students who are identified as needing special education must have an Individual Education Program (IEP) approved by the parents. This IEP includes objectives that will be met by the educational program, materials to be used, times for implementation of services, and the name of the person responsible for implementing and evaluating the program. The IEP must be evaluated yearly.

- Each child is to be placed in the "least restricted environment." The least restricted environment may vary from child to child. The intent for this mandate is to allow all students the same opportunities. Therefore, a student with a handicap may not be restricted to an isolated place or separate classroom without first being given the opportunity and interventions necessary to be successful in the regular classroom with other students.

- Due process is guaranteed for every child and family. This mandate allows parents the right to sue the district if they perceive the child has been inappropriately placed.

- Assessments must be done with evaluation tools that are nondiscriminatory in terms of race and ethnicity. A child must be tested in his or her native language if he or she is non-English- or a limited-English-speaking student.

- There are provisions for a surrogate to be appointed in cases when a parent refuses to participate or is unable to participate.

As is true with many federal laws, changes occur over time. It is important that the regular classroom teacher keep updated on these changes.

The category "specific learning disability" is a challenge to diagnose as well as treat. Parents are often unwilling to label a child with a learning disability for fear that he or she will be singled out by other children as well as by teachers. Labels under this category can include attention deficit disorder (ADD), attention deficit hyperactive disorder (ADHD), and students who have been born to mothers who were substance abusers.

Working with students with learning disabilities may be challenging for a new teacher. There are many resources available to you, and you should feel comfortable consulting with those individuals who have been specifically trained to work with a disabled student who may be placed in your class. As was mentioned in Chapter 3 issues of safety should be thoroughly thought about and proactively planned. Using an inquiry-based science program can be motivating to many students who do not function in traditional classrooms. On the other hand, some types of disabilities may interfere with a child's ability to make progress, and you may have to step in and be more directive. Another critical element is that all educators involved on behalf of the disabled student learn how to effectively work together to benefit the student's educational, social, psychological, and physical needs.

Many of the strategies suggested in this chapter are helpful in dealing with special needs students. Involving parents in their children's program can be helpful for both parties. It is important to keep a perspective on the needs of all involved when interacting with parents of special needs students. Just as we know that each child is unique, we also know that each set of parents and each teacher will be experiencing unique stresses, resources, and coping strategies in educating a student with disabilities. As the teacher, you can provide practical recommendations and programs that support and maximize each child's potential.

The Gifted Child

Recent research has brought to light the special needs of another group of "special children": those considered to be *gifted*. Although we can often describe certain characteristics that seem evident in special children we have thought to be gifted, the term is difficult to define because of the various types of giftedness we all perceive. As we know, Gardner and his multiple intelligences research states that all children can be gifted according to certain criteria. For many educational institutions, giftedness has come to mean those students whose performance is significantly above average in intellectual and creative areas. They are students who are usually quick to catch on, begin to read and write early, and may have a more sophisticated vocabulary than the other students in the room.

Some students' giftedness is seen through special talent in art, music, or another creative area. Many times for these students, the traditional classroom and class work can be extremely frustrating. These students can process information and share this information in ways other than writing and speaking if given the opportunity. Once again, the strategies and methods suggested in this chapter are helpful in designing programs for these students. Also, an inquiry-based science program can provide the opportunity for these students to advance their skills and knowledge at a pace that is more in line with their learning ability.

Gifted students need a wide variety of challenging and rewarding work along with developing a healthy attitude about school and learning. In some instances, students may be academically gifted but socially and emotionally may need supportive guidance. Just like all the different learners in your class, they will need exposure to novel, diverse, and enriching activities that move them forward in their educational pursuits.

Perhaps some of the strategies you mentioned in this activity will be explained in further detail in this chapter. Perhaps you will see strategies listed here that were on your list of those you wanted to find out more about. Perhaps you will be introduced to some new strategies that you can incorporate with your previous learning.

Suggested Activity 4.2

Adapting Science Curricular to Meet Learner Needs

1. With a partner, design introductory activities that you could use to start a unit on simple machines that addresses the use of multiple intelligences. Present these to the rest of the class.

2. In small learning groups, select one of the researched learning style inventories and administer it to the members of your class. If several learning groups are involved, compose a matrix of the various learning style inventories and list their commonalities, differences, and how they could be useful in the classroom.

3. There are many research studies, articles, and books available on recent brain research. Select one and share findings with your class members. Relate the research to how it will promote effective science teaching and learning.

4. Find a multicultural trade book that is linked to a science concept and prepare a lesson for your class.

5. Interview a classroom teacher and a special education teacher about successful strategies to use with students with disabilities.

METHODS AND STRATEGIES

Suggested Activity 4.3

Identifying Strategies That Promote Inquiry-Based Science

In groups of four to six people, complete the following process:

1. Use "post-it" notes or index cards and individually brainstorm two to five strategies or methods you think would promote a constructivist inquiry-based experience for learners (you will have 5 minutes).

2. Share your individual ideas and cluster them into similar categories, posting them on chart paper. Finally, write the names of your categories above the "post-it" notes or index cards.

3. Rotate clockwise around the tables, viewing what other groups have done.
4. Return to your table and discuss the following with your small group:
    *What items need clarification or elaboration?
    *What strategies did you find interesting or intriguing?

    *Were the ideas new to you?

    *Were any ideas mentioned that you would like more information about?

In any event, you will be "constructing" your knowledge about various ways to organize inquiry-based science experiences that help students construct and retain useful concepts, develop effective thinking skills, and implement lessons that apply scientific concepts to the "real world" of the students.

The Learning Cycle

The learning cycle is viewed by many constructivist educators to be one strategy to assist learners in constructing knowledge. It is a tool that helps teachers organize science experiences so that students see science "as a process of inquiry rather than as a body of knowledge."

The learning cycle was first introduced in the early 1960s as the strategy used in the Science Curriculum Improvement Study (SCIS; sponsored by the National Science Foundation), a complete program that focuses on giving students a hands-on approach to life and physical science concepts. There are essentially three phases to the learning cycle. Numerous name changes have occurred over time, but the essence of each cycle has remained the same. For our purposes, we will use the terms exploration, concept introduction, and concept application.

The first phase starts the process of learning by allowing for free exploration and is called the stage of *exploration*. Students learn through their own actions and interactions. This is their time to manipulate and interact with one another. Students exploring should be able to raise questions and verbalize conflicting or inadequate prior knowledge. This analysis may lead to the students' generating alternate ways to view, test, or hypothesize their ideas. There can be debate and analysis either alone or among students.

During this phase, the teacher remains the "guide on the side." While in the background, the teacher will observe and occasionally insert a comment or question. The teacher's knowledge about the students' stage of development facilitates the choice of materials and how they are presented to the students during this exploratory phase. For example, in an early elementary classroom conducting an exploratory lesson about feathers, the teacher might set out a variety of feathers, a

FIGURE 4.3   Learning Cycle Beginning Stage: Exploration

magnifying glass, and a microscope (young children really get excited about using a microscope). Students are told to explore the materials and to share with one another what they are discovering. In a later elementary class, students could be given a box with 1.5-volt batteries, a few pieces of wire, a few bulb holders, some 1.5-volt light bulbs, a light switch or two, and a 1.5-volt electric motor. Using very few directions, instruct the children to figure out something they did not know before they explored the contents of the box. Students are able to connect what they are doing in the classroom with what they already know. They are able to share their discoveries and conceptualize their own information. These kinds of activities promote the first phase of exploration.

During the next phase, *concept introduction,* terms for the patterns that students have discovered can be introduced. At this point, the teacher can begin direct instruction by eliciting the information students discovered during their explorations. If appropriate data can begin to be collected and children can record information, the direct instruction from the teacher can be in the form of explanations, print materials, guest speakers, use of technology, and other available resources. For example, the children exploring the feathers might notice that there are "pointy" ends or something holding the feathers together. At that time, the teacher can introduce the terms "shaft," "barb," and "barbules," as well as "pliant."

Students could classify different sizes, shapes, and textures of feathers. Students could separate feathers into down or contour classifications, and together they could explore which parts of the bird would have downy feathers and which would have contour feathers. In the later elementary classroom where children were exploring the batteries, wires, motors, and bulbs, the terms "open," "closed," "short circuit," "series circuits," and "parallel circuits" could be developed. As students share their explorations, the appropriate label could be given to the students and reproduced in a schematic drawing on the board or in individual student journals.

In the final phase of the learning cycle, *concept application,* students apply the new term or thinking pattern to additional examples. This phase allows the learner the opportunity to integrate and evaluate his or her new ideas with old ideas to form additional ideas. This application can be directed by the teacher, by the student, or by both. In our example of the early elementary classroom, students could identify different types of feathers as belonging to different types of birds. Children could place down feathers and contour feathers on the appropriate body parts of the bird and identify their function. In the later elementary classroom, students could be given different drawings of various arrangements of batteries and bulbs and asked to predict and then prove which drawings were accurately wired and which ones were incorrect. Students could also generate ways "short circuiting" occurs in everyday life (e.g., kites in electric lines or metal placed in wall sockets). This would make their concept of electricity meaningful and related to their life experiences.

The learning cycle is a flexible instructional model. Teaching all lessons in this manner may not be appropriate. There are times when exploration and observation might be the whole lesson. Some lessons need more, and data collection and interpretation are important. It is also important to remember Piaget's stages of development and realize that the children's view of the world are not the same as the teacher's. Remember the students are constructing their perceptions from their own experiences. Misconceptions occur frequently and need to be dealt with developmentally and with many experiences. The learning cycle is one tool to use that meshes with Piaget's theories of cognitive development.

Cooperative Learning

Cooperative learning is a research-based strategy to help organize small-group interaction and instruction and differs from traditional small-group work. By working constructively in a group, learners can share their understandings in their own words, expose any misconceptions, strengthen concepts, and help one another succeed.

Cooperative learning groups differ from traditional small-group work in some specific ways. Simply placing students in groups is not doing cooperative learning. There are four key principles that should be evident when using cooperative learning: positive interdependence, individual accountability, use of social/collaborative skills, and group processing.

Positive Interdependence

Students must believe that they need one another in order to succeed. This belief can be created by having two goals for each group member, making sure that they complete their task, and ensuring that all the other group members understand the task. Sharing resources and assigning particular roles to certain group members also encourage positive interdependence. By using activities that build a sense of team, students can develop respect for one another and the ability to work together so that all can succeed. Students need to learn to promote one another's learning through encouragement and assistance and face-to-face interaction. For this reason, it is advisable that group size be kept small, ranging from two to six members. There are many inquiry-based science experiences that effectively promote the work of students in pairs or small groups.

Individual Accountability

Student performance should be assessed individually within the group. Learners need to know that while they are working in a group, they are ultimately responsible for their own learning. By using individual accountability, group grades are eliminated, and each student receives specific feedback related to his or her level of development or accomplishment. This eliminates some of the concern over "gifted" students being punished if they are in a group with learners who are not at their level. Positive interdependence can still be encouraged through the use of joint rewards, such as team improvement points. This can also be encouraged by allowing students to work alone and then bring their work to the group. This is an extremely important concept for constructivist activities. Encouraging students to construct their own meaning first and then sharing with a group allows for each student to construct his or her meaning on the basis of personal experiences and prior knowledge.

Social/Collaborative Skills Taught

Many children, as well as adults, have not had learning experiences that have taught them skills in leadership, communication, decision making, trust building, and conflict resolution. Without developing these social skills in students, the benefits of cooperative learning will be diminished. Since we do not have the innate ability to effectively interact with one another, we should practice skills such as listening, praising, encouraging, paraphrasing, and summarizing. When students have practiced and learned these skills, they will be able to be productive members of a group. These skills are extremely important as students are sharing new learning, discussing previous misconceptions, and building and expanding existing knowledge.

Group Processing Skills

Groups should periodically assess how well they are working together. This can be done in a reflection time when members discuss productive and nonproductive behavior of individuals and/or of the group. Once the reflection has been completed, plans should be designed to correct the inappropriate actions and reinforce the appropriate ones.

In the traditional system of cooperative learning, there is encouragement to assign roles to members within a group so that there is a division of labor. In a constructivist inquiry-based learning experience, you might want to modify this suggestion. Remember in constructivist learning that the emphasis is on each child doing the activities so that all the children can become immersed in the process of doing and developing the process and inquiry skills needed to construct their own concepts. However, before students can assume all those roles, they should have specific practice, modeling, and feedback about each of them.

During that instructional time, care should be taken to rotate the roles so that all students have the opportunity to experience each one of them. It is a good idea to use activities that are not content specific when teaching the various roles, such as recorder, materials manager, leader, reporter, facilitator, and so on. Once the skills needed to accomplish these tasks have been internalized, students will be able to transfer that knowledge to tasks they will perform when they are placed in a group situation in a specific content area.

Another area of cooperative learning that might need to be altered from time to time is the grouping pattern of placing students heterogeneously in groups. A few studies have found that students in science classes scored better in reasoning skills and content achievement when grouped homogeneously. On the other hand, research studies have shown the opposite. Once again, the teacher, as decision maker, needs to carefully consider the complexities of the learning cycle with other learning strategies to make the best choices for the situation and his or her students.

There are various cooperative learning structures. The most used and researched are Student Team Achievement Divisions (STAD) and Teams-Games-Tournament (TGT). Basically, they are similar in design, the major difference being that STAD uses individual quizzes at the end of the unit and TGT uses a tournament game at the end. However, TGT can be followed up with an individual quiz at the end after the tournament play.

STAD and TGT. Prior to beginning cooperative learning, the teacher needs to do the following preparatory work: presentation of material to be studied, formation of student teams, and a base score for each student.

Material. Information in STAD and TGT is presented to the students in a traditional direct instruction format. Of course, this presentation can include audio or visual materials, but the idea here is mainly to give students the resources and information they need to be able to conduct their own work study sessions.

Teams. Teams should be composed of three or four students and should be a cross section of the class in terms of academic performance, gender, and race and ethnicity. The function of the team is to work with and prepare one another to take the quiz at the end of the learning experience. The teams work together by problem solving, comparing answers, correcting misconceptions, studying data, conducting investigations, and any other technique that they or the teacher designs to learn presented concepts and information. You can put students into groups by ranking them from highest to lowest in terms of past performance and then assign groups so that each team has high-, average-, and lower-performing students. For the purposes of demonstration, look at the following list of 17 students and their group assignment:

Student's Name (by rank ordering from high performing to low performing)	Team Assignment Number
Kristy	1
Jeff	2
Nick	3
Jordan	4
Shea	4
Bill	3
Lizzy	2
Eric	1
Sandy	Teacher Decision
Deanne	1
Dan	2
Dorin	3
Sheila	4
Vern	4
Dave	3
Lorraine	2
Steve	1

Because we wanted four teams, four people on a team, and four teams in the total class, we used the numbers 1 to 4. If you have 32 students in the class and wanted eight teams of four, you would use the numbers 1 to 8. Starting at the top of the list, we numbered the students 1, 2, 3, and 4; went to the bottom of the list and numbered the students 1, 2, 3, and 4; and then continued to number to the middle of the list. This method ensures equitable groups according to ability. The leftover student can be placed with any team, making for a five-member team. (Their scores at the end will be pro-rated for five members instead of four.) Once the groups have been formed and are equal in ability, the teacher needs to check for gender and ethnic and race balance. **(Students do not see this list. It is only for teacher planning.)**

Base, or Individual Improvement, Scores. The concept with base scores is to assign each student a goal that he or she can reach by working and performing a little bit better than in the past. Each student can contribute 0 to 10 improvement points to the total team score. They earn these points by doing better on their quiz than their base score. The base scores represent students' average scores from past work. For example, Kristy has probably been getting mostly 90s or above in her work, so her base score would be 90. Lorraine, on the other hand, has probably been receiving scores closer to the 50s, so her base score might be 52. In order for each of them to contribute improvement points to her team, she will have to improve her quiz score to exceed her base score. If Lorraine scores 85 on her quiz, she will have earned an excellent individual grade and will also be able to contribute 10 points (because she improved 10+ points) to the collective improvement points for her team. The rule is that no student can earn less than 0 or more than 10 improvement points. The individual scores are the grade he or she receives on the quiz, and the improvement points go toward his or her team points to determine which team was most effective in working with one another. There should be some sort of celebration or recognition for teams that achieve the criteria that have been set by the teacher. For example, the teacher may want to award the teams by setting the following goal:

Total Team Improvement Points	Award
20	Good Team
25	Awesome Team
30+	Quality Team

You can provide recognition in a variety of ways. You may want to have certificates to honor students. You could take pictures and display winning team members. If you have a newsletter, mentioning the winning teams and any 10-point winner is also very motivating. If you want, you can use extrinsic rewards, but more important here is the process of rewarding success on the basis of cooperation.

Students should be aware of how the team improvement scores work. It should be emphasized that the process is to try to give everyone a minimum score that he or she can beat that has been based on past practice. (Using real-world examples like bowling averages, batting scores, or golf handicap scores usually helps students understand the concept.) It is important that students see how valuable every team member is and that everyone on the team can contribute the same amount to the team improvement points because everyone has his or her own individual scores to beat. It is not necessary to post student base scores. Inform students that you have averaged their previous scores to determine their base score. As the students become more familiar and sure of the process, they can keep track of their own base score and watch them get higher and higher. Remember that the student's grade is not determined by averaging the team scores. Each student receives his or her own score on the basis of his or her own quiz. This eliminates much of the concern that some students, as well as parents, have about only one person doing the work for the entire group. If you wish, you can add "extra points" to student individual scores if you feel that the members of the team have worked really well together. If your school has grades for effort or citizenship, you may want to use the improvement scores in this area. The important concept is to reward cooperation, have individual students still be accountable for their own learning, and allow students the opportunity to practice the real-life skill of working with others who learn differently.

Once the students have been instructed and practiced their group skills and you have set up the groups and the base scores, you are ready to begin. STAD consists of the following steps:

The use of good questioning increases student involvement, assesses knowledge, and promotes higher-level thinking.

Teach	Present the lesson.
Team Study	Students work in teams on assignments.
Test	Students take individual quizzes.
Team Recognition	Team scores are computed and a celebration is held (students also receive their own individual score).

TGT would follow the same process, but in place of a test, a tournament would be held. If you are interested in trying this approach, you can find the directions for setting up the tournament in the works of Robert E. Slavin (1977) or Johnson and Johnson (1999).

In addition to the formal structures that have been developed, there are some simple cooperative structures that can be used in the classroom that encourage co-operation and keep students active in their learning. Spencer Kagan (1989/90) has identified at least 52 such structures. These structures are tools that work together with multiple intelligences and different learning style models. They promote active learning for the student. For example, the co-op structure called *Inside/Outside Circle* has students in concentric circles rotate to face a partner to answer the teacher's questions or those of the partner. Another structure, called *Numbered Heads Together,* has students huddle to make sure that all can respond. Each student has a number, the teacher picks that number, and the student with that number responds. Another version, titled *Paired Heads Together,* has the students in pairs huddle to make sure that both can respond. An "A" or "B" is called, and, the student representing that letter responds. For further information, you can access Kagan's work at http://www.KaganCoopLearn.com.

Questioning Strategies

Effective questioning is an art. In order to help you acquire the skills involved in effective questioning it is necessary to examine the role of questioning in the learning process. With a partner, discuss the various reasons teachers ask questions. When you and your partner have compiled a list, find another pair of students and compare your lists. Save your newly compiled list, as you may want to add to it as you read through this section.

Questioning is one of the oldest and most common teaching strategies. To be effective, a teacher uses the method of inquiry to guide the students in the appropriate direction of their investigations and thinking. Planning and reflecting about questions before, during, and after a planned science experience helps improve teacher effectiveness and student thinking. The use of good questioning strategies increases student involvement, preaccesses prior knowledge, assesses student understanding during the science experience (check for understanding), assesses knowledge, encourages higher-level thinking, checks for understanding of directions, and fosters creativity, just to mention a few.

During the course of any inquiry-based learning experience, teachers and students will be asking a variety of questions for a variety of purposes. It has been said that teachers in elementary and middle school ask between 64 and 348 questions a day. There are two broad types of questions: convergent and divergent. Convergent questions usually have only one answer and are content specific and seek right or wrong answers. During this type of questioning, thinking is usually at a low level, requiring students simply to repeat information that was provided. They may include questions like, What is the definition the book gives of an open circuit? or What causes the molecules of a liquid to move? Many objective tests and standardized test items emphasize the convergent level of fact and recall. Content questions are necessary for student understanding and thinking; however, questions need to go beyond the low level of recall. When questions go beyond the low level, they are called divergent.

Divergent questions are open ended and have many acceptable responses. Divergent questions encourage creativity, independent, and critical thinking. They promote reflection, generalizations, and inferences. In addition, divergent questions promote discussion and exchanges of ideas—both higher-level thinking processes. Examples include What might have caused that? Or, how can we find out if heat affects the time it takes for a substance to dissolve in water? The use of divergent questioning strategies connects thinking to knowledge. Divergent questions encourage students to integrate the "pieces or bits" of information they have been learning.

Careful planning will help you decide when to use divergent or convergent questions. Both types are useful to use in an inquiry-based planned science experience. Convergent questions can be valuable if they help students analyze a situation, find or correct an error, or clarify a misconception or point of confusion. Divergent questioning strategies fit the learning cycle, as they encourage students to own the process, expand their prior knowledge, and build new schemata that are meaningful and different for each learner.

In addition to the two types of questions, there are various classification systems for describing levels of thinking and questioning. You are probably most familiar with **Bloom's Taxonomy of Objectives (1956).** The taxonomy is used both in the planning of lesson objectives and in designing questions to encourage higher-level thinking. The six sequential levels provide the teacher with a framework for formulating questions that will encourage students to engage in a specific level of thinking in responding. Table 4.1 presents each of the six levels of thinking as identified by Bloom. The intended student behavior for each level and some examples of questions that could elicit that intellectual behavior are also included.

Bloom's six levels represent a hierarchy. In order for a person to be able to think at higher levels, he or she must have the basic information to think with. Students need to have the facts, comprehend them, and then apply them to new situations. But the learning should not stop there. Once they have the preceding information, students can then analyze, synthesize, and evaluate if given the opportunity and encouragement. The thinking must be encouraged in a planned science experience through stimulating activities, planned higher-level questioning, and listening to responses to understand how students are constructing information so that they can be guided in their learning. Beware that asking questions designed to elicit thinking at a specific level does not mean that the learner will automatically respond at the level.

You must consider the students' prior knowledge and developmental levels when you are planning your questions. As a teacher, you must provide many opportunities for students to experience, gather, organize, analyze, and evaluate information. These planned science experiences provide the necessary schemata that students need to draw on when responding to questions. Without these kinds of experiences, students are unable to operate at the higher levels of thinking. Young children especially need many concrete experiences prior to being asked higher-level questions. Then, when asked these questions, they should relate directly to the concrete inquiry-based science experiences. Another important factor to remember is that, when asking higher-level questions at all levels, students need **time** to formulate their thoughts.

Research has documented that it takes 5 minutes longer to respond to higher-level questions. Often teachers, as well as students, become uncomfortable with periods of silence. Practice waiting for students to respond to questions. One of the strategies suggested by Mary Budd Rowe is to count 15 seconds to yourself before saying anything else or calling on students. Increased wait time can lead to a more effective discussion and higher-level responses and, therefore, should be part of the overall questioning strategy.

Another role of questioning pertains to assessment. It is important here to emphasize the importance of assessing students throughout the learning cycle. *Diagnostic assessments* occur prior to planned inquiry-based experiences to assess students' knowledge and to determine any misconceptions that may exist. *Formative assessments* occur

TABLE 4.1   LEVELED QUESTIONS USING BLOOM'S TAXONOMY

Level 1:	Memory—The student is asked to recall or recite information	1. To which group of animals do frogs belong? 2. What are the four developmental stages of a moth? 3. What is the young underdeveloped baby plant in a seed called?
Level 2:	Comprehension—The student is asked to describe, summarize, or understand information	1. In your own words, how would you describe the four developmental stages of a moth? 2. Explain how fish are able to breathe underwater. 3. We have been involved in gathering data concerning the amount of time a candle continues to burn when a beaker is inverted and placed over it. We have used three of four beakers and found that under beaker 1 (100 ml), the candle continued to burn for 11 seconds; under beaker 2 (220 ml), the candle burned for 22 seconds; and under beaker 3 (300 ml), it burned for 33 seconds. How do you think it will burn under beaker 4 (400 ml)?
Level 3:	Application—The student is asked to solve or show ideas and apply them to a specific concrete situation	1. What would happen if you placed a fish in a covered container of cooled, boiled water? 2. How would you prepare an environment to grow frogs? 3. How would you use a balloon to demonstrate how our lungs work?
Level 4:	Analysis—The student is asked to separate the whole into component parts, to infer and compare	1. Why do you think people are not more concerned about pollution problems? 2. Jeff, can you explain how Jim's conclusion is consistent with yours? 3. How are plants and animals alike/different?
Level 5:	Synthesis—The student is asked to create or predict something new or unique	1. How would you describe life on earth in the year 2090? 2. Suppose you lived on a faraway planet. Draw a plant that would grow on that planet. How would you prove that? 3. What could you do to find out how much water the bucket of snow would make?
Level 6:	Evaluation—The student is asked to judge or choose by making well-reasoned decisions	1. What is the best way to find out if water is a good conductor of heat? 2. What do you see as the best solution to the energy problem? 3. Do you think there should be a law to limit the number of landfills that can be used in a given county? Why? Why not?

during directed teaching and are aimed at providing feedback, reinforcement, and motivation to the student as well as way of keeping the teacher informed about student progress. *Summative assessments* occur after the instructional process. They can provide the teacher and the student with information about the learning that has occurred, or they can be the springboard to further inquiry-based activities. In some instances, they are used for reporting results in the form of grades to students and parents.

Taba's Questioning Strategy

Hilda Taba and colleagues (1971) devised a questioning strategy that involves learners in a step-by-step process aimed at encouraging effective thinking. In the first step, the teacher uses an opening question that requires only low-level cognitive responses, thus allowing most learners to enter the discussion. To be effective, an opening question should involve general knowledge but permit a wide range of responses within specific parameters. A question such as "What are the four basic parts that most plants have?" is considered a closed question and would be inappropriate as an opening question. It has a "right" answer and does not encourage other meaningful responses once the right answer has been given. Using the same general theme, a teacher might ask, "How do the roots from a carrot, turnip, and beet differ?" Providing that students have seen a carrot, turnip, and beet, this question allows for more students to enter the discussion since there are several possible responses.

Another criterion of an opening question involves establishing a focus for the discussion. The teacher must decide beforehand the discussion's purpose and guide the student in that direction. Consequently, the opening question should set the general direction for the discussion. This does not mean that the teacher should attempt to control the content of the students' responses. It does mean, however, that he or she guides the students to engage in certain thought processes. For example, if the purpose of the discussion is to compare and contrast the roots from different types of plants, the teacher must guide the students in that direction. The question that opens the discussion must be worded so that it relates to the initial purpose of eliciting low-level, factual responses as well as to the overall purpose of using this needed data in the high-level cognitive process of inferring and generalizing.

In the second step of Taba's scheme, the teacher attempts to raise the students' thinking from that of low-level memory or factual knowledge to a higher level in which they are required to look for relationships among data. Such questions are known as "lifting" questions and should be designed to encourage students to respond with tentative opinions rather than more qualified ones. Questions that include phrases such as "what seems to be," "what might be," and "what do you think?" are suggested in promoting open, tentative questions. The following are examples of lifting questions:

1. What factors might account for the difference in the size of your bean plant and your partner's bean plant?

2. Steve, what seems to be the best environment for growing bread mold, based on our findings?

3. What do you think will happen when we drop the raisins into the liquid in this beaker?

Not all students will be able to initiate a response at this level, so the teacher must attempt to involve as many students as possible by asking for other examples. In this way, a student who cannot raise the level of the discussion with an original response can participate once the level has been established by offering responses and examples similar to the initial response or with a thought that is correct but incomplete. When this happens, the teacher should continue with that student in order to permit him or her to develop the idea, provided that the rest of the class can be kept mentally involved as well.

The third step of Taba's strategy requires that these students combine relationships and make generalizations about them. During this phase of the discussion, the teacher guides the students into thinking and speaking in abstract terms. Supporting questions that require the learners to clarify, extend, and synthesize are used during this phase. These questions should encourage the learners to (1) build on the ideas already presented, (2) use gathered data as the basis for statements, and (3) establish a rationale for their opinions. Questions such as "What evidence have we gathered that would support our hypothesis that gases expand when heated?" or "Explain why the balloon in the ice-cold water changed shape," or "What is the purpose of leaving one of the three balloons at room temperature?" permit learners to infer and generalize, thus operating at a higher cognitive level.

Taba also suggests that the teacher may find it helpful to let the students in on this step-by-step process of becoming more effective thinkers. The students can then be more directly involved in assessing their ability and their classmates' ability to respond at a higher level to different questions.

The Taba strategy uses questions to direct the students' thinking step by step, from low-level, specific concrete ideas to more abstract, generalized concepts. It suggests that both the nature of the class and the purpose of the discussion are important factors and must be considered when planning questioning sequences. Again, as the students gain more experience, the teacher's role should become more indirect, and the students will be able to structure their own questions.

It is important in a constructivist classroom for the teacher and the students to work together in creating a classroom climate that allows for differences of opinion. The teacher should take the lead in offering support to students whose ideas are rejected or proven incorrect, as it is important that learners feel comfortable and secure enough to reenter the discussion. Once again, the students themselves can also learn this supportive role.

The questioning strategies of both Taba and Bloom provide the classroom teacher with helpful guidelines in formulating a workable plan for effective questioning. No one series of questions will work every time or with all learners. It is up to the teacher to determine the specific purpose of a planned science experience and to devise effective questions to accommodate the learners and to make the learning meaningful to them. In addition, there are several other factors to consider. These include using verbal and nonverbal congruence, providing appropriate feedback, and avoiding teleological and anthropomorphic questions.

Verbal and Nonverbal Congruence. Another factor to consider in implementing a questioning strategy is that of verbal and nonverbal congruence. As students are engaged in inquiry-based experiences, the teacher should pay particular attention to the nonverbal cues that the learners are receiving. While the lessons are to be child centered, the learners need to feel that the teacher is interested and listening to what they are discovering or saying. Facing the student who is speaking and maintaining eye contact is one way to let the student know that you are interested. Nodding and making facial gestures that encourage and motivate indicate involvement with the discussion and demonstrate interest.

When addressing the student, the teacher's nonverbal and verbal cues need to be coordinated so that the students are not confused by words that indicate an involvement in the dialogue and body language that clearly indicates detachment. When conflicts between verbal and nonverbal cues occur, the nonverbal action tends to be taken by students as the more reliable of the two. Therefore, in order to facilitate effective interaction, the teacher must demonstrate both verbal and nonverbal involvement.

Providing Feedback. The most common responses are those that accept or reject a reply. Research has shown that the most common teacher response is praise. However, praise can be misused. The response of "good" can be overused and provides very little feedback. Praise can also mislead students and end creative thinking, as students may interpret the comment as getting the correct answer. Continually giving accepting or rejecting kinds of responses is usually indicative of low-level questioning. Questions that require the learner to engage in higher-level thinking call for a teacher's response that encourages continued thinking and discussion, such as "That's one possibility; can you think of another?," "Everyone think of another example and be ready when I call on you," "Who can add more to Jeff's explanation?," or "Why do you say that?"

When a student gives an incorrect or incomplete answer, the teacher needs to help the student with an acceptable response rather than ask another student to help. A Canadian researcher, J. W. Powell, says that by analyzing a learner's "wrong" answers, we can discover meaningful information. Many times, the wrong answers fit a pattern or can tell us something about the way the learner processes information. Take, for example, the following dialogue that occurred in a classroom. The teacher asked the students what 1/2 of 8 would be. One student's answer was 3. Can you figure out why the student answered that way? What does that answer tell you about the way the student approaches problems?

When answers are incomplete, it has been suggested that the teacher affirm the correct part of the question and then use probing or extending questions. In the event that a student continues to have a difficult time completing the question, the teacher can provide the answer and then ask the same child to repeat in his or her own words the additional information. This strategy sets up the expectation that all students are capable of learning and answering questions. Many students learn that if they do not answer, the teacher will call on other students. For many students, it is easier to say nothing than risk being wrong or embarrassed. Remember that, for learning to occur, students need to be active and interactive with the knowledge being presented.

Avoiding Teleological and Anthropomorphic Questions. The teacher should avoid science questions that attribute purpose or will to nonhuman things and those that imply that natural phenomena have human characteristics. These teleological and anthropomorphic questions are not consistent with scientific attitudes and promote many misconceptions. When asking questions about natural phenomena, do not suggest or imply that nonhuman things think or feel in the same way that humans do. Questions that do, such as "How do you think a plant feels when it doesn't get enough water?" or "Why do some animals like to hibernate in the winter?" are misleading and do not help students understand natural phenomena. See Chapter 3 for further information about misconceptions and the use of children's literature.

Suggestions for Developing Your Skill in Asking Questions

Listed here are suggestions for you to think about as you move toward developing your question techniques:

- Make sure that questions are brief and clear. Plan your words carefully to avoid questions that are ambiguous and long.
- Ask only one question at a time. Stay away from the desire to ask for multiple pieces of information in one question. Many times, students are overwhelmed and do not know where to begin in answering.
- Beam the questions to the entire class. Avoid calling on a student and then asking the question. It produces more activity if you ask the question, give wait time, and then call on a student.
- Use a variety of questions at different levels of thinking. Remember that there are many different levels of abilities and prior experiences in the classroom, and you increase participation by having different types and levels of questions.
- Give appropriate feedback. Using praise alone does not always work. Students need specific and appropriate feedback. Have high expectations for all students and keep them all accountable.
- Provide a mistakes-OK, "safe" classroom climate for questions and answers.
- Utilize team and group cooperative responses.
- Give students the opportunity to get a partner or learning buddy to serve as a consultant to discuss the answer before offering it to the class.
- Provide mini white boards, student response cards, hand signals, or private cues.

- Encourage students to ask questions. As students refine their inquiry-based constructivist science activities, they will have the opportunity to ask and pursue their own questions and answers in order to make knowledge meaningful for their own learning.

Brain-Based Problem Solving

What is the best way to teach problem solving? In recent brain-based learning, it is with real-world problems, with real people under real conditions. This should sound familiar to you by now, as we have been stating throughout this book that inquiry-based planned science experiences need to allow the students to construct or build their *own knowledge*. Students have to take an active role in their learning. Unfortunately, only 5% of all 11-year-olds have developed formal reasoning skills; by age 14, that number is 25%. For most of us, that number is only 50%. Learners need to be taught the strategies used in problem solving in order to be able to seek solutions. Allow students to solve problems in both a creative and a structured way.

The steps for problem solving are to (1) identify the problem; (2) collect reference material and information related to the problem; (3) hypothesize solutions while analyzing the tasks necessary to solve the problem; (4) evaluate, synthesize, and/or experiment to check the hypothesis; (5) conclude by offering an answer, generalizations, or alternatives to the problem; and (6) communicate the finding of the investigation.

Remember that students can solve a problem on paper, with a model, with an analogy or a metaphor, by discussion, with statistics, or through artwork, music, or demonstration. Therefore, students need exposure and experiences in these areas. When using problem solving with students, it is important to continually monitor students' progress and help keep them on task. As you think about the previous steps, you can see that problem solving requires time. If you use a problem-solving strategy, allow enough time for students to work through the process with the needed materials. Your results will be well worth the time. As Eric Jensen states in his book *Teaching with the Brain in Mind* (1998), problem solving is the "single best way to grow a better brain."

Visual Tools: Concept Mapping

The concept map is a valuable constructivist tool to use in science education. It enables learners to show how meaning is being constructed within their mind. This strategy has been shown to increase student achievement in science. Concept maps are developed by writing words related to a key word in categories around the key word; the categories are labeled, and linking words are placed along the lines connecting the categories. This gives the students (and teachers) a visual comparison of relationships among and misconceptions about ideas. Concept mapping should not be confused with semantic webbing. Concept maps differ in that they show both hierarchical arrangement and meaningful interconnectedness. Concept maps are not linear, so they differ from outlines and flowcharts. It is important to note that there is no one right way to arrange a concept map. Many commercial companies have prepared concept maps ready for student use. Many of these maps already have the arrangements drawn, and all the student does is fill in the "correct" word in the circle. These would not be considered effective concept maps, as the students are not able to make their own connections and draw their own arrangement; in other words, they would not be constructing their own knowledge. Let's try making a concept map by following these directions:

1. Write each of the following words on a small "post-it" note:
   teachers, students, teaching, caring, colleagues, collaborating, parents, sharing, resources, encouraging, informing, behavior, field trips, helping, academics, "tips of the trade," materials

2. Arrange the "post-it" notes in an order so that
   a. The most important items are at the top
   b. The related items are underneath
   c. The examples follow underneath the related items
   d. Important topics are on the same level

   Remember that this is your concept map. There is no correct or incorrect way of arranging them. It is your interpretation.

3. Once you have your "post-it" notes arranged, transfer the information to a sheet of paper and draw a circle around each word.

4. Compare your arrangement with a neighbor next to you. In your comparison, talk about how and why you arranged your words as you did. Listen to how other people interpreted the relationship of the provided words. Once again, remember that theirs is not right or wrong, just as yours is not right or wrong. Remember that in using a constructivist approach, each person will put together these ideas in a way that makes sense to him or her because of prior knowledge.

5. Once you have completed your sharing, the next step is to link lines between the concepts on your diagram that relate to each other and to write one or two words on each line that describe the relationship. These words are called "linking" words and show the relationship between the concepts. Concepts can be linked up, down, or sideways. The assumption is that the linking lines go from the upper word to the lower word. If you are linking sideways, you may want to use arrows that show the direction of relationship.

6. When you are done, share your concept map with a partner. Remember to talk through the map and explain your relationships and your linking words.

As was stated earlier, concept maps can be used by learners to help organize the information they are learning and to express how this information is being processed and connected to previous learning. In other words, you can see how information is being constructed. The use of concept maps can also show if misconceptions are beginning to develop. When you notice this occurring, use the opportunity to question the student and make any corrections that may be needed. As students share their maps and compare them with others, they may also become aware that they have some misconceptions or uncertainties about the way they are constructing their information and can modify or change these ideas prior to being stored incorrectly in long-term memory.

Teachers can also use concept maps to plan their teaching by organizing the sequence and scope of lessons. Also, they are helpful tools to use when integrating or doing thematic planning (See Figure 4.4). You will be learning more about this in the next section. When you start to prepare your unit, review the previous steps and do your preliminary planning using this method. You will find it a lot easier to organize and see the connections.

Responding to the Needs of All Learners

The methods and strategies outlined so far are but a few of the ways to meet the exciting yet challenging task of responding to differences in learners. When we attempt to meet all these needs in an inquiry-based constructivist approach, we are adding even another dimension to the learning process as well as the teaching process. In a book written by Carol Ann Tomlinson (1999) for the Association for Supervision and Curriculum Development, the terms *differentiated classroom* and *differentiated instruction* are

FIGURE 4.4

Concept Map

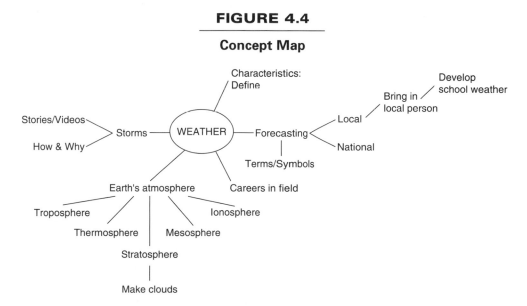

used to represent those practices that teachers use to increase learning regardless of socioeconomic background, cultural differences, and background experiences.

In a differentiated classroom, the teacher makes persistent efforts to respond to students' learning needs. He or she does that by using many of the strategies and methods suggested in this book. It is not entirely possible to differentiate everything for everyone every day. Through the use of appropriate assessment, both formal and informal, you can be ready to modify your instruction as you see the need. You can make the learning as meaningful as possible by structuring your inquiry approach in a way that makes it meaningful to students and to their previous learning.

You can also differentiate by allowing students time to work alone as well as time to work together and allowing for differences in learning styles. In other words, organize your room to remain proactively flexible to meet students where they are and help them achieve optimum growth as learners. Review the concept maps (Figure 4.5) to get an idea of what differentiated instruction entails. Remember that this is just one way to look at a differentiated classroom. As you begin your teaching career, begin con-

FIGURE 4.5

Concept Map Depicting Differentiated Classroom Instruction

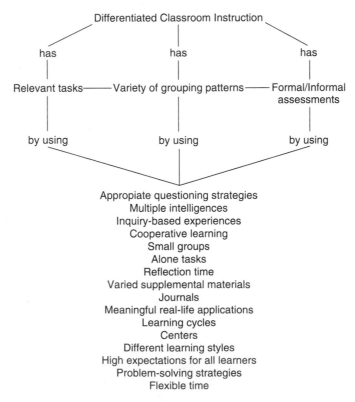

structing your own map of how you want your classroom to be so that you can meet the needs of your students in your inquiry-based planned science experiences.

The information presented in Figure 4.5 is meant not to be inclusive but rather a beginning for you as you think about the many different ways you can support student learning by making your classroom a differentiated classroom.

Suggested Activity
Using Ideas from This Section
4.4

The activities that follow will help you use the ideas presented in this section of the chapter. As you complete these activities, keep in mind that they have been designed to help you assimilate and build new concepts into schemata you currently hold. You should try to analyze the purpose of each activity, relate it to what you previously knew, and add any new information that was presented.

1. Using the learning cycle as a guide, prepare a science lesson.

2. Research TGT and present it to your classmates.

3. Contact Dr. Kagan's Web site and select five co-op structures you could use with students. Share them with your classmates.

4. Formulate several science questions designed to elicit higher-than-rote-memory responses from elementary students. You may select a central theme or concept and relate all your questions to the same topic.

5. Write some questions designed to stimulate convergent and divergent thinking. Find a partner and see if he or she agrees with you. Discuss the purposes for using convergent and divergent questions. Where in the learning cycle would you most likely use either type of question?

6. Find some prepared materials that use children's literature to teach a science concept. Examine the resources provided and see if you can discover any teleological and anthropomorphic activities and questions. How would you alter these activities so that students would not form misconceptions?

7. Select a science topic and construct an appropriate questioning strategy as part of a planned science experience. Use either of the two strategies presented (Bloom or Taba). Outline your strategy on a separate sheet of paper using the guide that follows. Give examples of questions that could be used. Limit your selected topic or content area so that it can be dealt with effectively in 20 to 30 minutes.

Outline Guide for Questioning Strategy

Science topic:

Approximate grade level:

Brief description of lesson (purpose, content or concepts to be explored):

Description of questioning strategy:

8. Make your own concept map of what a **"differentiated classroom"** means to you.

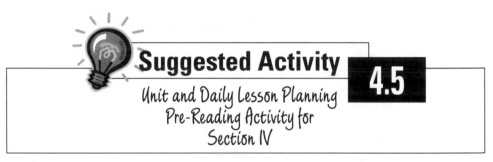

Suggested Activity   **4.5**

*Unit and Daily Lesson Planning
Pre-Reading Activity for
Section IV*

In order to teach effectively, teachers must organize what they plan to teach. Use of an inquiry-based constructivist science experience does not alter this premise. Chapter 3 provided you with the criteria for making curricular decisions that should be of value as you begin your own planning. We have also stated that prepared curricular resources are excellent tools to utilize when planning. But one of the best ways to meet the specific needs of your students is for **you** to plan their inquiry-based experiences by doing your own planning. Of course, you will use many different resources to help you accomplish your goals and objectives. But you will be the best judge of your students' prior knowledge, learning styles, cultural needs, and available resources.

Assess your prior knowledge. How would you define the following curriculum designs: traditional, thematic, integrated, integrative? After reflecting, jot down your thoughts about the four designs and then share with a neighbor. As you go through this next section you may want to reflect on your notes and modify, extend, delete, or refine your notes. Then, with your knowledge, you will be able to select an appropriate design and begin the exciting work of designing a unit.

There are many different models of unit designs. Table 4.2 summarizes four curriculum designs and their effect on student learning.

In response to student needs, school district policies, and other related factors, you will probably find yourself using parts of each of the models shown in Table 4.2. You have probably had previous experience in designing traditional and thematic lessons or units. They can be effective designs for planning but may need modification

TABLE 4.2   UNIT DESIGN MODELS

Traditional	Thematic	Integrated	Integrative
Each subject discipline is taught separately, in isolation from each other. A fragmented curriculum.	Central theme identified. Some or all of the disciplines contribute to theme. An interdisciplinary curriculum.	Common areas of curriculum correlated. Subject areas disappear. A correlated curriculum.	Themes identified that focus on broad concepts. Content skills and objectives built around theme without regard for subject areas covered. Identification occurs after design. Students contribute their ideas. A student-centered curriculum.
Effect on Students			
Sees no connection between content areas. Limited sense of the "connectedness" to real life.	Connections begin to develop. Relationship between content areas taught to students.	Students develop sense of wholeness instead of separation. Begin to lose sense of subject areas.	Delineate any sense of subject areas. Students expand their understanding of their world by using skills and objectives they identify.
Curriculum Used			
Prepackaged curriculum, mainly textbook oriented.	Teachers identify theme. Develop curriculum from predetermined set of objectives that are related.	Teachers or teams develop curriculum by integrating knowledge and skills reflecting their content areas.	Students and teachers cluster their questions into common areas, develop key questions, and plan activities to address each question. Objectives are identified after planning is complete.
Effect on Student and Teacher			
Teacher control limited by textbook. Students limited to information in textbook. Little input by teacher or student.	Teachers begin to "own" curriculum. Make choices they feel appropriate. Students begin to connect ideas.	Teachers and students begin to see meaning and application of skills as they relate to a meaningful context.	Develops concept of democracy in planning. Curriculum is relevant and meaningful for students and teachers.

in implementation so that student inquiry can be accommodated. Remember that the national standards and benchmarks for science education endorse active learning, inquiry, problem solving, and cooperative learning. They also promote the need for students to go beyond observing, inferring, and experimenting by using these skills with scientific knowledge as they use scientific reasoning and critical thinking to construct their meaning. For those very reasons, an integrated or integrative unit plan may help you with your planning needs.

The steps listed below employ one method in designing an integrative unit. These steps are meant not to be inclusive but rather to expand your approach to planning so that you can meet the needs of your learners, your school district, and state and national standards. This approach may create a bit of "cognitive dissonance" with some of your prior planning experiences, as it reverses the traditional planning process. It has been called by some the "backward design process," as it begins with the end in mind.

When the "end" or final outcomes have been established, interventions or inquiries can be planned that will allow students to use the learned information in ways that are meaningful for them. An integrative approach varies from an integrated approach in the major area of student involvement (see Table 4.2 for clarification). The use of student input is critical when using a constructivist approach and when designing an integrative unit. However, the age, level, and ability of the student will determine the degree of the involvement. This is one of many critical decisions that are part of the planning process.

The following section provides the steps that can be used to design an integrative unit with examples from an integrative unit on the environment. This particular unit was designed for students in grades 4 through 8. Listed here are the six steps suggested for designing an integrative unit. Each step will be explained and examples provided for strategies you might want to use as you design your unit.

Step I: Select a topic

Step II: Teacher/student brainstorming

Step III: Design focus question(s)

Step IV: Culminating activities

Step V: Daily lesson planning

Step VI: Match unit/lesson plans with curriculum objectives for all content areas. If your district does not have a list of objectives, you may use state or national core curriculum objectives. If the textbook is all you have available, you can use the list of objectives provided in the teacher's edition.

Selecting the Topic. The emphasis in a constructivist-based science classroom is on student involvement. This involvement can start right at the beginning of your planning. Involve students in the selection of your topic. If you are obligated to teach certain concepts, provide students with a list of the concepts and let them choose a topic that appears to be the most motivating. If you must use a textbook to guide your instruction, let students select the topic from their textbook. If neither of these resources is mandatory, review the national science standards and benchmarks that are age appropriate for your students and together select a topic. Listen to your students. Many times, students are interested in certain scientific concepts because of a current event or an occurrence happening nationally or locally; use that interest to select your topic.

Teacher/Student Brainstorming. This step can be thought of as investigating through free discovery. Once the topic has been selected, the teacher and students decide what is important for them to learn, what learning activities they would like to perform to learn about the topic, and how the inquiry will be conducted. It is helpful to guide students in this process, as many of them will not have had the prior experience necessary to "construct" their learning. You can guide students by providing a planning sheet like the example shown in Figure 4.6 used by students who were interested in studying the topic "environment-quality and how to preserve." As you can see, many concepts and activities were generated.

These ideas can be generated by placing students in small brainstorming groups. Also, if you are part of a team of teachers, you might want to use this sheet as well to include their ideas. Better yet, teachers and students could work in brainstorming groups together.

Design Focus Questions. These are questions designed around the brainstorming and inquiries the students and teachers have been generating. They are questions that will guide the teaching and will unmask the key inquiries and the core ideas of a concept. They are a method of inquiry that demands that the students use analysis, synthesis, and judgment to answer. They also should be designed so that they have no obvious "right" answer. It is suggested that a reasonable number of key questions be used for each unit (between two and five). There are various sources and researchers that have identified criteria for designing effective questions. These criteria are frequently mentioned:

- They go to the heart of the discipline.
- They are thought provoking and personalized to students.
- They allow for creativity.
- They are higher order in cognitive function, requiring synthesis, analysis, and evaluative judgment.
- They provide the avenue for content knowledge, identifying a series of lessons.
- They have no obvious "right" answer, and they encourage more inquiry and research as well as controversies and different perspectives.
- They cause the student's learning to uncover and review important ideas.

FIGURE 4.6

Student/Teacher Brainstorming Template

UNIT Environment **TEAM MEMBERS** Mrs. Daigh, Eric, Mackenzie, Bill

IDEAS/CONCEPTS	SORT	ACTIVITIES, RESEARCH PROJECTS, TO DO'S	MATERIALS/RESOURCES NEEDED, CONTACTS
What is an environment?		Make an environment	List of speakers
Animals		Take field trips to:	Contact places to visit
Smog		• zoo	Order videos
Is our water safe?		• water plant	Write to zoo, fish hatchery
How do you know it's safe?		• sewage plant	Get list of governmental agencies
Is the air bad?		• recycling plant	Lorax video
Garbage dumps		• park	Plan field trips
Ozone layer		• fish hatchery	List of organizations for protecting environment
Endangered animals		• ship school	Look at magic school bus shows
Endangered insects		Have guest speakers	Get books on environment
Endangered flowers		Go in woods, explore	Find experiments on
Can trees be endangered?		Interview people	• water cycle
Rain forest		Read books—write poems	• building environments
Dinosaurs		Watch movies, videos	Demo food chain
Recycle		Do experiments	
Earth Day		Create an environment	
Cars—smog		Make posters	
Sewage		Learn about animals	
Can we do anything?		Study parts of world that are polluted	
How many environments are there?		Clean-up	
Are oceans polluted?		Learn about rain forest	
What is acid rain?		Recycle in school	
Are fish safe to eat?		Raise money to save animals	
How do they recycle paper?			

THE ITEMS IN THESE COLUMNS DO NOT NEED TO MATCH. JUST WRITE AS MANY IDEAS DOWN AS YOU CAN THINK ABOUT.

The important thing to remember about the key questions is that they frame the learning, involve the learner, encourage inquiry, and provide a path for students to construct meaningful learning.

Key questions for our environmental unit could be the following:

1. What is the environment?
2. How does each environmental system work (air, land, and work)?
3. How do environments become polluted? Who contributes? Who doesn't? Is it necessary to have some pollution? Is all pollution bad?
4. What does "endangered" mean?
5. What can people of all ages do to save the environment?
6. What careers and related fields of study would be motivating for someone interested in the life sciences?

Generate Culminating Activity. Once the brainstorming has been completed and the key questions have been designed, the next step is to design some performance tasks that demonstrate that students understand the key concepts and can use the knowledge correctly in their everyday world. The terms "understanding" and "use knowledge" have provided the stage for much research on the topic of understanding. One of the best summaries comes from Wiggins and McTighe (1998). They have identified six facets of understanding. A student who understands can do the following:

1. Explain: demonstrates sophisticated explanatory power and insight
2. Interpret: offers powerful, meaningful interpretations, translations, and narratives
3. Apply: uses knowledge in context and has know-how
4. See in perspective: criticizes and justifies, infers the assumption on which an idea or a theory is based, knows the limits and power of an idea, and sees through language that is biased, partisan, or ideological
5. Demonstrate empathy: has the ability to sensitively perceive
6. Reveal self-knowledge: recognizes own prejudices, uses metacognition, self-assesses, and accepts feedback and criticism

Using these guidelines, the culminating activity should involve the student in demonstrating real-world application through some type of observable performance. At this step, we are asking, What would we see that would show that students have learned information related to the key questions and can use that information in a novel way that is meaningful to their world? It is also motivating to the students if the wording used in the culminating activity is understood by the students. For example, our environmental unit could have the following culminating activities:

- Time: 2993. You have been hired as a paleontologist as part of a scientific expedition searching for fossil remains in North America. Your area of study is the ancient 20th-century extinct animal life and their environment. You have uncovered the fossil remains of a polar bear, a crocodile, a chameleon, and an eagle. In order to qualify for further archaeological funding, your scientific team is scheduled to present the following information to the Chicago Natural History Museum's board of directors:

  - Location of fossil bones on North America map
  - Reassembling of fossilized bones (paper, clay, paper mâché)
  - Illustration of environment animal lived in
  - Written explanation of adaptation to environment
  - Scientific prediction of when and why animal became extinct

- You are to prepare a campaign that will help save the local environment. You will need to devise a plan and be ready to present it to the city commission. The commission will want to know the names of organizations that will be involved; what support from local, state, and federal agencies you have garnered; and a proposed budget for your plan.

- Write a play or sing a ballad describing the layers of earth's atmosphere or the water cycle.

For each of these activities, assessments should be designed that reflect all areas of student performance (see Chapters 6 and 7).

Daily Lesson Plans. Using the key questions, the next step is to design lessons that will lead students to the answers to their questions and prepare them to have the information they need to complete the culminating outcome. You can also use student ideas during this phase of the planning. Identify the key question, share the culminating activities, and allow students the opportunity to ask their questions and design their own activities. An example from our environment unit looked like the following:

Key question	What do you want to know?	How could you find out?
What does "endangered" mean?	How do we save an endangered species? What animals and insects are endangered? Can land and trees be endangered? What does government do? How high does a tree grow? Things about the rain forest.	Go to a zoo Write a report Interview people Use the Internet Adopt an animal Don't buy fur coats Debate ideas Invite a speaker Make posters Start a campaign

After the students have provided input, you are ready to take each key question and design your daily plans. As this is an integrative unit, you will be including other content areas with your planned science experiences. Therefore, we are suggesting that you use the format given in Figure 4.7 to accommodate this type of planning.

FIGURE 4.7

Daily Lesson Plan

Mrs. Daigh	4	Environment	00-00-00
TEACHER	GRADE	CLASS/SUBJECT	DATE
	DAILY LESSON PLAN		

Objectives: Students will write their own definition of pollution. Will find evidence of pollution in their immediate environment and generate solutions to control.

#	(Content/What?) TASK ANALYSIS	(How?) TEACHING STRATEGIES	(Student Performance/Do?) CHECK FOR UNDERSTANDING	(With?) RESOURCES/MATERIALS
1	Introduce concept of pollution (anticipatory Set)	Read book to the class: *The River Ran Wild*, by Lynne Cherry	Students will listen to book.	Book from Library: *The River Ran Wild*, by Lynne Cherry
2	Define "pollution" (Verbal Discussion, input)	a. Discuss the book. b. Brainstorm with the students examples of pollution found in the book and examples of their own. c. List ideas on the board or overhead. d. Instruct students to formulate a definition of pollution in their own words in their science notebook. e. Share definitions.	Participate in large-group teacher-directed discussion. Write their definition of "pollution." Share with a partner. If called on, share with the whole class.	Overhead/Blackboard Science Notebooks
3	Pollution Patrol (Investigation)	a. Review Activity: Pollution Patrol in Pollution Solution Booklet (pp. 2–3). b. Copy Copycat Page. Pollution Patrol for each student or group. c. Take students outside for a pollution patrol (around school grounds). d. Complete activity in classroom, discussing observations.	Listen to directions. Walk around school grounds looking for evidence of pollution. In small groups, list what was observed and generate solutions to share.	Pollution Solution Books Copies of Copycat Page
4	Closure	Ask students to share with a neighbor one thing they learned about pollution during today's class that they can share with others when they get home today. Randomly check with a few students.	With a partner, discuss one thing they learned. If called on by teacher, share information.	

The important elements of an inquiry-based science lesson should be present re-gardless of what model you are using. Also, the important elements of a lesson will be included.

The task analysis column breaks apart the key question. What inquiries, investi-gations, observations, data collections, and other activities need to occur so that the student can answer the questions? What concepts, skills, and knowledge need to be mastered so that students can use the information in their culminating activity? These are all teacher decisions and tasks that need to be analyzed and presented to the students for investigation. Your job is to plan for these tasks, whether they are teacher generated or student generated. Many science concepts need to build on one another, so sequencing the tasks is a salient teacher decision. Place these tasks in the column labeled "Task Analysis."

Once the task has been defined, the next step is to define the teacher behavior that will facilitate student learning. Will the teacher set up an investigation for the students to pursue? Will you use small groups, large groups, or a pair-share strategy? Should you show a video to the entire class, play a song, or role play? This column accommodates the planning that tells how the teacher will employ methods or strategies to meet the needs of the various students. Each task identified will need a teacher behavior to show how the task is going to be accomplished.

In addition to the task and the teacher behavior, a plan must be developed to as-sess student performance. In other words, what will students do to demonstrate that they have indeed "understood" the task that was identified? If possible, the student per-formance should be visible to both the learner and the teacher, and feedback should be immediate. There are many student behaviors, such as signaling, discussing, sum-marizing, drawing, developing choral responses, creating a mind map, holding up an-swer cards, turning to a neighbor and explaining, and creating short quizzes. The key ingredient is that the student is actively engaging in proving that learning is occurring and is making a connection to previously learned patterns in the brain. Many miscon-ceptions can be stopped if the learner exhibits problems as the learning is building. That is why it is important to check for understanding with each piece of the task.

Finally, the last column provides a space to list the needed resources and mate-rials that will be used for the various tasks that will be performed.

As you can see, thus far there has not been any delineation as to subject area anywhere in the planning process. In the example provided in Figure 4.7, students have not been told that they are doing a reading and science activity but are actively engaged in a meaningful task. Also, students have had the opportunity to generate, explore, and answer their own questions. As you can see, this does not mean that the teacher does not have to plan or facilitate the learning. What it does mean is that by carefully planning, we may be more free to listen to how students are learn-ing instead of thinking about what we are going to do or say next. For inquiry-based lessons, this is certainly an advantage, as we can listen for weak insights or miscon-ceptions that can cause problems with future learning.

The final step in this planning process is to identify the objectives that have been learned from the various content areas involved. As previously stated, these can be selected from district curriculum guides, textbooks, or state and national standards and benchmarks.

Components of Effective Lesson Planning

A necessary component of the unit is the lesson plan. No matter what format you use to write your plan, there are some salient elements that should always be present. These are general information about the class, topic/concept, objective, instructional components, resources and materials, and assessment strategies.

- *General class information:* Include name of teacher, what class is being taught, grade level of students, and any other demographic and logistic information that may be important.

- *Topic/concept:* This is not the objective; it is more abstract or generic. In order to focus your teaching on the major concept, you need to ask yourself what part of science you will be working with. You might ask yourself a questions like "What do I want the students to know about the atmosphere and weather?"

- *Objective/s:* Once you know what concept of science you are working with, you can then ask the question "What do I want the student to *do* to facilitate his or her understanding of the water cycle and its relationship to weather patterns?" The objective consists of the process and the content. Many teachers find it helpful to use the words "The student will be able to . . ." to help his or her write objectives. For example, "The student will be able to draw a diagram of the water cycle" or "The student will be able to record and chart weather changes over a period of three days using the necessary weather tools." It is important when writing objectives to include a variety of cognitive levels. Refer to the section on use of Bloom's taxonomy found in this chapter. One cannot expect students to operate at higher levels of thinking if they, the higher levels of thinking, have not been planned. Particularly with a constructivist approach to students' planned science experiences, it is important to challenge students to ask the next questions and for the teacher to be prepared to facilitate the next level of learning for the student. Also, objectives need to focus on the three dimensions of scientific literacy:

  - Using scientific knowledge by describing, explaining, predicting, and designing
  - Constructing scientific knowledge by asking questions, solving problems, interpreting text, and reconstructing knowledge
  - Reflecting on scientific knowledge by justifying, criticizing, describing limits, making connections, taking perspectives, and describing interactions among science, technology, and society

- *Instructional components:* This is the body of the lesson. The components are the following:

  - Content: The information to be learned. The teacher has to decide what information will be presented or what information students will need to explore or develop questions for further investigation and discovery. Information is selected on the basis of objectives developed, developmental level of student, and requirements of the curriculum.

- Instruction: What instructional methods and strategies will be used to meet the objectives and to match all the learner differences discussed previously in this chapter?
- Lesson introduction (set): To begin a lesson, you must, of course, first get the students' attention and then motivate them so that they experience the need to continue with their learning. The following techniques are a few ways that can be used:

1. Discrepant events: Piaget's theory on equilibrium, discussed earlier, relates to this technique. A discrepant event can be an effective technique only if it relates to the learner's past experiences. That is, a learner must have some background to enable him or her to perceive the event as discrepant or inconsistent. By using this instructional technique to begin a lesson, a teacher is able to capitalize on the learner's natural curiosity and need to resolve the inconsistency. The remainder of the instructional sequence would be used to provide the learner with the necessary materials and guidance to resolve the inconsistency.

2. Use of anticipatory set or advanced organizer: This provides a framework for capturing student attention and can be brief. It can be a question designed to stimulate previous information, a humorous story, a guided imagery lesson, a personal story, or a recent experience related to the topic.

3. Verbal discussion: One of the most used beginning techniques is verbal discussion. The teacher can provide background information through the presentation of material or question-answer sessions designed to discover the students' past experiences. For example, to begin a lesson on magnets, the teacher might hold up a horseshoe magnet and ask the children to identify it. Further discussion would continue, and opportunities would be given for students to express their personal experience and knowledge of magnets. Also, the teacher could assess for misconceptions as well as connection for further study.

4. Demonstration/investigations: Presenting a live demonstration or experiment. These demonstrations can be either teacher or student led. They can provide the basis for further investigations and planned science experiences. If they lead to data-gathering techniques, you will need to plan carefully for these experiences. Also, you will need to assist the students in use of data-processing techniques. With the use of modern technology, there are many methods of collecting and analyzing data. Many commercial products need some advance setup time.

- Activities and procedures: Activities selected must be purposeful and meaningful to the students. Students need to be actively engaged in the learning. You can accomplish this by organizing activities around student-generated questions and problems. Other kinds of motivating activities include involving students in solving real-world problems, presenting puzzles for them to solve, and raising questions and not answering as many of theirs. Finally, students like to perform. Find ways in which they can present information (e.g., oral presentations or graphic displays).

- Closure: How will you bring the lesson to an end? You should plan your lesson so that you effectively utilize the entire amount of time available for student learning. It is extremely important for student management as well as student learning to make effective use of the beginning period of time and the ending period of time. If these times are planned effectively, there will be little dead time, and students will be engaged in quality one-task behaviors. A closure provides students with a sense of completeness and, with effective teaching techniques, a sense of understanding the concepts and objectives learned. A closure activity can consist of a summary by the student or an opportunity to practice the learned material.

- *Resources and materials:* In order for the students to manipulate materials, they must be available prior to the class activities. Resources can include audiovisual materials, textbooks, computers, library books, and other supplies needed to accomplish the objectives. Teachers also need to plan how students will access and use these resources during their planned science experiences.

- *Assessment/evaluation:* Evaluation refers to the difficult task of assessing the extent to which the students were able to attain the specified objectives. It is difficult, if not nearly impossible, to effectively plan the next lesson without feedback about what the student understood in the previous lesson. By assessing, we are trying to find out what learning took place before, during, and after interventions by the teacher. Many ideas were presented in Chapter 6 and 7. In addition, the format used with the integrative unit design in this chapter addresses the idea of assessment

Suggested Activity 4.6
Planning an Integrative Unit

You are now ready to perform the exciting task of planning an integrative unit. If you are not able to survey a whole classroom of students, you can still get direction by finding a few students at the level your are planning for and ask for their input or have your classmates role play the part of the students. For your first attempt, you should try and limit the size of your unit and plan for approximately three to five days. Your unit plan will include several daily lesson plans. Your instructor will provide the criteria for designing a quality unit plan.

with each piece of the task analysis. Teachers who break apart their objective into the essential tasks or "pieces" have identified key learnings that can be used to check for student understanding during instruction. There is no one "best" format to use; what is important is that assessment is occurring and used to further student learning.

REFERENCES

American Association for the Advancement of Science. (1993). *Benchmarks for science literacy.* New York: Oxford University Press.

Bloom, B. S. (1956). *Taxonomy of education objectives: The classification of educational goals. Handbook 1: Cognitive domain.* New York: Longman.

Caine, G., & Caine, R. N. (Eds.). (1994). *Making connections: Teaching and the human brain.* Menlo Park, CA: Addison-Wesley.

Covington, M., & Berry, R. (1976). *Self-worth and school learning.* New York: Holt, Rinehart & Winston.

Dunn, R., & Dunn, K. (1978). *Teaching students through their individual learning styles: A practical approach.* Reston, VA: Reston Publishing.

Gallimore, R., & Tharp, R. (1990). Teaching mind in society: Teaching schooling, and literate discourse. In L. C. Moll (Ed.), *Vygotsky and education* (pp. 175–205). New York: Cambridge University Press.

Gardner, H. (1983a). *Frames of mind: The theory of multiple intelligences.* New York: Basic Books.

Gardner, H. (1983b). *Multiple intelligences: The theory in practice.* New York: Basic Books.

Gardner, H. (1995, November). Reflections on multiple intelligences; myths and messages. *Phi Delta Kappan,* 200–203, 206–209.

Gardner, H. (1999). *The disciplined mind: What all students should understand.* New York: Simon and Schuster.

Jensen, E. (1995). *Brain-based learning and teaching.* Del Mar, CA: Turning Point Publishing.

Jensen, E. (1998). *Teaching with the brain in mind.* Alexandria, VA: Association for Supervision and Curriculum Development.

Johnson, D. W., & Johnson, R. T. I. (1999). *Learning together and alone: Cooperation, competitive, and individualistic learning* (5th ed.). Boston: Allyn and Bacon.

Jung, C. G. (1971). *Psychological types.* Princeton, NJ: Princeton University Press.

Kagan, S. B. (1989/90). The structural approach to cooperative learning. *Education Leadership, 47*(4), 12–15.

Karplus, R., & Their, H. (1967). *A new look at elementary school science.* Chicago: Rand McNally.

Lawrence, G. (1987). *People types and tiger stripes.* Gainesville, FL: Center for Application of Psychological Type.

McCarthy, B. (1981, 1987). *The 4MAT system: Teaching to learning styles with right/left mode techniques* (rev. ed.). Barrington, IL: Excel.

Michigan Board of Education. (1991). *Michigan essential goals and objectives for science education (K–12).* East Lansing, MI: Michigan State University Press.

Myers, I. B. (1962). *The Myers Briggs type indicator.* Palo Alto, CA: Consulting Psychologists Press.

National Institute for Science Education. (1997, May). Facts on working women. http://gatekeeper.dol.gov/dol/wb/public/wb_pubs/hotjobs/htm

National Research Council. (1996). Washington, DC. National Academy Press.

Path Finders 4. (1989). *Minority scientists and inventors.* Detroit: MICHCON.

Piaget, J. (1962). The stages of the intellectual development of the child. *Bulletin of the Meninger Clinic, 26*(3), 120–145.

Piaget, J. (1977). *The development of thought: Equilibrium of cognitive structures.* New York: Viking Press.

Rowe, M. B. (1973). *Teaching science as continuous inquiry.* New York: McGraw-Hill.

Slavin, R. E. (1977). *Student learning team techniques: Narrowing the achievement gap between the races* (Report No. 228). Baltimore: Center for Social Organization of Schools, The Johns Hopkins University.

Sternberg, R. J. (1990). *Beyond I.Q.: A triarchical theory of human intelligence.* New Haven, CT: Yale University Press.

Sternberg, R. J. (1996). Myths, countermyths, and truths about intelligence. *Education Researcher,* March 11–16.

Taba, H., Durkin, M., Fraenkel, J., & McNaughton, A. (1971). *A teacher's handbook to elementary social studies* (2nd ed.). Reading, MA: Addison-Wesley.

Tomlinson, C. (1999). *Differentiated classroom and differentiated instruction.* Alexandria, VA: Association for Supervision and Curriculum Development.

Vygotsky, L. S. (1962). *Thought and language.* New York: John Wiley & Sons.

Webster's New Twentieth Century Dictionary, unabridged. (1983) Prentice Hall Press, New York, NY Second Edition.

Wiggins, G., McTighe, J. (1998). *Understanding by design.* Baltimore, MD: Association for Supervision and Curriculum Development.

Witkin, H. (1954). *Personality through perception: An experimental and clinical study.* Westport, CT: Greenwood Press.

Witkin, H., & Goodenough, D. R. (1981a). *Cognitive styles: Essence and origins.* New York: International Universities Press.

Witkin, H., & Goodenough, D. R. (1981b). *SCIS teacher's guides.* Berkeley: University of California Press. (now supplied by Delta Education, Nashua, NH).

CHAPTER 5

Using Instructional Technology to Enhance Science Teaching and Learning

Dr. Raymond W. Francis

What we refer to as "instructional technology" is becoming commonplace in the home, office, and some schools. However, even as teachers are using e-mail to communicate with friends and identify lesson plans and resources on the Internet, they may be missing a great opportunity to impact student learning in science through the ongoing student use of instructional technology. Instructional technology, as a tool for student learning, has the potential to help students improve their performance at solving problems, answering questions, communicating their views, and demonstrating their understanding of a given science concept or idea. Instructional technology appears to be poised to play a major role in how students learn about science, and as teachers we must become comfortable with the various tools of instructional technology to better enable our students to learn now and in the future.

This chapter is intended to help you realize the power that instructional technology has in delivering a science curriculum to meet the needs of students and promote increased student performance and learning. Throughout the following sections, the benefits of using instructional technology and practical activities for students are presented to guide you through the incorporation of instructional technology into the science curriculum. Information in this chapter is focused on three areas. First is defining instructional technology and making connections to the national standards in science from the classroom perspective of teachers and students. Second is the use of instructional technology to collect and organize science information. Finally, the use of instructional technology by teachers to impact learning in the science classroom will be explored.

Take a few minutes and think about how instructional technology has impacted your learning experiences and your preparation to become a science teacher. Have you had many experiences with instructional technology? Have those experiences resulted in your learning about a concept or topic? It is hoped that you will keep these questions in mind as you move through this chapter.

DEFINING INSTRUCTIONAL TECHNOLOGY FROM THE SCIENCE TEACHER'S VIEWPOINT

Effective science teaching includes many factors. According to *the National Science Education Standards* (*NSES*) developed by the National Research Council (1996), teachers must manage the learning environments that provide students with the time, space, and resources needed for learning science (Standard D). This includes "making available the science tools, materials, media, and technological resources to students." In fact, as you examine the *NSES* document, it becomes clear that instructional technology must play a major part in the education of our students if they are to develop into what is referred to as "scientifically literate" citizens. Have you, as a future teacher, reviewed the *NSES* document? If not, you should take the time to examine the *NSES* and become familiar with the changes in the ways science education is changing.

Instructional technology has in many instances redefined the way we teach science. Recent years have seen the television, VCR, and computer become commonplace in our schools. It can be a powerful tool focused by the teacher and used by the student.

Instructional technology can allow students to spend more time using their own critical thinking and problem-solving skills while spending less time with the physical manipulation of data. Instructional technology can allow students to visit places and see events not normally possible from the public school classroom. Students can visit a museum hundreds or thousands of miles away or be a part of a NASA space shuttle mission without leaving their classroom.

What is your definition of instructional technology? How can you use instructional technology to better deliver the science curriculum and promote student learning in science? Instructional technology is defined in many different contexts. The definition we will use here is *the use, by a student or teacher, of any electronic device to assist in completing a task or locating information that promotes student performance or student learning.* This definition includes such traditional instructional technologies as overhead projectors, television, and audio- and videotape recorders. It also includes nontraditional tools such as calculators, graphing calculators, computers, electronic probes and sensors, video camera recorders, laser-disc players, compact discs, and of course the Internet. How many of these forms of instructional technology have you used in completing science-related tasks? How competent did you feel in using these items?

With these tools at our disposal and the courage and skill to use them effectively, we will be well prepared to deliver a curriculum that addresses the national standards, state goals and objectives, and local expectations. These existing tools allow teachers more flexibility and information than has ever been available in the classroom. They also allow the student more freedom and opportunity to demonstrate their understanding and knowledge of a specific scientific skill or concept.

Connecting With the National Science Education Standards Through Instructional Technology

In *Project 2061: Science for All Americans* (American Association for the Advancement of Science [AAAS], 1990), the authors specify that information processing will play an important role in science education. The very process of word processing and the use of charts and graphs necessitate that the learner make use of a method for doing science and utilize a variety of higher-order thinking skills and scientific process skills. These activities encourage students to organize their thoughts and data and to design effective ways of approaching a problem. It further requires students to make decisions about how information should be analyzed and effectively communicated.

National groups interested in science education across the United States have indicated that the use of instructional technology is a necessity if students are to be successful in their education and their future. That implies that, as teachers, we must be able to teach effectively and incorporate instructional technology into the science classroom. Simply stated, there is no one best strategy to promote the student use of instructional technology. In *Project 2061: Benchmarks for Science Literacy* (AAAS, 1993), instructional technology is included as a component for understanding the designed world. The AAAS indicates that students should not only understand what technology is but also develop an understanding of how instructional technology works as it relates to speed, transmission, coding, and protocols. The Internet provides an outstanding opportunity to teach students through and about instructional technology. This example of the expectation of the use of instructional technology is mirrored by the goals and objectives for other states in science education at the middle school level.

Second, the *NSES* and *Benchmarks for Science Literacy* have a keen focus on science process skills. Instructional technology is an effective tool for use in promoting student learning and enhancing their use of science process and problem-solving skills. Actually, instructional technology may be used as an effective tool in enhancing all science process skills, including observing, classifying, measuring, communicating, inferring, predicting or hypothesizing, experimenting, interpreting, and concluding answers about a given activity or experiment. As noted later in this chapter, all science process skills can be addressed through the use of instructional technology.

A third consideration in connecting the use of instructional technology with the national standards and benchmarks is the idea that all students can learn science. Instructional technology may provide the avenue through which student interest can be increased on a regular basis. Instructional technology provides the opportunity for students to learn and participate in their education through a variety of intelligences (Beckman, 1999). Through instructional technology, students can learn through those intelligences where they are dominant and still increase their ability to learn through other intelligences.

The Importance of Instructional Technology in the Science Classroom

The use of instructional technology in the classroom is important because it allows students more time on higher-level thinking and problem-solving skills than traditional methods of instruction. Examine the two examples in Table 5.1. It becomes relatively easy to determine that the example in the table involves a great deal more thought and application by students. They are spending more time doing science than doing the tasks related to doing science. Once students have gained the skills necessary to use instructional technology, they are able to incorporate these skills in learning and applying information and concepts they have learned in an effective and efficient manner.

Without instructional technology, students are limited in their creativity and their demonstration of their understanding of the science concept. With instructional technology, students are limited only by their understanding of the concept of speed or velocity. Instructional technology is a tool that allows the students to complete all the same tasks as with any effective hands-on, minds-on science activity and then extends their learning and performance through addressing a variety of learning styles. Students spend less time on lower-level tasks, such as collecting data and plotting graphs, and spend more time on higher-level tasks, such as analyzing data, organizing information, and communicating results.

In a series of lessons, students can learn about geological faults from a lesson titled "A Model of Three Faults" (http://www.usgs.gov/education/learnweb/ESLesson1.html) available from the U.S. Geological Survey (USGS). Students may then explore

TABLE 5.1   ENHANCING INSTRUCTION WITH INSTRUCTIONAL TECHNOLOGY

Without Instructional Technology	With Instructional Technology
Objective: The learner will determine the relationship between the distance traveled and the elapsed time to determine the speed of the object.	Objective: The learner will determine the relationship between the distance traveled and the elapsed time to determine the speed of the object.
Description: Students use a stopwatch to measure the elapsed time it takes a marble to travel 2 meters over several trials. The students then average their collected data and plot a graph by hand, using 1-centimeter-square graph paper. The students then examine their graph and write a lab report detailing their findings and establish or confirm that the speed of an object is equal to the distance traveled divided by the time.	Description: Students use a photo-gate sensor connected to a computer to measure the elapsed time it takes a marble to travel 2 meters. They then use the computer to chart and eventually plot their data and spend most of their time interpreting the graph. These same students then import their graph into a word processing document and develop a laboratory report in the format specified by the teacher. The students then examine their graph and write a lab report detailing their findings and establish or confirm that the speed of an object is equal to the distance traveled divided by the time. These same students then develop a presentation using PowerPoint (Microsoft) or other multimedia presentation software that makes use of their graph and also uses pictures of real cars and objects downloaded from the Internet to demonstrate that they are making the connection between the classroom and the concept in the real world.

the impact of geological faults by conducting an Internet search using a search, and finally they can actually communicate with a geologist from the USGS by sending a message to Ask-A-Geologist@usgs.gov. This type of lesson involves students looking at real-world examples, asking questions, making predictions, and finally asking a real scientist about their predictions. This type of activity has much more power to promote student learning than the traditional reading about geological faults, watching a video or movie, and then simply drawing pictures.

In the attempt to bring the real world into the science classroom, teachers in the past have talked about or shown pictures of a NASA shuttle launch or talked about advanced microscope methods. These may seem very abstract to students looking at pictures or using a simple light microscope. Today students can use the Internet to find out about a current NASA shuttle launch or mission by visiting the NASA Internet site (http://www.nasa.gov) and track the preparation, launch, and mission through daily reports and images. Students can also view enhanced microscope pictures and images at sites like the one posted by the Stevens Institute of Technology (http://k12science.ati.stevens-tech.edu/microscope/images/). These sites can enhance the understanding that students have of space and of the use of microscopes in all fields of science.

USING INSTRUCTIONAL TECHNOLOGY TO COLLECT AND ORGANIZE INFORMATION IN THE SCIENCE CLASSROOM

There are many strategies you can use to incorporate more instructional technology into the science classroom to help students collect and organize scientific information. The use of instructional technology can provide you and your students with access to materials and resources not readily available or affordable to schools in the recent past. Some of the strategies to collect and organize scientific information include the following:

- Taking a virtual science field trip on the Internet
- Exploring current science events on the Internet
- Conducting historical and content area research in science
- Using word processing and computer graphing for scientific concepts
- Using electronic probes to collect and display scientific data
- Making science presentations
- Communicating with scientists

Each of these strategies has specific strengths and promotes student learning and performance in a unique manner. However, in each instance, instructional technology is being used to gather information and then organize that information use in a planned science learning activity in the classroom.

How many experiences have you had in the previously listed areas? Do you feel comfortable in each area? The next section will provide you with the opportunity to review and revisit your skills in each of these areas so that you can provide your students with many exciting science activities.

Brief Overview of Using the Internet to Identify Science Information

The use of the Internet to gather information has become common in our personal lives. Currently, most public libraries and public school media centers report that routine access to the Internet is available to patrons. If you are skilled at searching for information on the Internet, then you will be able to access resources and materials for the science classroom on a regular basis. If you are less familiar with the Internet, then you need to review some important information and first steps. To search for information on the Internet, you need to remember that the computer you use will make use of a program called a browser. Some common Web browsers available at this time are Netscape, Mosaic, and America Online. These systems make the Internet accessible to you in your search for information.

Once you have located a suitable computer, you will need to select a search engine. That is the term given to a computer program that searches out information across all the computers on the Internet and reports back where specific information can be found. These search engines are usually accessible through a no-charge provider. Some of these no-charge search engines include the following:

- Altavista: http://www.altavista.digital.com/
- Infoseek: http://www.go.com
- Magellan: http://www.mckinley.com
- Google: http://www.google.com
- HotBot: http://www.hotbot.lycos.com
- Excite: http://www.excite.com
- Lycos: http://www.lycos.com
- WebCrawler: http://webcrawler.com

Many other search engines are available, and more are being published all the time.

You should try several different search engines to see which format you are most comfortable with and then begin your search. Internet search engines search throughout the Internet and identify sites, or Web pages, where specific information can be found. For example, let's say you want to find out information about amphibians. You will need to determine the descriptors you will use to look for information. In the search shown in Figure 5.1, the focus was made to locate middle school lesson plans about amphibians. On the HotBot search engine, the terms "middle school lesson plans amphibians" were entered in the Search box. Then the Search icon was selected, and HotBot returned over 160 sites where information about middle school lesson plans about amphibians could be located.

Each location identified, or hit, provides a brief description of the site, the likelihood that the site matches the identified criteria, the date the site was most recently updated, and the URL, or Internet address. The 10 sites listed in Figure 5.1 provided some wonderful information related to amphibians. The information included rare photographs, movies, descriptions, classifications, life cycle information, predator-prey relationships, geographic ranges, and much more. Most sites included specific lesson plans and activities related to amphibians as well as other sites where more information could be found. In order to use this information effectively with students, teachers must visit each site and explore on their own. It is only then that you will know the value of each site and decide how students could make the best use of the available information. The most common strategies, related to science content and concepts, are located in the following sections. For more information about downloading information and reasonable use policies, you should discuss the topic with your instructor, or contact your local system manager or district technology administrator. They will be able to quickly fill you in on the specific processes related to the Internet on your specific computer system.

FIGURE 5.1

A Top 10 List of Information About Amphibians

1. AITLC Guide to Amphibians and Reptiles: The ACCESS INDIANA Teaching & Learning Center Guide to Amphibians and Reptiles. . . .
99% 6/24/99 http://tlc.ai.org/amphibia.htm

2. The Rainforest Workshop: The Tropical Rainforest Back to the Rainforest Workshop. To the Temperate Rainforest. Toucan graphic © by MediaClips Welcome to the Tropical Rainforest! To Lesson plans The purpose of this page is to help teachers and students learn more. . .
98% 7/3/98 http://kids.osd.wednet.edu/Marshall/homepage/tropical.html

3. Thematic Units Index: Elementary lesson plans and activities arranged by theme Over 300 thematic unit links from all over the web are organized here by theme. . . .
98% 6/23/99 http://www.atozteacherstuff.com/themes/index.html

4. Thematic Units Index: Elementary lesson plans and activities arranged by theme Over 300 thematic unit links from all over the web are organized here by theme. . . .
98% 6/23/99 http://atozteacherstuff.com/themes/index.html

5. IXI: Educator's Resources: Educational Resources Contents Internet Basics Technology in the Classroom Curriculum, Lesson Plans & Projects Virtual Field Trips Events Electronic Magazines & Newspaper Kid Stuff Arts English & Literature Math Music Science Social Studies Health. . . .
98% 4/18/98 http://www.iximd.com/er7.htm

6. Birds: Birds, Butterflies & Insects Resources Lesson Plans Handouts Web Based Activities Connecting Students Through Themes and Units Resources Animal Omnibus Amphibians, birds, fishes, mammals, reptiles, etc. Audubon Online Activism. . . .
98% 4/17/99 http://www.conectingstudents.com/themes/birds.htm

7. k12 Internet Resources: K-12 Previewed Internet Resource
98% 6/1/99 http://dent.edmonds.wednet.edu/IMD/k12index.html

8. JASON X: RAINFORESTS CONTENTS:Project JASON Sites Locations Related Sites About Rainforests Flora (Plants) Fauna (Animals) Rainforest Conservation Other Sites CONTENTS: Project JASON Sites Locations Related Sites About Rainforests Flora (Plants. . . .
98% 3/10/99 http://www.lamphere.k12.mi.us/CyberLibraries/Elementary/jasonx.htm

9. The Science Editor's Jump Page: Herpetology links The Science Educator's Jump Page Herpetology links: Legend: (5 apples).Specially for Teachers. Sites designed for use by teachers, usually include complete lesson plans. . . .
97% 8/11/97 http://home1.gte.net/jwagner/herpetol.htm

10. Wildlife Links, Education: Education Academic Programs in Conservation Biology The purpose of this site is to function as a clearinghouse for information on academic opportunities in Conservation Biology, and in doing so, increase the likelihood that mentor and mentee will. . . .
97% 6/9/99 http://www.selu.com/~bio/wildlife/links/education.html

Suggested Activity 5.1
Virtual Field Trip

Now would be a good time to apply some of the information furnished so far in this chapter. Locate a computer; then, using a search engine listed earlier in the section, pick a topic to research. Pick the descriptors as in the example. They might include anything from "ancient dinosaur bones" to "jet powered planes" and everything in between. Complete the instructions for the search and look at the sites you have identified. Visit the sites and examine the information available to you through the Internet. Next, think about the ways in which you can have your students use this information to help them learn more about science in the classroom.

TABLE 5.2   VIRTUAL FIELD TRIP POSSIBILITIES

Museum or Exhibit Name	Internet Address
The Discovery Museums	http://www.ultranet.com/~discover/
National Air and Space Museum	http://www.nasm.edu/
The Franklin Institute Science Museum	http://sln.fi.edu/tfi/welcome.html
Northern Lights Planetarium	http://www.uit.no/
Honolulu Community College	http://www.hcc.hawaii.edu/dinos/ dinos.1.html
The Hands On Children's Museum	http://www.hocm.org/
The Children's Discovery Museum of San Jose	http://www.cdm.org/

Taking a Virtual Field Trip on the Internet

As you know by now, the Internet has become an outstanding resource for identifying science information to be used by students in the classroom. One of the first and most interesting things students can do on the Internet is take a virtual field trip. Students can work with materials from The Magic School Bus (Scholastic, Inc.) or visit a planetarium. They can look at a dinosaur exhibit or see enhanced images from microscopes. All these are possible by using the Internet. Several locations particularly interesting to students are listed in Table 5.2.

This type of information collection activity helps students gain confidence in using instructional technology and gives them the opportunity for success at the assigned tasks. Students routinely discover that they have learned many things from taking a virtual field trip.

One safety tip to remember about having students use the Internet as a resource is that *you, as the teacher, should always visit the site before sending students to review or explore information on the Internet.* It needs to be noted that when students are using the Internet, they need to be well supervised, informed about potential hazards on the Internet, and aware of local school protocols for student use of the Internet. Teachers also need to be constantly aware of the sites students are using and the information they are viewing. This is extremely important.

Suggested Activity 5.2
Create a KWL Chart

Establish a KWL chart related to a topic such as amphibians. Ask students to fill in the chart with the things they know about amphibians under the K (Know) heading. Then have students visit two or three museum or exhibit sites on the Internet to fill in the W (What do you want to know?) section of the chart. Next, ask the students to complete the L (What have we learned?) column of the chart. KWL charts are commonly used in educational programs, such as Activities Integrating Math and Science (AIMS). The chart may take the following form:

K	W	L
What do you know about amphibians?	What do you want to know about amphibians?	What have you learned about amphibians?

Exploring Current Science Events on the Internet

Exploring current science events in science via the internet has become a great way for students to explore our world and become aware of how people are interacting, both good and bad, with the environment. Students can participate in a NASA shuttle launch, review science news of the day or the week, or see information about science-related television broadcasts and series. Table 5.3 shows several Internet sites that provide outstanding information on a regular basis.

Activities can be developed around general or specific topics. Current event topics may include such items as space exploration and the recent mission to Mars. They may include monitoring the changes in the ozone layer or in pollution in groundwater and ocean water around the world.

This type of activity addresses the *NSES* (Science Teaching Standard D) through the idea that "the school science program must extend beyond the walls of the school to include the resources of the community" and that an "effective science teaching depends on the availability and organization of material, equipment, media, and technology."

TABLE 5.3 EXPLORING CURRENT SCIENCE EVENTS

Source or Organization Name	Internet Address
Discovery Channel Online and The Learning Channel	http://www.discovery.com/sched/domestic/learning/learning.html
MSNBC	http://www.msnbc.com
National Aeronautics and Space Administration	http://www.nasa.gov
Science News Online	http://www.sciencenews.org/
Popular Science Online	http://www.popsci.com/
Scientific American	http://www.sciam.com/

Suggested Activity 5.3
Internet as a Research Tool

Working in a small group, select a current science topic, such as hurricanes in the Atlantic Ocean. Then use the Internet to monitor the events leading up to and following the developing hurricanes. Have groups develop written presentations that describe the conditions needed to create a hurricane, describe how hurricanes are classified, and explore how scientists monitor and learn about developing hurricanes. As a teacher, you need to consider some of the following ideas:
- What research do my students need to be successful?
- What is the essential information my students need to have about the topic?
- How will my students be able to show me what they know about the topic?
- Is the topic appropriate for the grade level of the students?

Incorporating this type of data collection activity into the science classroom helps bring the real world into the classroom and helps students connect the classroom with their environment. This type of activity also promotes the process of students gathering and organizing information on a specific topic. They address what has been referred to as allowing the learner to "potentially function at a level that transcends limitations of his or her cognitive system" (Salomon, Perkins, & Globerson, 1991). With this in mind, how can we, as teachers, afford to miss the opportunity to help our students through the use of a tool with the potential to have such a powerful impact?

Science Content and Historical Research on the Internet

The Internet can also be a great source for students to discover or identify information about people, places, or things related to the science curriculum. Students can

TABLE 5.4 BACKGROUND INFORMATION AND HISTORICAL PERSPECTIVES

Information Topic and Source	Internet Address
History of the Light Microscope, by Thomas E. Jones	http://www.utmem.edu/personal/thjones/hist/hist_mic.htm
History of Modern Science, Kansas State University	http://www.ksu.edu
The Faces of Science: African Americans in the Sciences, Louisiana State University Libraries, Baton Rouge	http://www.lib.lsu.edu/lib/chem/display/faces.html
History of Flight, Ohio History of Flight Museum, Port Columbus International Airport, Columbus, Ohio	http://www.aeroweb.org.brooklyn.cuny.edu/museum/oh/ohfm.html
Plate Tectonics and Geology University of California Museum of Paleontology (UCMP), Berkeley, California	http://www.ucmp.berkeley.edu/museum/firsttime.html

explore the history of the light microscope, rockets, or the nuclear age. Students can identify sites where they can learn about topics such as plate tectonics, rock and mineral formation, the history of flight, and how the internal combustion engine works.

Teachers should also be aware *that much of the information posted on the Internet is not reviewed for quality, accuracy, or content. Any individual with a home page on the Internet can post information he or she feels is appropriate.* Most professional organizations continue to use the same types of review processes for on-line works as they do for traditional print material. You can be more confident using information from these professional sources than individuals; however, all sources need to be reviewed by the teacher. Some sites that provide particularly good background information and historical perspectives include those shown in Table 5.4.

Still, much more can be done with the exploration of history and science content by students using the Internet. Most professional organizations involved in scientific research maintain an active Internet Web site. These organizations include the Center for Polymer Studies (http://cps-www.bu.edu/); the National Chemical Society (http://www.ncs.org); the NSTA's Scope, Science, and Coordination Project (http://www.gsh.org/NSTA); the Association for the Education of Teachers of Science (http://science.cc.uwf.edu/aets/aets.html); and many others. Each of these organizations can serve as an outstanding source of information and resources for both teachers and students seeking to obtain information by using the Internet.

Using Word Processing and Computer Graphing

One of the most basic ways your students can use instructional technology to collect and organize information is to write about their experiences and to create graphs using a word processing program. Most word processing programs available today have the capacity to develop and insert graphs and charts into the text of a word processing document. This type of activity provides the student with the structure needed to complete scientific investigations and also allows the student the opportunity to determine the way data should be organized and eventually presented.

Using Electronic Probes to Collect and Display Data

The use of electronic probes and sensors allows science students to use the computer, or a graphing calculator, to collect data and then import the information into a word processing program. In this manner, they can collect accurate scientific data and complete multiple trials in a timely manner and spend more time analyzing their results, not plotting graphs by hand. This type of instructional technology is becoming less expensive and in some cases is becoming routine in the science classroom.

Suggested Activity 5.4

Person/Concept Exploration on the Internet

Select a person or concept to explore through the Internet. For example, use a common search engine such as available on HotBot (http://www.hotbot.lycos.com) or Excite (http://www.excite.com) to search for information on famous African American scientists. Then print out selected information about the person. Compare your information with the information identified by other members of your group and develop a presentation about these important individuals. Think about how you might use this type of activity in your own classroom. How would you approach this idea to make it work for you?

Suggested Activity 5.5

Data Collection

Answer the question, Is there a relationship between a person's height and his or her arm span? First, have the students make a prediction about the outcome of the activity. Next, have the students measure, in centimeters, the height of 10 of their classmates and the distance from fingertip to fingertip on their outstretched arms. Then, using a word processing program, describe their data collection process, make a table of their results, and create a graph of their findings. They should then use their graph to determine if in fact their initial prediction was correct.

Think about how this type of activity gets students to explore their world and make use of the process skills essential to developing a scientific mind.

One such instance is Kanawha County Schools in West Virginia. There, all 10th-grade students are required to take a course titled "Coordinated and Thematic Science." All students in the course participate in cooperative activities related to problem solving through the use of instructional technology. Students spend more time analyzing data and solving problems than collecting data. By the end of the course, all students have become more comfortable with instructional technology and have had extended periods of time working with the analysis of data. This type of program is becoming more popular and is being implemented with increasing frequency at the middle and elementary school levels.

Suggested Activity 5.6
Mapping the Motion of Moving Objects

Using a motion detector probe, the appropriate software, and a computer, students will map out the motion of moving objects. Students move a variety of objects in front of a motion detector probe and determine the instances of acceleration and change in direction from the data collected and the graph plotted. Objects might include a rolling ball, a walking student, and a bouncing ball.

Think about the ways you, as a teacher, could use this technology to help your students learn about science. How could your classroom be an interesting and effective science class through the use of this type of technology? How would your curriculum change? How would your students benefit from the consistent use of instructional technology in the science classroom?

Making Presentations

An effective use of instructional technology is in the area of student-made presentations on scientific topics. One type of presentation software suitable for students to use is called PowerPoint. This software is available in both Windows and Macintosh formats and allows students to create a series of slides on the computer that can contain text, graphs, links to the Internet, pictures, sounds, and movies to demonstrate their understanding of a given concept. This is easily accomplished by students working in cooperative groups, even with limited access to computers. This type of activity allows students to teach one another about a topic or concept. Students can be creative and demonstrate their understanding of a topic in many unique ways and meet the objectives set forth by the teacher and the curriculum.

These presentations can be saved on a disk and used for future reference by other classes of students and will prompt them to expand on the work and research completed by their peers.

Take this information and locate a computer that has the PowerPoint program already installed. Use the program to develop a seven- or eight-slide presentation that you could use in a classroom to share information about a scientific topic. If you are uneasy about trying an unfamiliar program, talk to a local media specialist or your instructor for help and ask he or she to help you get started with your presentation.

Communicating With Scientists

Perhaps one of the most interesting ways science students can use instructional technology is to use e-mail to communicate with scientists who are working in a specific field. This can be accomplished by contacting a local college or university and asking them to collaborate with your particular classroom project. Another way to accomplish this communication and bring what students call "real science" into the classroom is to make use of an established Web site. Some of these locations request a subscription fee, while others are free. However, all provide quick responses to student questions. Some popular and effective sites are shown in Table 5.5.

Another project, called *Science Mentors,* helps Texas students use the Internet to find information and conduct research. Terry Antoine heads the project funded by a minigrant through the Texas Educational Network. The project matches middle school students involved in conducting research with experts in corresponding scientific fields via e-mail. In this setting, the teacher acts as a guide to show students how to find information for their project. The address for this project is http://tenet.cc.utexas.edu/minigrants/antoine/html.

Another way to create ongoing communications with scientists is through contact with a local or regional company involved in product research and development. By contacting organizations such as chemical companies, petroleum refineries, foundries, mines, or engineering organizations, you can establish an important link between your classroom and the real world.

In each of these instances, the real world in which our students are living and are going to live is being brought into the classroom and then explored by students. Students will gain knowledge and grow from their experiences into the "scientifically literate" citizens needed to succeed in our dynamic world. The age of information will not pass them by. Rather, they will be active participants in their own learning and understand more of the world around them.

Other Uses of Instructional Technology

In addition to the uses previously listed, there are many other ways to make use of instructional technology in the science classroom. CD-ROMs have become common

TABLE 5.5   RESOURCES FOR SCIENCE STORIES

Name of Site	Internet Address
Ask a Scientist	http://www.halcyon.com/sciclub/kidquest.html
	or
	http://www.hmsc.orst.edu
Ask the Space Scientist	http://image.gsfc.nasa.gov/poetry/ask/askmag.html
MAD Scientist Network	http://www.madsci.org
WhaleNet	http://whale.wheelock.edu
Windows on the Universe	http://www.windows.ucar.edu

Source: Koch (1999, p. 281).

and in many schools have replaced the traditional set of school encyclopedias normally found in the library or media center. These resources provide a quick and visual resource for students to explore a specific topic or event. Another outstanding way CD-ROMs are used is in the area of simulations. These programs allow students to explore variables and set parameters and discover the impact that change has on an environment or a planet.

Still other forms of multimedia programs make use of laser-disc technology connected to the computer to give the student and teacher control of a situation. These programs link a laser-disc player to the computer to allow for high-speed location and viewing of information.

IMPACTING STUDENT LEARNING THROUGH INSTRUCTIONAL TECHNOLOGY IN THE SCIENCE CLASSROOM

Instructional technology has become an important part of the educational system. During the 1998 fiscal year, it was estimated by the Westchester Institute for Human Services Research (1999) that national spending on instructional technology exceeded $5 billion and is expected to increase by at least $1 billion each year. Instructional technology has become a big business, and as teachers we need to be able to take advantage of this outstanding tool for student success.

In order for instructional technology to have an impact on student learning in science, students must be involved in using the instructional technology in the science classroom. It is not enough for students to see the technology; they must use the equipment and become comfortable with its use related to science and experimentation. The more we explore classroom applications of instructional technology, the more it becomes clear that instructional technology can have a positive and powerful impact on student learning. Students can spend more of their time focused on higher-level skills and problem solving rather than routine tasks used frequently in the traditional classroom. This approach to the use of Instructional Technology aligns with the vision set forth in the *National Science Education Standards* (National Research Council, 1996) and *Project 2061: Science for All Americans* (AAAS, 1990).

FIGURE 5.2

1. Identify the types of instructional technology available in the classroom or in the school.

2. Identify the goals and objectives that your students are expected to learn during a given unit or lesson.

3. Determine how students will demonstrate their understanding of the identified goals and objectives.

4. Examine your unit plans and existing material to determine the assignments you believe to be the most effective in helping students learn science through the use of instructional technology.

5. Use instructional technology in a consistent and ongoing manner in the classroom.

A Process for Utilizing Instructional Technology in the Classroom

In order to impact student learning, we must identify a method for ensuring that we include instructional technology as a meaningful tool in the science classroom. The most logical place to do this is during the unit or lesson planning stage of teaching. If we stop to explore all our options related to instructional technology while we are planning to teach science, we have a much better chance of incorporating instructional technology into the classroom.

A simple but effective process for incorporating instructional technology into the middle school science classroom involves five steps, shown in Figure 5.2.

Step 1. *Identify the types of instructional technology available in the classroom or in the school.* This includes your classroom, team member classrooms, other science and mathematics classrooms, computer laboratories, resource rooms, and the library or media center. If you accomplish this step prior to establishing your plans for teaching, you have this information available to use while you are planning to teach your science lessons.

Step 2. *Identify the goals and objectives that your students are expected to learn during a given unit or lesson.* As you work through the identification of goals and objectives for your students, you can see the places where instructional technology can play an effective role within your comfort zone as a teacher. You will also be able to begin envisioning the ways in which instructional technology will be able to be used by students in an effective manner. Keep in mind those strategies for using instructional technology noted earlier in this chapter.

Step 3. *Determine how students will demonstrate their understanding of the identified goals and objectives.* In place of a traditional set of questions, think about how students could complete a project using instructional technology to demonstrate their understanding of the same goals and objectives. Think about using alternatives to traditional forms of assessment; these could include instructional technology through student presentations, research projects, experimental design, and portfolios related to what students have learned.

Step 4. *Examine your unit plans and existing material to determine the assignments you believe to be the most effective in helping students learn through the use of instructional technology.* It is here that you can begin transforming your curriculum into a more effective one through the use of instructional technology. As you plan your lessons related to science and other content areas, you can keep in mind the ways in which instructional technology can be used by students to demonstrate their understanding of science content and concepts. Students can use cooperative groups to research a topic and then develop a presentation using available presentation software. They can develop graphs and tables using graphing calculators to demonstrate and confirm their comprehension of formulas and scientific relationships, and they can create projects using information from the Internet and make the connection between the classroom and the real world.

Step 5. *Use instructional technology in a consistent and ongoing manner in the classroom.* The more students use instructional technology, the more comfortable you and your students will become at using instructional technology. As you and your students become more comfortable, you both will gain confidence in the use of instructional technology, and you will be amazed at the creativity and ingenuity demonstrated by your students in showing you what they know about science and how it relates to the world around them.

If you follow these five steps, you will become confident in the use of instructional technology, and your science students will begin their journey into the information age of the new century. Students will be able to locate and use information. They will be able to solve problems and use science process skills to predict and test situations and then make their own decisions on the basis of information that they have collected. In short, your decisions about using instructional technology will have an impact on your students that will last their entire life.

Addressing Science Process Skills Through Instructional Technology

Think about how you could use instructional technology to identify and prepare a curriculum that stimulates students to think and develop understandings of concepts in a setting where the learner is active and involved in developing his or her own understanding of science. Science process skills can be addressed by the learner by using instructional technology in a consistent and ongoing manner. From Table 5.6, it becomes apparent that teachers can organize and successfully encourage students to make good use of instructional technology.

Addressing Multiple Intelligences Through Instructional Technology

Instructional technology is a tool that can also be used to address the multiple intelligences exhibited by all students in the science classroom. They can use the Internet or other tools to participate in a variety of activities where the focus is on learning through a variety of intelligences. Some sample activities are shown in Table 5.7.

TABLE 5.6   ADDRESSING PROCESS SKILLS USING TECHNOLOGY

Science Process Skill	Classroom Use of Instructional Technology
Observing	• Taking a virtual field trip on the Internet • Exploring current events on the Internet • Using word processing and computer graphing • Using electronic probes to collect and display data
Classifying	• Taking a virtual field trip on the Internet • Exploring current events on the Internet • Using word processing and computer graphing • Using electronic probes to collect and display data • Communicating with scientists
Measuring	• Taking a virtual field trip on the Internet • Using word processing and computer graphing • Using electronic probes to collect and display data • Communicating with scientists
Communicating	• Using word processing and computer graphing • Communicating with scientists
Inferring	• Exploring current events on the Internet • Using word processing and computer graphing • Communicating with scientists
Predicting or Hypothesizing	• Exploring current events on the Internet • Using word processing and computer graphing
Experimenting	• Using word processing and computer graphing • Using electronic probes to collect and display data • Communicating with scientists
Interpreting	• Taking a virtual field trip on the Internet • Conducting historical and content area research • Using word processing and computer graphing • Communicating with scientists
Concluding	• Conducting historical and content area research • Using word processing and computer graphing • Communicating with scientists

TABLE 5.7 ADDRESSING MULTIPLE INTELLIGENCES USING TECHNOLOGY

Intelligence Addressed	Instructional Technology Activity Starter
Linguistic	Establish a daily journal using a word processing program and the Internet on a current event at the local or national level.
Logical-Mathematical	Collect data and, using a word processing program, create a data table and graph as a part of a laboratory or activity report.
Musical	Use the Internet to search out the connection between the scales used in music and the pitch made by an instrument.
Spatial	Use the Internet to explore the coordinates of sites in different places in your state, country, or the world.
Bodily-Kinesthetic	Conduct a physical fitness test and, using a word processing program, create a data table and graph as a part of a laboratory or activity report. Share this information with a local hospital or medical care agency.
Interpersonal	Participate in a group project to design or redesign a product. Contact scientists or engineers and share your design changes with them and other members of the class through a multimedia presentation.
Intrapersonal	Establish a word processed journal to help students explore their own understanding of a given concept or topic.
Naturalistic	Identify locations on the Internet that help students explore the role of technology in society and address the issues of society versus nature.

SUMMARY

Instructional technology may be the tool we use to ensure that students are consistently involved in their own education. As we change from a traditional classroom to one in which instructional technology is used on an everyday basis, we will also find that our students begin to change. Their use of process and problem-solving skills may increase, their ability to learn through a variety of intelligences may improve, their retention of information may increase, and their performance in the science classroom may improve as their familiarity with instructional technology is promoted. We may also find that teachers who use instructional technology and the strategies outlined in this chapter consistently provide their students with a learning environment in which learning, and not necessarily teaching, is emphasized. These teachers are facilitating learning in the truest sense of the word, and are enabling their students to learn now and in the future.

Teaching through the use of instructional technology is in fact transforming the local classroom into a global classroom where students learn and relate to the world in which they are living now and in which they will be living in the future.

REFERENCES

American Association for the Advancement of Science. (1990). *Project 2061: Science for all Americans.* New York: Oxford University Press.

American Association for the Advancement of Science. (1993). *Project 2061: Benchmarks for science literacy.* New York: Oxford University Press.

Beckman, M. S. (1999, June). *Multiple ways of knowing: Howard Gardner's theory of multiple intelligences extend and enhance student learning.* http://www.earlychildhood.com

Kent, T. W., & McNergney, R. F. (1998). *Will technology really change education?* Thousands Oaks, CA: Corwin Press.

Koch, J. (1999). *Science stories: Teachers and children as science learners.* Boston, MA: Houghton Mifflin.

Michigan State Board of Education. (1991). *Michigan essential goals and objectives for science education (K–12).* East Lansing: Michigan State University.

National Research Council. (1996). *National Science Education Standards.* Washington, DC: National Academy Press.

Salomon, G., Perkins, D. N., & Globerson, T. (1991). Partners in cognition: Extending human intelligence with intelligent technologies. *Educational Researcher, 20*(3), 2–9.

Sinclair, A., & Coates, L. (1999). Teaching multiple intelligences. *Science Scope and Sequence, 22*(5), 17–18.

Westchester Institute for Human Services Research. (1999, July). *The balanced view: Educational technology. A report prepared for the New York State Department of Education.* http://www.sharingsuccess.org/code/e1/ms_mst.html

Woodbury, J. (1992). *Adventures of Jasper Woodbury.* Learning Technology Center. Vanderbilt University. Nashville, TN.

CHAPTER 6

The Multiple Roles of Assessment

Dr. Leonie M. Rose

FIGURE 6.1

"Assessments are the primary feedback mechanism in the science education system. They provide students with feedback on how well they are meeting expectations, teachers with feedback on how well their students are learning, school districts with feedback on the effectiveness of their teachers and programs, and policy makers with feedback on how well policies are working."

(National Research Council, *National Science Education Standards,* 1996, p. 5)

In this chapter, you will learn how assessment has changed since you were in elementary school. Why you need to assess before, during, and after teaching science lessons will be explained. You will also discover how the national science assessment standards affect assessment in the classroom and reasons why experts in the field of science education are recommending moving away from traditional testing to authentic assessments.

Suggested Activity

Assessing Science Learning

6.1

1. In your journal or on a sheet of paper, write about what you remember about how you were tested in science in elementary or middle school. Share your thoughts with those in your collaborative group.

2. What do you know about assessment in science classrooms? Jot down your thoughts and share them with others at your table.

3. Create a web or list of science assessments with others in your group or at your table. Select the ones you feel you might use in your classroom and explain why you chose them.

CURRENT SCIENCE ASSESSMENT THEORY

Diagnostic, Formative, and Summative Assessment in Science

Assessing student learning before, during, and after instruction is a necessary part of effective teaching in science. It is important that you understand that assessment is **ongoing or embedded** in the instructional process. Assessment is **not limited to some sort** of evaluation *after* instruction has taken place. Feedback based on the information gathered as part of the assessment process should be provided to students to help them grow in their understanding of science concepts, skills, attitudes, and processes. Teachers can use assessment information in a number of ways.

Before beginning instruction, teachers need to be aware of what students already know. This is referred to as *diagnostic* assessment. Effective learning occurs most often when new knowledge is built on and connected to prior learning. There are several ways for you to assess students' prior knowledge before beginning instruction specific to a targeted science concept. Strategies such as KWL (Ogle, 1986), interviews, pretests, self-assessments, and science journals are commonly used to measure prior knowledge.

You are probably already familiar with the KWL strategy used by many teachers at all grade levels in various curriculum areas. As part of the instructional process, the teacher asks the learners what they know or think they know (the **K**, or *know*, part of the KWL strategy) about a specific topic area, for example, dinosaurs. Typically, the teacher will lead the discussion, calling on a variety of children to share what they know about the selected topic. Responses are accepted without evaluation and usually written down on the chalkboard or on chart paper. The teacher's reaction to each shared bit of information is something like "Jason thinks that dinosaurs don't exist anymore" or "Courtney told us that some people kept dinosaurs as pets."

Sometimes children's responses will contradict each other. When this happens, the teacher does not try to resolve the contradiction at that moment but instead points out the issue in this way: "Cory Lynne says that people and dinosaurs did not live at the same time, so they can't be someone's pet." Let's list that as one of our questions that we want to answer as we learn about dinosaurs (the **W**, or *want to know*, portion of the KWL). As we complete our unit on dinosaurs, we will look at all these ideas again to find out which of them are supported by what we learn and which are not. How will we write our first question? Alisha asked whether dinosaurs lived at the same time as people. Let's write that down: "Did people and dinosaurs live at the same time?" The teacher would then continue to list the students' questions about dinosaurs. Some questions the class may wish to explore might be "Which dinosaur was the largest?" "What did they eat?" "Where did they live?" "What happened to the dinosaurs?" or "Why don't dinosaurs exist today?"

Diagnostic assessment allows teachers to assess knowledge that children already possess, measure students' interest in the concept, and become aware of misconceptions that are present. The teacher then uses this information to plan for, guide, and facilitate learning. During instruction, the teacher observes students while they are involved in the planned science experience and offers on-the-spot help in the form of feedback and reinforcement. This is referred to as ***formative assessment.*** Formative assessment is an essential part of effective instruction. It provides immediate individual feedback that is used to guide the learner in completing the task at hand. Constant feedback allows the teacher to measure students' progress and to determine an individual student's needs.

Formative assessment gives the teacher an emerging picture of who understands key ideas and who can perform targeted skills at what level of proficiency with what degree of interest. Effective science teachers use this information to plan for tomorrow's lesson by structuring instruction in a way that assists individual students in building on their current level of competency (Tomlinson, 1999). Teachers also use formative assessments to help them make on-the-spot decisions about their instruction. For example, if the students look puzzled or their science journals reveal misconceptions, you can go back and review a concept before you introduce more in-depth information or add new information related to the concept.

This might be called the "honest appraisal" approach. The teacher does not rely on a test score. Rather, he or she may obtain feedback from the observations of a student's behavior, work habits, attitudes, and classroom participation. Written work on lab sheets or in a student's manual can provide clues along with the student's responses to the teacher's questions. Such formative assessment information may come from small-group discussions with the teacher and a few students, whole-class discussions, journal entries, portfolio entries, exit cards, skill inventories, pretest homework assignments, student opinion, or interest surveys. This is a more subjective method of assessment, but if the teacher is conscientious, it probably is the most accurate and most helpful. In fact, when Black and William (1998) surveyed the research on science achievement for children with mild handicaps, they found that improved formative assessment helps the students who are struggling the most and therefore raises achievement levels overall.

During the dinosaur unit mentioned earlier, the teacher can use formative assessment in several ways. One choice would be to listen to student discussions as they work in cooperative learning groups designed for learning about different dinosaurs. How do the students categorize them? Are there any misconceptions that need to be discussed? While monitoring the class and noticing Jerome's ongoing list of information that he has been recording about dinosaurs in the **L** column (*what was learned*) of his KWL sheet, the teacher might ask him what evidence he has for

Teacher questioning can facilitate a student's demonstration of his or her science understanding.

writing "Dinosaurs are birds today." The teacher may ask self-reflection questions about instructional decisions while teaching this unit. Sample questions include "What examples of information are students placing in their science journals that demonstrate their learning?" "What are their attitudes about dinosaurs?" and "Do I need to spend more time on this unit by clarifying information?"

Assessment that occurs after instruction of a lesson or unit of study is called ***summative*** assessment. In summative assessment, the results are not used to plan for further instruction, as is the case with diagnostic and formative assessment. Thus, the main difference between these forms of assessment is in the use of the results or data gathered in the assessment as well as when they occur during the science lesson or unit. In diagnostic and formative assessments, the results become a part of the instructional process; therefore, students and teachers are able to use them. In summative assessment, the results are not usually used for instructional purposes because the learning process is essentially over, a grade is given, and the class proceeds to another area of learning.

At the end of the dinosaur unit, the teacher would have the students work together as a class to share the information that they have learned about dinosaurs. The teacher places the information gathered by the class on the chalkboard, on a chart, or on an overhead transparency. At the end of the unit, it is crucial for the teacher to make sure that the items listed represent accurate information about dinosaurs. One way to do this is to have students explain how they know the information is correct.

First, the teacher would return to the information listed under the **K** column to have the class check the items on the list that were supported and those that were not. "Based on what we learned, could dinosaurs have been people's pets? What do you think, Michael? How many of you agree with what Michael said?—Because dinosaurs lived on earth before people did, they could not be people's pets—what evidence do we have to support this? Good. Let's cross this one off our list. Under our *What We Learned* column, we can write two facts: People and dinosaurs lived during different times, and dinosaurs lived before people."

Then the teacher would lead the class in checking to see if their questions from the **W** column of the KWL were answered. When the class comes to the question about what happened to the dinosaurs, there might be conflicting information. At this point, the teacher needs to resolve the issue: "Jerome found that there is some evidence that dinosaurs have evolved into the birds we see today. Jerome, can you explain what evolved means? Yes, it would be the same as turned into over a long period of time such as thousands or millions of years or maybe even more time. Maisha found a different answer to this question. She found that there is evidence to suggest that a large meteor struck the earth. This caused large clouds of dust to block out the sun, and the dinosaurs died because their climate changed. Let's talk about what this tells us. Jeff, you are right—at this time we do not know exactly why the dinosaurs became extinct. Let's place that on our list and write down the two major theories or ideas about what happened to them." The process continues until all the relevant information that the class has learned about dinosaurs is written under the **L** column. If all the questions have not been answered, perhaps some students may want to research them more on their own and report back to the class at a later time.

Assessment Versus Evaluation

Often the terms *assessment* and *evaluation* are both used to describe diagnostic, formative, and summative means of collecting data, interpreting the results, and providing feedback about students' science learning. Although the terms are sometimes used interchangeably, they are two distinct approaches to designing a plan that assists teachers in determining how well each student is performing in science. According to the elementary school edition of *NSTA Pathways to the Science Standards* (National Science Teachers Association, 1996), *evaluation* compares and ranks what students have learned at a specific time, usually in the form of scores and grades. This is the most common and traditional approach because it uses tests such as multiple choice, true or false, or short answer that are simple to administer, score, and grade. Evaluation measures usually include a value judgment of the student's recall knowledge. On the other hand, *assessment* is a systematic, multistep process involving the collection and interpretation of science educational data (NSTA, 1996). Assessment plans use a variety of formats to determine information about what students understand, what they are able to do, and how they can use their new information/knowledge (NSTA, 1996). Assessment has these two important features:

1. It is more prescriptive than judgmental. Feedback is provided to enable both the teacher and the student to know what was done well and what needs to be improved. Rather than just noting in an evaluation that a report was "poorly written," an assessment would tell why with notations such as "You may want to revise your information in this report to lead to a stated conclusion to show your understanding of the concept. The way you have the report organized at this point makes it difficult to decide what your main idea is and what conclusions you are trying to reach."

2. Assessment places understanding as the key to learning rather than simply noting whether the answer is correct. For example, the ability to explain the problem-solving steps the student used to answer a question is just as important as the final answer.

SCIENCE EDUCATION ASSESSMENT STANDARDS

American education has been undergoing reform or change in how assessment is viewed. Assessment and learning are currently believed to be two sides of the same coin. In this paradigm, instruction and assessment must be related. New methods of data collection along with new ways of judging data quality are being used in all areas of the curriculum. Another shift is from using a more traditional approach of sampling one variable or aspect of learning with a single measure to using a variety of multiple assessments to measure an assortment of variables. Students are also being involved in assessing their learning. This enables them to learn from the process as well as to become more responsible for their own learning.

In the vision described by the *National Science Education Standards* (National Research Council, 1996), all aspects of science achievement should be measured by using multiple methods, such as performances and portfolios, as well as conventional paper-and-pencil tests. The assessment standards view assessment as a process that consists of the following four components that must interact for decision making and actions based on the data to occur: how the data will be used, what the data collection will be used to describe and quantify, which methods will be used to collect the data, and who will use the data.

How can data be used? Some possible science classroom uses for the data include: planning teaching, guiding learning, calculating grades, and making comparisons. Building or district uses of data include determining access to special or advanced education, allocating resources, and evaluating the quality of curricula, programs, and teaching practices. Policymakers may want to use the data to create standards to credential and license teachers, to develop educational theory to inform policy formulations, to monitor the effects of policies, and to allocate resources.

What can data collections describe and quantify? Science teachers may want to collect data to describe and quantify student achievement and attitudes while a district may want to examine teaching performance, program characteristics, and resource allocations as well as student achievement and attitudes. Those who make policies may collect data to examine all these areas plus teacher preparation and policy instruments.

What methods can be used to collect data? There are several methods for collecting data. Some examples include paper-and-pencil testing, performance tasks, interviews, portfolios, performances, rubrics, observations, and expert reviews. Classroom work samples, such as science journals, projects, concept mapping, and drawings, can also provide useful information about students' science learning.

Who will use the data? Those who may use the data include the people who are most closely involved in the classroom, such as teachers, students, and parents. Other groups further removed from daily science learning but who also need to use the data include educational administrators, the public, institutions of higher education, members of business and industry, policymakers, and government agencies.

Assessment Standards for Science Education

The standards for science education define what teachers should teach and what students should learn. They also include assessment standards that cover five important areas:

- Consistency of assessments with the decisions they are designed to inform
- Assessment of both achievement and opportunity to learn science
- Matching the technical quality of the data collected and the consequences of the actions taken on the basis of these data
- Fairness of assessment practices
- Soundness of inferences made about student achievement and opportunity to learn (*National Science Education Standards,* 1996, p. 5)

As a science teacher, you will be collecting information about students almost continuously and making adjustments to your teaching based on your interpretation of that information. To become effective in using science assessments, you need to become aware of issues that relate to these standards at the elementary and middle school levels. Once you are comfortable with the standards and a wide variety of science assessments, you will be in a position to put assessment data to powerful use in your classroom. The issues and teaching messages provided for each standard in the following paragraphs are a synthesis of information provided in the *National Science Education Standards* (1996) and the elementary edition of *NSTA Pathways to the Science Standards* (1996).

Assessments must be consistent with the decisions they are designed to inform. Designing assessments is not an easy task. *Each assessment tool should be constructed in a way that can measure clearly stated outcomes accurately.* Good teachers assess their students continually, not just at test time, to help them pace instruction. You will need to make sure your science lesson or unit objectives and assessments match. As a science teacher, you will use assessment data to make decisions about your students and your science curriculum. Answering the following questions will help you gather appropriate data:

- Will the students be interested in this content?
- Are these activities effective in producing my learning outcomes?
- Are my selected examples effective for student learning?
- What understandings and attitudes do my students need to have so that they can benefit from my selected activities and examples?
- How developmentally appropriate is the science content for this lesson or unit?
- Which assessment tools will provide me with the best measure of whether my students have attained my learning outcomes?

Assessment must measure both achievement and opportunity to learn. Science assessments must measure rich and varied outcomes. Some possible science outcomes include the ability to inquire; the ability to understand and to know scientific facts, concepts, principles, laws, and theories; the ability to reason scientifically; the ability to use science to make personal decisions and to take positions on societal issues; and the ability to communicate effectively about science. At the classroom level, one of the most powerful indicators of opportunity to learn is your professional knowledge or, in other words, your knowledge of science content, your teaching methods, and your understanding of students. Another indicator of opportunity to learn is the time you have available to teach science and how much time you provide for your students to learn it. The amount of resources that you have available to use for student inquiry is another strong indicator. You need to consider the quality of your science education materials. A final factor is the extent to which you and your school district have coordinated content, teaching, professional development, and assessment.

Students cannot be held accountable for achievement unless they are given adequate opportunity to learn science. Therefore, you will need to assess both your students' achievement and their opportunity to learn science equally. It is very important for you to look at *every* set of assessment results or test data for what they tell you about learners and what they tell about the *opportunities you* have provided *for* the learners. The assessment tasks you select to use in your classroom also provide important clues to students about what is important to learn.

There must be a match between the technical quality of the data collected and the consequences of the actions taken on the basis of these data. The content and form of an assessment must be congruent with or match what it is supposed to be measuring. In other words, *the assessment must be valid.* This means it measures what it is designed to assess. For example, if an assessment needs to be designed to measure students' ability to create questions to investigate magnetism in a scientific inquiry, having the students write possible questions and design an investigation to address them would be a more appropriate task than a short-answer question that requires them to explain how to write such a question. However, if the purpose of an assessment task is to measure the student's recall knowledge of characteristics of magnetism, then a multiple choice test may be the most appropriate. Your choice of assessment tools should be consistent with what you want to measure and infer.

In addition, *assessments must be reliable.* Students should score similarly on tasks that claim to measure the same aspect of student achievement. A student who is successful in classifying types of dinosaurs should be successful in classifying rocks once the types of rocks have been taught. Consistency of performance must also be part of assessment. This can be established through repeated observations and by using more than one type of assessment tool to measure student learning related to your objectives.

Finally, *assessment tasks must be authentic.* When students are engaged in assessment tasks that are similar in form to tasks that they will engage in their lives outside the classroom or are similar to the activities of scientists, great confidence can be attached to the data collected. Such assessment tasks are authentic. These types of assessments take time to create, administer, and interpret. They may look very different from the ones that are familiar to your students and their parents. You will need to explain why you are using the assessments you have chosen and how they measure your outcomes. There are several ways to ensure that your students have had the opportunity to demonstrate their full understanding and ability. *Your assessment tasks will need to be developmentally appropriate.* They must be set in contexts that are familiar to your students. Make sure that your assessments do not require reading skills or vocabulary that is inappropriate to the student's grade level or abilities.

Assessment practices must be fair. In assessment, as in teaching, you must make every attempt to avoid bias and stereotypes. Just as the styles of learners differ, their perspectives will vary, depending on their backgrounds, environments, strengths in the various intelligences, or areas of ability. Your assessment practices will need to accommodate diversity. *Assessment data must always be examined for signs of bias or stereotyping.*

Bias may appear in the procedures used to develop assessment tasks, in the content and language of the assessment tool, in the processes that you use to assess the students, and in the analysis of the data. When using authentic assessment in context, the likelihood that all tasks have some degree of bias for some population increases. For example, some contexts will have more appeal to males and some to females. One way you can avoid bias is to use a variety of tools rather than relying on one way to measure outcomes because the data will then be "equally unfair" to all.

As in teaching, fairness in assessment requires that your *assessment tools make provisions for students with physical or learning disabilities and those with limited English proficiency.* These students also need to be able to demonstrate their full knowledge, skills, and understanding of science content.

The inferences made about student achievement and opportunity to learn must be sound. Because your assessments will influence the plans that you make for students, your lessons, units of study, and science programs, it is crucial that you are aware of the strengths, weaknesses, assumptions, and inaccuracies inherent in every assessment as you decide which to select for each situation and how you will use the resulting data. Some assessments are more appropriate for use during different times and for different purposes in science instruction. *The information from any one assessment is only one piece of the puzzle that makes up instruction.*

Recommended Shifts in Assessing Science in the Classroom

The *National Science Education Standards* (1996) envision change throughout the system in science education. Less emphasis needs to be placed on assessing what is easily measured, discrete knowledge, and scientific knowledge. A shift to more emphasis on assessing what is most highly valued, rich well-structured knowledge, and scientific understanding along with reasoning is strongly recommended. We should assess to learn what students do understand rather than what they do not know. Assessment should emphasize not only achievement but also the opportunity to learn. There should be less emphasis on end-of-term assessments by teachers and more emphasis on having students engaged in ongoing assessments of their own work and that of others. In addition, the development of external assessments needs to have teacher involvement as well as that of the measurement experts.

Meeting the Needs of Diverse Student Populations

As noted earlier, the *National Science Education Assessment Standards* require that assessment practices be fair to all students. Fairness in assessment means that your assessment tools must make provisions for students from culturally diverse backgrounds, of both genders, with different intellectual learning styles and intelligences, with physical or learning disabilities, and with limited English proficiency. All students need to be able to demonstrate their full knowledge, skills, and understanding of science content.

Teachers must be able to assess their students in ways that allow them to demonstrate their learning and that provide the information teachers need to guide their future learning. You need to know how to make accommodations and adaptations that are congruent with classroom instructional practices. As noted in the *National Assessment for Science Standards,* you can avoid bias by using a variety of tools rather than relying on one way to measure outcomes because the data will then be "equally unfair" to all.

For culturally diverse students, Barba (1998) recommends using authentic assessment tools such as oral interviews, portfolios, concept maps, and drawing to assess changes in their knowledge structures in the affective, cognitive, and psychomotor domains. Group performance is a more comfortable means of displaying knowledge than individual testing situations for many culturally diverse students. However, care must be taken with group work to provide individuals the opportunity to be accountable for their portion of the project.

Performance-based tasks that require students to perform a science process and then justify or explain their answers are appropriate for gaining insights into the ways that culturally diverse students engage in problem-solving skills. Clarkson (1991) maintains that these tasks allow bilingual students to demonstrate computation, measurement, and mathematical language abilities far better than other assessment instruments. Additionally, these instruments are well correlated with students' language ability in their first language or English. For culturally diverse learners, performance-based tasks may provide an alternative form of assessment that provides the teacher with an understanding of the ways that students have constructed knowledge of science.

Portfolios are another assessment tool that offers limited-English-proficient students an opportunity to perform in nontraditional media that do not rely on

Performance-based assessments can facilitate culturally diverse students' ability to perform science processes.

language. Videotapes, audiotapes, drawings, and projects may be used to show evidence of learning in science. Additionally, electronic portfolios are multimedia tools for storing students' documents in an electronic format that is appealing to students with diverse needs.

Armstrong (2000) recommends that teachers accommodate differences in learning styles and multiple intelligences. One way to do this in assessment is to allow students to choose their own format for demonstrating what they know by signing a contract that allows them to use their strengths. Some students may be most comfortable writing a report, while others may want to build a model. Other options include putting on a demonstration, creating a chart, developing an interactive computer presentation, developing a simulation, drawing diagrams or sketches, setting up an experiment, writing and performing a song or rap related to the topic, or teaching it to someone else. Teachers can also provide activities and assessments that build on students' strengths in intelligences.

Suggested Activity
National Science Assessment Standards
6.2

1. In your collaborative groups, clarify why the National Science Standards for Assessment are important for teaching science at the elementary and middle school levels.

2. Demonstrate your understanding of the main features of the National Science Assessment Standards by choosing to do one of the following:

   • Create a detailed outline of the standards and their implications.

   • Create a concept map that shows the relationships among the standards.

   • Develop a diagram, matrix, or data chart containing the important information that shows your understanding of the standards.

   • Write an essay in which you explain the assessment standards in your own words and describe how this will affect science teaching in your classroom.

3. In your journal, explain your perspective concerning diverse needs of students.

A RATIONALE FOR CHANGES IN SCIENCE ASSESSMENT PRACTICES

Why have the *National Science Education Standards* (1996) and science educators as well as experts in the area of educational measurement recommended a shift from using mostly traditional testing to using more authentic assessments? You may be thinking, if traditional tests were good enough for me, why shouldn't I continue to use them as the main way to measure my students' science learning? After all, testing is a tried and proven method for assessing learning that has been used by teachers for centuries. They do provide a simple, direct, and impersonal way to find out something about a student (Hein & Price, 1994).

In the past, many teachers have received little guidance on how to develop assessment systems, so they have relied on textbook tests and standardized tests for much of their science assessment program. Since traditional tests have often been the only assessment tools that are readily available, teachers who use them teach to these tests, which in turn drives or determines the curriculum. As noted by Smith, Ryan, and Kuhs (1993), many teachers have tended not only to teach the way they were taught but also to test the way they were tested, which has largely been through paper-and-pencil tests consisting of a combination of true or false, multiple choice, matching, short essay, fill in the blank, and circle the correct picture items.

Unfortunately, most traditional science tests generally are not consistent with changes in current science education goals and curriculum content. There have also been changes in the nature of science teaching methods and strategies that are difficult to assess traditionally. Finally, there are additional concerns about measuring students' science understandings and capabilities when using traditional testing. On the other hand, there may be times when you determine that a paper-and-pencil test is the most appropriate assessment tool for your measurement purposes.

Changes in the Content of the Science Curriculum

One reason teachers need to rethink science assessment is that content in the science curriculum has changed. In the past, vocabulary, definitions of scientific concepts, and facts were considered to be more important than the applications of the concepts. Therefore, tests most often measured these areas. This was similar to "learning all of the vocabulary of a foreign language without ever taking time to actually speak the language or converse with others using the language" (Gega & Peters, 1998, p. 161). Science teachers now know that immediate, corrective feedback is necessary to teach scientific concepts effectively. This feedback can be gained through a combination of procedures, including traditional and authentic assessments.

New science curricula are qualitatively different in form and content from the commercial textbooks frequently used as the curriculum in the past. The current emphasis is on a combination of "hands-on" and "minds-on" science. Active participation of children doing science rather than simply learning about science is stressed. Teachers involve students in learning the content of science while engaging in its processes. In addition, students are expected to think scientifically, to act like scientists, to investigate science concepts or problems, and to have positive feelings about science. Science educators and experts in the field agree that the vast amount of knowledge that is constantly growing has made it futile to require students to memorize large quantities of discrete facts that will quickly become outdated. In our information age, labor force experts are calling for students who can learn to solve problems, make decisions, learn how to learn, collaborate with others, and manage themselves.

Paper-and-pencil tests simply are not sufficient to assess all the components of a modern, comprehensive science education program. A broader approach is needed. One objective of most science programs is that children learn some facts and concepts about science. Hein and Price (1994) note that while it is feasible to assess such learning through multiple-choice tests, it is more difficult to assess conceptual knowledge than factual knowledge, and it becomes very difficult to nearly impossible to measure skills and processes or attitudes with traditional multiple-choice tests. Being a scientist and engaging in doing science is impossible to measure in this way.

Changes in the Nature of Teaching Science

These new educational science goals, standards, and curricula also require changes in the way science is taught. Do you remember science lessons that involved you in various combinations of reading a chapter in a text either as a homework assignment or by taking turns reading sections orally in class, writing answers to questions at the end of sections or at the end of the chapter, listening to your teacher's lecture about the material you read, taking turns answering the teacher's questions in class, watching the teacher demonstrate an experiment, viewing a film or video, and then taking the end-of-the-chapter or unit test? Effective science teaching methods have changed considerably since many of you were in both elementary and middle schools.

Today, effective science teachers begin by activating and examining students' prior knowledge about the scientific world and how well learners understand its major concepts through diagnostic assessments. Science educators also view knowledge as something that helps students analyze a question, solve a problem, or conduct an investigation in a way that is meaningful to them. Teachers not only teach learners how to do the strategies but also model them in their teaching. Active and integrated strategies such as collaborative learning are stressed. Science teachers also value discussion, student-generated questions, and reflection as ways to facilitate learning.

Using and teaching problem-solving skills such as observing, comparing, classifying, measuring, hypothesizing, analyzing, and concluding are part of effective science lessons. Interpersonal skills used in daily life such as communicating, resolving, and solving problems are essential to collaborative investigation in inquiry-based science. Students are encouraged to ask questions, become excited about investigations, remain open minded about new ideas, be thorough in their inquiries, stay fair in their conclusions, and be honest in their presentation of evidence. Students need to understand how they have arrived at an answer, transfer knowledge to real-life situations, and think critically as well as document, communicate, analyze, and synthesize information. Effective science teachers model how to use these strategies, create a learning environment that lends itself to exploring science, and facilitate students' learning.

Practices that assess these learning strategies and teaching methods need to be holistic and complex. As a science teacher, you will need to measure knowledge, skills, and attitudes to solve problems, make decisions, and collaborate. Although traditional tests can be structured to measure deep, understanding of concepts and some of the teaching strategies described previously, they frequently are not. Students can easily memorize terms and guess at correct answers based on shallow and disconnected understanding of material to answer many items on traditional paper-and-pencil tests (Krajacik, Czerniak, & Berger, 1999).

Additional Concerns About Traditional Testing

As noted previously, one difficulty is that traditional testing tends to measure the recall of facts and neither the broader goals of student understanding nor the use of science concepts or process skills. Many experts in science education and educational measurement agree that paper-and-pencil tests usually request low-level, factual answers and do not often measure higher-level thinking or assess depth of understanding.

Traditional science tests usually have only one acceptable response for each question. Requiring students to choose one of a few given answers or to fill in a blank measures only a fraction of what you need to know about students' science learning. These test formats focus on right or wrong answers, limiting classroom activities to those that can be easily measured and limiting student involvement, expression of creativity, development of original solutions to problems, and ownership of learning.

Another way to judge the quality of traditional science tests is to ask what they tell you about what children know or do not know. Baskwill and Whitman (1988) maintain that traditional assessments do not allow teachers to view the child's learning processes. The data derived from many pencil-and-paper tests provide no information about how the result was achieved or what to do next to assist the students' learning. Many factors such as testing conditions, the assessment items themselves, and a student's frame of mind can influence the reliability of the single snapshot taken at the end of a lesson or unit; therefore, the results are not always trustworthy indicators of a student's science learning.

In addition, traditional assessments are based on the assumption that individual knowledge or learning traits are what should be measured. The focus has been on studying individuals in isolation and often in artificial environments. In recent years, this notion has been challenged. Critics of traditional testing contend that constructing knowledge is a profoundly social process and that focusing on individual achievement actually distorts what individuals can do. Many educational researchers recommend a shift toward studying individuals in classroom settings and activities where they can draw on their peers and the environment around them to create their responses to assessments (Wineburg, 1997).

When considering the diverse needs, interests, and abilities of students in our country, traditional paper-and-pencil tests are limited in their usefulness as science assessments. This is especially true for females, minorities, those from culturally diverse backgrounds, students with disabilities, and individuals with limited English proficiency. These tests tend to overlook the prior experiences, learning styles, multiple intelligences, and interests of our diverse population. Neill (1997) notes that while traditional tests have presumed that assessing all students in the same format creates a fair situation, the process of test construction, determination of content, and use of only one method that is usually multiple choice all build in cultural and educational biases that favor some ways of understanding and demonstrating knowledge over others. Sometimes ambiguous words, unclear questions, or vague sentences make it difficult for some students to even respond during these types of traditional science tests.

A final difficulty is that traditional testing often fosters false competitiveness and values comparisons. Students are often rank ordered by their scores after science instruction has occurred. They are challenged to get high scores or grades rather than being challenged to learn to think, to solve a problem, or to understand a concept. Assessment should be used for measuring and enhancing science learning rather than solely for the purpose of providing grades.

Benefits of Traditional Testing

On the other hand, Marzano, Pickering, and McTighe (1993) maintain that while the emphasis on new formats for gathering assessment and evaluation information is a necessary change, it does not imply that traditional forms of assessment are obsolete because *there is no one answer to the issues of assessing learning*. The challenge for science teachers is take the best that current research and theory have to offer and combine this with the best of what has been successful and useful in traditional testing. You need to be aware that a test, in and of itself, is neither valid nor invalid; it is up to you as the teacher to decide whether a certain test is valid for use in a particular situation with the students you have in your science classroom.

Multiple choice, true or false, short answer, and short essay questions are the primary means that many teachers use to assess student knowledge in the cognitive domain. These kinds of test items are commonly used in science assessment because most teachers view them as being easy to administer, less time consuming, easy to score, and flexible, or, in other words, an easy way to assess a wide range of declarative science knowledge. Teachers also tend to use them more because students and parents are more familiar with these types of assessments.

Traditional science tests do have value in offering insight into students' abilities to perform in testing situations, to recall and/or apply information, and to respond to carefully crafted questions while using critical thinking skills on essay items. Open-ended questions can also provide valuable information when you provide students with your expectations. If you are simply interested in discovering what facts students know, then a fact-finding test is appropriate, but if you want to discover whether students understand what they have learned, questions that require them to use the information studied are more useful (Baskwill & Whitman, 1988). These questions go beyond simply providing the correct answer to using higher-level thinking questions such as the following:

- If the following facts are true, what would happen if . . .
- In light of what you know about . . .
- What would you do if . . .
- Based on what you have learned, what would you do in this situation . . .

Traditional tests also lend themselves well to pre- and posttesting when you want to use the same format to compare results before and after teaching facts and concepts. Hein and Price (1994) maintain that matching pre- and postassessments can demonstrate that the students know more about the topic at the end of the science unit than at its beginning. Comparable results are best achieved when identical assessments are used, and this is easiest to accomplish with paper-and-pencil tests. *Remember that pretests should be used as a measure of what you need to teach rather than being graded.*

You will want to make sure that the formative assessments that you choose to use explore children's ideas, determine how much of the teaching has been effective and with which children, and identify what concepts need to be reexamined and explored further. Sometimes this can be done with traditional paper-and-pencil tests, and sometimes you will need to use authentic assessments to reach these goals.

Suggested Activity 6.3
Pros/Cons of Traditional Testing

1. Working as a collaborative group, use the information provided in the chapter thus far to create an essay, a chart, or a graphic that depicts reasons for and against using traditional paper-and-pencil testing.

2. As a group or individually, write a rationale for answering a parent who wants to know why you are not using multiple-choice and short-answer tests to measure all the science units that you have been teaching in your classroom. Be sure to base your rationale on the information provided in the previous sections of this chapter. Choose whether you want to respond as a primary, upper elementary, or middle school teacher.

AUTHENTIC ASSESSMENT

Educational measurement experts such as Grant Wiggins (1989) have proposed an alternative to using traditional assessments in the classroom. The term *authentic assessment* has been coined by Wiggins to meet this need to expand assessment to include a broader view of student learning than that allowed by traditional testing. According to Herman, Aschbacher, and Winters (1992) and the National Research Council (1996) several characteristics define authentic assessment.

Implications of Authentic Assessment Characteristics

The following paragraphs explore the implications of authentic assessment characteristics applied to teaching science in elementary and middle school classrooms.

Applications that measure students' science understandings, skills, and motivation in real-life situations. Authentic assessment requires applications that measure students' science understandings, skills, and motivation in situations that resemble those used by society at large rather than just those needed for success in school. In the real world, employees in the workforce and those involved in the field of science are seldom asked to perform on a test. They are, however, often expected to perform tasks that require integration of knowledge, science processes, problem-solving skills, inquiry skills, and motivation to get the task done alone or, more often, by collaborating with others. *When your students are engaged in assessment tasks that are similar to tasks that they will engage in their lives outside the classroom or are similar to the activities of scientists, you can be fairly certain your assessments are authentic.*

Tasks, materials, and contexts involving students and teachers in daily classroom instruction. Authentic assessments are embedded or anchored in tasks, materials, and contexts involving students and teachers through all phases of classroom instruction. *When you use assessments that ask students to perform tasks you have modeled in your teaching, such as how to design a science experiment or how to investigate the answer to a science problem through inquiry, you are using authentic assessment.*

Performance-based, realistic, and instructionally appropriate assessment. When a fourth-grade teacher gives groups of students a bag containing common kitchen substances such as baking soda, sugar, and starch and has them test the contents to determine which ones are in the bag, that teacher is using authentic assessment. When a middle school science teacher provides students with a set of minerals and requires them to test the minerals for known attributes and to create a classification system using the results, this is another example of authentic assessment (Solano-Flores & Shavelson, 1997). These examples describe authentic assessments that are performance based, realistic, and instructionally appropriate. *The assessment requires students to perform a task that reflects what scientists do and that fits into classroom science instruction.*

Integration into ongoing classroom life and assistance for teachers. Authentic assessments are integrated into ongoing life in the science classroom and help teachers plan instruction, determine students' impressions of science, revise curriculum, and teach accordingly. The performance tasks described in the previous paragraph would be part of the normal science curriculum and teaching in these two classrooms rather than a test that is separate from what is going on in daily classroom instruction. Teachers can observe students, read their laboratory notes or science journals, and examine their work to determine whether they understand targeted science concepts or whether they need more instruction to clarify these concepts or to correct any misconceptions. The fourth-grade teacher could then review how to test for various kitchen substances, while the middle school teacher may clarify how to create a classification system if students are confused about these science process skills.

Embedded assessments designed to monitor student progress. Authentic assessments are designed to continuously monitor student progress because they are embedded throughout the instructional process. When teachers use diagnostic, formative, and summative assessments such as those described in the KWL lesson about dinosaurs presented at the beginning of this chapter, they are using authentic assessments that are a part of instruction to access their students' understanding throughout the lesson or science unit. *Authentic assessments are never simply an end product of teaching or learning but are used during all stages of instruction.*

Something that students and teachers do together rather than something teachers do to students. In traditional assessment, the teacher is the one who is totally responsible for testing the individual student's knowledge by creating a teacher-made test, testing with a commercial science text's end-of-the-chapter or unit test, monitoring students taking a state-mandated science test, or administering a national standardized science test. Students are not involved in the creation of the tests or in assessing what they have learned. *In authentic science assessments, students and teachers become partners in the assessment process as students become involved in establishing their learning goals, in setting up tasks, in creating rubrics with teachers, in evaluating their peers, and by engaging in self-assessments.* With the introduction of these techniques, assessment becomes something that students and teachers do together rather than something that teachers do to students.

Self-reflective, self-regulated learners who monitor their own learning. Since teachers and students work together at each stage of the assessment process to collect data, make decisions about individual progress, document progress, and set goals, this collaborative process helps students become reflective, self-monitoring learners who regulate and take responsibility for their own science learning. When you ask students to describe which parts of a project they enjoyed most, what was hardest for them to do, or what they believe they have learned, you are having your students engage in authentic assessment tasks.

Student performances or products. Rather than simply choosing a correct response or filling in a blank, authentic assessments require students to perform something or to produce a product. For example, students can participate in performance tasks such as testing for kitchen substances or classifying attributes of specific minerals. Other performances might include acting out a scientific concept, taking part in a performance of a report to a community agency such as the electric company, or presenting the results of an investigation at a science fair. Products are often a result of a science project or an inquiry. These products can take a variety of formats, such as posters, songs, artwork, diagrams, models, or videotapes.

Higher-level thinking skills and problem-solving abilities. Because science learning does not happen in small, discrete steps, assessment should measure holistic knowledge and abilities. Authentic assessments encourage students to demonstrate the use of higher-level thinking skills and problem-solving abilities. Higher-level thinking skills such as planning, inventing, and making conclusions are measured by stressing open-ended answers rather than a single "correct" one. Students engage in higher-level reasoning when they discuss concepts with their peers and teacher. Creating projects, working on a scientific inquiry, or completing a performance task are complex assessments that require learners to construct knowledge and are more engaging than simply repeating memorized information that they may not be able to apply. *When students participate in authentic assessments, they are demonstrating a wide variety of knowledge, concepts, skills, and attitudes that they have learned rather than just recalling isolated facts.*

Variety in assessment techniques and sources of materials for measuring academic progress fairly and accurately. Authentic assessments measure academic progress in science fairly and accurately by using a variety of assessment techniques and various sources of information. *Using a variety of assessment formats accommodates differences in students' learning styles, interests, attention spans, or types of intelligences. Authentic assessments allow students to demonstrate abilities that may be academic, artistic, verbal, or social.* Students are provided with more than one chance to demonstrate their capabilities, are allowed to revise work and show improvement over time, and are given enough time to complete tasks.

A focus on progress of individual students in regular classroom contexts. Authentic assessments assess the progress of individual students rather than group norms or comparing students to one another after contrived special test situations. The focus of authentic assessment is students' science learning rather than measuring students' rank against peers in a classroom or school. Students are encouraged to meet classroom standards for learning and to compete against themselves rather than others. *Authentic assessments provide science teachers with information about what individual students have learned as well as how they can apply what they have learned.* Students are often provided with choices in how they wish to demonstrate their understanding of a science concept. Some students are more comfortable creating a concept map that demonstrates their knowledge, others may want to demonstrate their learning through creative drama, while still others prefer to create a rap or draw and label a diagram. Students' science learning is the goal rather than the grades that students may receive.

Subjective judgments based on teacher knowledge and experience. Authentic science assessments use subjective judgments based on teacher knowledge and experience. Traditional assessments are considered to be objective because they are administered to individual students under the same conditions with predetermined correct responses. Authentic assessments are administered to individuals or groups of students, under a variety of conditions with open-ended tasks that have more than one acceptable response. *Teachers' knowledge of and experience with the students in their classrooms, knowledge of science content, and science instruction are valued in authentic assessments.* Teachers are both qualified and expected to infer the results of a variety of assessment tools, to determine student learning, and to make decisions in daily classroom instruction based on student needs, curriculum demands, and assessment data gathered before and during instruction.

Now that you have a working knowledge of the characteristics of authentic assessment, you need to consider when you may want to use them and when it may be more appropriate to use more traditional paper-and-pencil tests. Since all assessment approaches have strengths and weaknesses, the following sections describe the benefits of and concerns about using authentic assessments in general.

Benefits of Using Authentic Assessment

Authentic assessments have many benefits for both teachers and students as well as for those further removed from daily science instruction. One of the greatest advantages of authentic assessments is that they are versatile in nature. This versatility lends itself to measuring the broad scope of current science educational goals and curriculum content. In addition, authentic assessments also match effective science teaching methods. With authentic assessments, you can measure whether students can solve problems, make decisions, collaborate with others, use strategies for learning, and manage themselves in your science classroom.

Since authentic assessments are used to monitor understanding, skills, and attitudes, science teachers using these techniques are less likely to blindly continue lessons without regard to how students are progressing. The goal is learning science rather than covering the curriculum. In other words, as you use this type of assessment, you will become a reflective practitioner. As a self-reflective teacher, you will think about, analyze, and mentally reconsider your science instruction practices. Ongoing reflection frequently results in science teachers changing the direction of their questioning, instructional strategies, choice of curriculum, and teaching materials.

If you use authentic assessments, it is less likely that your assessment data will result in biased conclusions or errors because authentic assessment focuses on more than simply the attainment of declarative knowledge, uses diverse sources of information, and involves the student in the assessment process. Authentic assessment techniques are more reliable because they give students many opportunities and ways to demonstrate their abilities, which helps eliminate variables that may alter results.

When you use assessments that are consistent with science learning, you will come to know your students better. Since you will be working with each student, you will be in a position to learn that child's capacity, styles of learning, and rate of learning. There will be less chance that students' needs are not being met because authentic assessments can help you achieve a deeper understanding of what they know, how they learned it, and how well they can apply it in various situations (Faulk & Ort, 1998).

Because teachers and students work together to determine which processes are most representative of a student's ability and how that work is evaluated, students can analyze the strengths and weaknesses of their own work and establish their own goals for improvement in science. This self-monitoring behavior or metacognitive thinking helps students develop intrinsic motivation to learn and strengthens their relationships with their teachers.

Authentic assessment also allows for individual differences in student abilities and cultural diversity since the focus is on student improvement rather than on comparison with others. Students are encouraged to chart their own improvement over time, which in turn tends to promote self-esteem. These assessment techniques provide a less threatening environment for assessment because they are an ongoing part of instruction in science rather than an occasional, anxiety-producing situation. Authentic assessment techniques also promote collaboration with peers. Students work with classmates to develop and share products, investigations, performances, and/or science portfolios. They also learn to seek suggestions for improvement. During this process, students develop important social skills. They learn to support and coach others while learning to work collaboratively and cooperatively.

If a school requires letter grades, authentic assessments provide teachers with a more honest and valid appraisal for students' learning that they can use as a basis for letter grades. Using diverse forms of assessment information will help you make more valid decisions about your students' science grades. Students also tend to learn concepts with a deeper level of understanding, so they are more likely to score well in other types of assessments that are often required in school districts.

While traditional tests provide parents with information about how their children compare to others and letter grades give them an approximation of what percentage of science information they mastered for a grading period, authentic assessments can offer rich, multidimensional information about their children's science learning. By examining samples of work over time, parents can learn a great deal about their child's science understandings and improvement. They can discover whether their child is interested in science, has developed scientific thinking and problem-solving skills, or has learned process inquiry skills. With authentic assessments, you can also involve parents in their child's science assessment through student-led conferences or by having them fill out checklists of science skills, attitudes, or abilities that they have noticed at home.

Concerns About Authentic Assessment

All assessments have weaknesses as well as strengths. Just as there are concerns about traditional assessments, there are also concerns about authentic assessments. Although concerns about individual types of authentic assessments vary, some of the more common issues deal with the technical aspects of validity and reliability, bias in testing, teacher difficulties, the complexity of many authentic assessments, time issues, storage problems, student concerns, and parental concerns.

Those who are more comfortable with testing individuals with traditional tests question the validity of using collaboration. They are concerned about determining individuals' true scores when these individuals receive different amounts of assistance in completing assessments. This line of thinking would make comparing the tests of two students impossible (Wineburg, 1997). When one wants to compare the results of individuals, traditional science assessments are a better tool. The purpose of authentic assessment is to measure individual growth rather than to compare that growth to the growth of others.

In addition, no single assessment approach will meet all the needs of current science educational curricula. Some authentic assessments are more valid for measuring an aspect of learning than others. When a teacher is interested mainly in learning how well students have learned factual or declarative knowledge, such as the characteristics or attributes of metals, a multiple-choice or matching test is the most valid and time-efficient assessment technique to use.

Another related issue deals with the technical aspect of *reliability.* In addition to students being able to perform at the same level on various assessments that measure the same science concepts, reliability also demands that a student's score will be consistent no matter who does the scoring. *Interrater reliability* is more difficult to achieve with authentic assessments because there is not a single correct answer. To solve this dilemma, teachers can be trained to score specific types of assessment, but this takes time and financial resources for the training. A related concern is that of *subjectivity.* When there are no longer single correct answers on an assessment, there is always the question of how can one be sure the interpretation of data is accurate. Even with scoring rubrics and training for interrater reliability, those who are more comfortable with standardized test results often question whether authentic assessments provide accurate data, especially in science classrooms where students have the option to select the type of assessments they will use to demonstrate learning because the results of various assessments are often not comparable.

All assessments are biased for some group of students because of differences in learning styles, preferences, cultural backgrounds, or ability. If teachers tend to use only one type of assessment, whether it is authentic or traditional, there will be bias for some students. As mentioned in the *National Science Education Standards* (1996), this is less of a concern when teachers use several different assessment measures to ensure that the chance of stereotyping or bias is equally distributed among students.

Assessment becomes more complex when students are allowed multiple ways to demonstrate what they have learned and can do. Science teachers must have the expertise to define high-quality work in a clear manner that lets students, parents, and the community know what variations on such quality look like. You will need clear scoring guides and examples of student work of varying kinds and degrees of quality. All these requirements create more work for the classroom teacher.

Authentic assessments usually take more time to plan, implement, and interpret than most traditional science tests. The time spent on the authentic assessments must be weighed against the possibility of taking too much time away from other areas of the curriculum. Setup time can become a problem when using some types of authentic assessment tools, especially when students need to move to other classrooms in a set amount of time or when the curriculum demands that a certain amount of time be allotted to various subjects each day. In addition, many authentic assessment tools require storage space. The issues then become finding room to store the necessary items, deciding who has access to them, and organizing these materials for easy access.

Most teachers need sustained support and professional development to begin to implement some of the more common authentic assessments in their science classrooms. Some school districts are unable or unwilling to provide professional development over a longer period of time because there is a lack of finances necessary to sustain the effort, there are differences in philosophy, or there are commitments to other curricular programs. Some teachers may be uncomfortable with moving away from more traditional testing systems that they have become accustomed to using or that they experienced in their own education. Others do not feel that they have the knowledge or expertise to implement authentic assessments.

In authentic assessments, students are given more responsibility for their learning. Sometimes students are reluctant to accept this responsibility and are more comfortable with taking traditional science tests. Before you can expect an increase in student motivation, content must be challenging, or changing the format of assessments and assignments will not be effective. You will need to take the time necessary to model how to use them and to teach students how to participate in their own learning and assessment before students can be active in authentic assessments (Khattri, Kane, & Reeve, 1995).

Although parents can receive a great deal of information about their children's science learning through authentic assessments, some parents are more comfortable with traditional testing and letter grades because they are more familiar with them. Teachers who use authentic assessments will need to be able to explain how these assessments measure children's learning, the rationale for their use, and what information parents can learn from them.

While these are valid concerns about using authentic assessments, they are not insurmountable. Most science educators and the *National Science Education Standards* contend that the benefits outweigh the concerns. With knowledge of the individual types of authentic assessments and traditional assessment tests along with their strengths and limitations, you will be able to choose a balance of appropriate assessment tools to use in your science program.

Suggested Activity
Traditional vs. Authentic Assessments
6.4

1. Based on the information provided thus far in this chapter, create a chart, a graphic organizer, or an essay that compares and contrasts traditional paper-and-pencil testing and authentic assessments. Compare your results with others in your group. How were they similar, and how were they different?

2. Working as a group or individually, create a rationale that you can use with parents to explain why you will be using a combination of traditional and authentic assessments in your classroom.

3. Prepare a letter or newsletter article that you could send home for your parents to read or a presentation that you could use at an open house at the beginning of the school year.

LARGE-SCALE ASSESSMENT

Large-scale assessments can be administered at the district, state, province, or national level. Those at the district, state, or province levels may be either traditional assessments or authentic assessments. Large-scale authentic assessments often include a combination of performance-based assessments, written logs, reports, or lab sheets. These assessments may also include portions of paper-and-pencil items such as multiple choice. Science tests that are developed for use across the nation are usually norm-referenced, standardized tests.

Norm-referenced, standardized tests are trusted by many in education and by the public as reliable and valid measures of student achievement. They have been a routine part of American students' school experiences since the mid-1900s. The appeal of norm-referenced tests is that they are considered to be objective, and they make quantitative comparisons possible. The test publishing industry is also aware of the economic power that such tests hold in education. Because of the continued public cry for accountability and economic gains for the test publishers, norm-referenced, multiple choice tests are commonplace and likely to continue to be used despite the trend toward performance-based methods of assessment.

Taylor and Walton (1997) maintain that teachers need to prepare students to perform well on these tests as well as on more authentic assessments. When teachers downplay the tests' importance with students, they are doing their students a disservice. The tests *do matter* in several ways because they are often used to determine placement in subject area tracks, remedial classes, or gifted education; and they may determine whether students are retained in a grade. Unfortunately, these decisions may actually have more to do with culture, style, gender, and test-taking skill than with what the student actually knows. They can also determine what is taught rather than a solid curriculum or student needs in science learning. As noted in the *National Science Standards for Assessment* (1996), this use of test scores to define learning and knowledge is questionable because of equity issues. In fact, Paris et al. (1991) found that repeated experiences with standardized testing, particularly for low achievers, result in three negative trends: disillusionment about tests, decreased motivation to give genuine effort, and increased use of inappropriate strategies.

Teachers who hold a constructivist theory of teaching science have difficulty teaching to these tests because they believe in collaborative and interactive methods that encourage children to question, consider multiple perspectives, and pool their combined resources to arrive at well-thought-out conclusions. The standardized, norm-referenced, multiple-choice tests, on the other hand, require students to work without collaboration, work under timed conditions, and seek one right answer from a list of prepared responses. Also, numeric test scores cannot tell what students think about material they are learning, how students feel about learning, what strategies students use, how students use information to make meaning of their world, whether students verify and revise their own thinking, and whether students have accepted ownership for learning. In addition to these issues, there is still the dilemma that even though the trend is toward performance-based assessments, norm-referenced tests will probably coexist with them for a long time.

The best solution to these problems is to provide students with the knowledge they need to be able to negotiate this form of assessment by teaching them how to take the test rather than teaching the information on the test. Let students actively explore how to take the tests in an active learning format rather than simply drill and practice interventions before a standardized test is given. Provide students with coping skills and problem-solving strategies to assist them in taking these types of tests so that norm-referenced tests will not become a barrier to academic opportunities and to make the tests less stressful to students (Taylor & Walton, 1997).

SUMMARY

This chapter provides a comprehensive view of assessment in the elementary and middle school science classroom. The chapter began by describing diagnostic assessments that occur before teaching to determine what students already know and their needs, formative assessments that take place during teaching to inform instruction, and summative assessments that measure what was learned after the instructional process is completed. Assessment was contrasted with evaluation, which usually occurs at the end of teaching and involves a judgment, while assessment is a systematic, multistep process involving the collection and interpretation of science educational data.

The *National Science Education Standards* (1996) recommend that all aspects of science achievement be measured by using multiple methods such as performances and portfolios as well as conventional paper-and-pencil tests. The assessment standards view assessment as a process that consists of four components that must interact for decision making and actions based on the data to occur: how the data will be used, what the data collection will be used to describe and quantify, which methods will be used to collect the data, and who will use the data.

Students with special needs must be provided the opportunity to perform equally well on science assessments. Selecting appropriate assessments for students with special needs must be done to provide equity in assessing all students. By becoming more knowledgeable about assessment in inquiry-based science classrooms, you can encourage students to develop into critical thinkers and effective problem solvers. When you take advantage of the many perspectives on assessment, you can make it possible for your students to demonstrate their best achievements in science.

There are many reasons for the recommended changes in science assessment practices. The content of the science curriculum has shifted from knowledge of vocabulary and definitions of scientific concepts and facts to the applications of science concepts. Methods of teaching science have also changed. Teachers no longer view the student's role as one of being a passive receiver of information. Effective science teachers value discussion, student-generated questions, problem solving, active investigations, reflection, and teacher modeling. While traditional assessments do have benefits, many concerns have surfaced about their dominance in science assessment, such as the difficulty of measuring higher-level thinking skills, science processes, and attitudes about learning science concepts using these assessment tools.

Authentic assessments have firmly established a role in science assessment practices. The characteristics of authentic assessments relate to instruction in the science classroom in several ways. Assessment must measure students' science concepts in real-life situations; be part of regular classroom activities; be realistic and instructionally appropriate; meet the developmental needs of diverse students; encourage student self-monitoring and collaboration among teachers, students, and peers; use student performance or products; measure higher-level thinking skills; and reflect teachers' abilities to use subjective judgments and self-reflection in their instructional and assessment practices.

Teachers have an obligation to prepare students to take large-scale assessments, whether these are authentic assessments created at the school, district, state, or province level or national norm-referenced standardized tests. When students are familiar with the format and procedures needed to perform well on tests, they are more likely to succeed in achieving the science standards reflected on the tests.

REFERENCES

Armstrong, T. (2000). *Multiple intelligences in the classroom* (2nd ed.). Alexandria, VA: Association for Supervision and Curriculum Development.

Austin, T. (1994). *Changing the view: Student-led parent conferences.* Portsmouth, NH: Heinemann Educational Books.

Barba, R. H. (1998). *Science in the multicultural classroom. A guide to teaching and learning* (2nd ed.). Boston, MA: Allyn & Bacon.

Baskwill, J., & Whitman, P. (1988). *Evaluation: Whole language, whole child.* New York: Scholastic.

Black, P., & William, D. (1998). Inside the black box. *Phi Delta Kappan, 80*(2), 139–148.

Brown, J. H. (1994, September). Science for everyone: New ways to measure what students know and can do. *Instructor,* 58–61.

Clarkson, P. C. (1991). *Bilingualism and mathematics learning.* Geelong, Victoria, Australia: Deakin University Press.

Ebenezer, J. V., & Conner, S. (1998). *Learning to teach science: A model for the 21st century.* Columbus, OH: Merrill.

Faulk, B., & Ort, S. (1998). Sitting down to score: Teacher learning through assessment. *Phi Delta Kappan, 80*(1), 59–63.

Gega, P. C., & Peters, J. M. (1998). *Science in elementary education.* Columbus, OH: Merrill.

Hein, G. E., & Price, S. (1994). *Active assessment for active science: A guide for elementary school teachers.* Portsmouth, NH: Heinemann.

Herman, L. J., Aschbacher, P. R., & Winters, L. (1992). *A practical guide to alternative assessment.* Alexandria, VA: Association for Supervision and Curriculum Development.

Khattri, N., Kane, M. B., & Reeve, A. L. (1995, November). How performance assessments affect teaching and learning. *Educational Leadership,* 80–83.

Krajacik, J., Czerniak, C., & Berger, C. (1999). *Teaching children science: A project based approach.* Boston: McGraw-Hill College.

Kulm, G., & Malcom, S. M. (1991). *Science assessment in the service of reform.* Washington, DC: American Association for the Advancement of Science.

Lowery, L. F. (Ed.). (1996). Exploring the assessment standards. In *NSTA pathways to the science standards: Guidelines for moving the vision into practice* (Elementary School Edition) (pp. 20–23). Arlington, VA: National Science Teachers Association.

Marzano, R., Pickering, D., & McTighe, J. (1993). *Assessing student outcomes: Performance assessment using the dimensions of learning model.* Alexander, VA: Association for Supervision and Curriculum Development.

National Research Council. (1996). *National Science Education Standards.* Washington, DC: National Academy Press.

Neill, D. M. (1997). Transforming student assessment. *Phi Delta Kappan, 79,* 34–40, 58.

Ogle, D. (1986). A teaching model that develops active reading of expository text. *The Reading Teacher, 39*(2), 564–570.

Paris, S. G. et al. (1991, June–July). A developmental perspective on standardized achievement testing. *Educational Researcher,* 12–20.

Smith, I. H., Ryan, J. M., & Kuhs, T. M. (1993). *Assessment of student learning in science.* Columbia: South Carolina Center for Excellence in the Assessment of Student Learning, College of Education, University of South Carolina. (ERIC Document Reproduction Service No. ED 358160.)

Solano-Flores, G., & Shavelson, R. J. (1997). Development of performance assessments in science: Conceptual, practical and logistical issues. *Educational Measurement: Issues and Practices, 16*(3), 16–25.

Taylor, K., & Walton, S. (1997). Co-opting standardized tests in the service of learning. *Phi Delta Kappan, 79*(1), 66–70.

Tomlinson, C. A. (1999). *The differentiated classroom: Responding to the needs of all learners.* Alexandria, VA: Association for Supervision and Curriculum Development.

Wiggins, G. (1989). A true test: Toward more authentic and equitable assessment. *Phi Delta Kappan, 70*(9), 703–713.

Wiggins, G. (1992). Creating tests worth taking. *Educational Leadership, 48*(6), 26–34.

Wineburg, S. (1997). T. S. Eliot, collaboration, and the quandaries of assessment in a rapidly changing world. *Phi Delta Kappan, 79*(1), 59–65.

CHAPTER 7

Types of Assessment Tools

Dr. Leonie M. Rose

In current science assessment, there are multiple ways of assessing students. This chapter acquaints you with a wide variety of assessment tools to use in your elementary or middle school science classroom. This chapter is divided into authentic assessment tools and pencil-and-paper tests.

Once you are familiar with the various assessment tools that are available for use in your science classroom, you will be the one who is ultimately responsible for selecting the ones that best meet your needs and those of your students. To make the most effective selections, you will need to consider the following factors as you select your assessment tools:

- The strengths and developmental needs of your students
- Your science goals and objectives for a particular science lesson or unit
- The match between the assessments and effective teaching methods
- The science curriculum in your school district
- State mandates
- The *National Science Education Standards* (National Research Council, 1996)

The most commonly used authentic assessment tools are performance-based tasks, portfolios, and scoring rubrics. Each of these is described in a section that also includes their uses, benefits they provide, and specific concerns about implementing them in the classroom. Next, a variety of assessment tools are presented that can stand alone or become part of a portfolio. These sets of assessment techniques are divided into three groups of authentic assessments: assessments for observing students, student work samples, and classroom activities. Paper-and-pencil or traditional tests are the final set of assessment tools described.

PERFORMANCE-BASED ASSESSMENT

Authentic assessments model the kinds of activities that usually go on during effective science instruction. As Brown (1994) noted, while teachers are usually comfortable with their science teaching methods, they sometimes wonder, How do I know if my students are learning from the activities I give them? How do I know if they can apply what they have learned to a new problem? In other words, they want to know if their students can do science.

Performance-based assessments can provide you with one way to measure what students know by watching what they do. This involves giving one or more students a task that will enable you to view not only an answer but also the process used to find that answer. Frequently, these types of assessment tools have children observe and manipulate objects, follow directions, design and carry out investigations, have more than one correct answer, and provide children with many ways of demonstrating what meaning they have of the science concepts discussed in the classroom.

Components and Scoring

According to Solano-Flores and Shavelson (1997), there are three components that define a science performance-based assessment: (1) a *task* that poses a well-developed problem in a specific situation that requires the use of concrete materials that react to the students' actions to reach a solution, (2) a *response format* that captures students' responses by providing a record of the procedures used to solve the problem, and (3) a *scoring system* that is used to score the accuracy and scientific reasonableness of students' responses.

Examples of products developed through performance-based tasks include models based on scientific concepts, written material, decisions, and applications of process skills such as investigations with definite or undetermined conclusions. Classroom activities that are a natural part of a lesson, such as observing something under a microscope or setting up equipment and asking students to assemble a slide and then focus a microscope, can be used to directly examine students' knowledge, skills, and dispositions.

Solano-Flores and Shavelson have developed four types of tasks that simulate conditions that are similar to those that scientists experience at work and that elicit the kind of thinking and reasoning used by scientists when they engage in problem solving. In *comparative tasks,* students are asked to conduct an experiment that compares two or more objects on some attribute. An example of a comparative task would be to provide students with three types of paper towels and have them discover which one holds the most water and which type holds the least. *Component identification tasks* require students to test objects to discover their components and/or how these components are organized. Asking fourth-grade students to identify which kitchen substances are in a bag is one example of this type of task. *Classification tasks* require students to classify objects according to critical attributes to serve a practical or conceptual purpose. The seventh-grade activity involving the identification of attributes of minerals along with the development of a classification system is an example of a classification task. Finally, in an *observation task,* students perform observations and/or model a process that cannot be manipulated. In an observation task, students could create a way to model the path of light from the sun as the earth rotates on its axis throughout the day from sunrise to sunset to solve location problems by using direction, length, and angle of shadows.

Different scoring systems would be appropriate for the four types of performance-based tasks. When using comparative tasks, a *procedure-based* scoring system checks the procedures students used to compare the objects to determine whether they are scientifically sound. You would use an *evidence-based* scoring system for a component identification task. The quality of the evidence the students used to confirm or disconfirm the presence of components would be the focus here. Classification tasks are scored by applying a *dimension-based* scoring system that focuses on how well the student-constructed classification system used attributes that are relevant to the purposes of the classification. Finally, an *accuracy-based* scoring system should be used for observation tasks. In this scoring system, accuracy of the student observations and their constructed models would need to be examined (Solano-Flores & Shavelson, 1997).

There are several additional ways you can interpret the data from performance-based assessments. The following examples demonstrate the wide variety of possibilities. You can observe how students go about problem solving and make notes about their process skills. You may want to interview students to find out how they framed their questions and selected a problem-solving strategy. You may wish to provide a written outline for the student to fill in. A student's daily journal entry in a science log can also be examined to gain detailed information about the student's process of scientific inquiry. You might want to develop a rubric as a scoring system to draw conclusions about selected indicators of science processes or inquiry skills.

Designing Performance-Based Assessments

Now that you know what performance assessments are, you may be wondering how you can design these assessments for classroom use. The following 10 steps can be used to guide you through this process. These steps are listed in a question format for quick reference in Figure 7.1.

FIGURE 7.1

Steps for Developing Performance-Based Assessments

When developing a new performance assessment, you need to ask yourself the following questions to complete the steps of the developmental process.

Outcomes: What do I want my students to understand and be able to do?

Indicators: What observable and measurable indicators will let me know what students understand and can do?

Assessment Tasks: What performance tasks will engage students in demonstrating what they understand and can do?

Characteristics: What are the key characteristics of the performance tasks?

Developing Tasks: How do I develop performance tasks for assessing student understanding and proficiency?

Criteria: What criteria will be used to evaluate student products and performances?

Valid and Reliable Tasks: How will I ensure that my assessment tasks provide valid and reliable measures of desire outcomes?

Standards: How will I establish performance standards for my learning outcomes and assessments?

Communication: How will I communicate results in ways that will lead to understanding of and improvements in student performance?

Student Support: How will I support my students to achieve desired levels of performance?

1. You will want to select the outcomes that include knowledge, processes, and skills that you want to measure with this assessment. Before continuing, you will need to decide whether a performance assessment is the best way to measure this particular set of science outcomes.

2. You will need to select observable and measurable indicators that will provide the data you need to show what students understand and can do. Determine whether your outcomes lend themselves toward measuring basic science processes or complex science processes. These processes are described in Chapter 1. They are excellent resources that you can use when you select your indicators as you design your performance tasks for assessing science processes.

3. You will need to determine the types of assessment tasks that will allow students to demonstrate what they know and can do. One possibility is using the four types of performance tasks recommended by Solano-Flores and Shavelson that were described in the previous section. Other suggestions include using experiments and investigations, creating products, and solving problems.

4. Next, you need to identify the key characteristics of these performance tasks. For example, what must be included in the task for it to be considered a comparative task or what would need to be part of an inquiry task?

5. Now you are ready to develop the specifics of your tasks. To do this, you will need to develop tasks that assess the students' understanding and proficiency in the areas you have selected. You will need to decide what it is the students will do, what materials and equipment you need, and how the performance assessment will be used.

6. Before you can present the performance tasks to your students, you will need to determine the criteria that you will use to evaluate the student products and performances (Wiggins, 1992). What will you be looking for in these products and performances to let you know their degree of understanding of the outcomes for this task?

7. You will also need to ensure that the assessment tasks provide valid and reliable measures of the desired outcomes. To do this, you will need to be sure that your task actually measures the outcomes you have selected consistently. One way you can test the assessment tasks is to let students try out the activity. Then revise the performance task based on the results of these trial runs.

8. Next, you will need to establish performance standards for your learning outcomes and assessments. You must decide what is acceptable performance at what levels and what indicates that the student needs further experience to learn the targeted science outcomes.

9. Before you use your performance-based assessments, you need to decide how you will communicate the results of the assessment. You must know who the audience will be, the format that will explain the information

that best represents an understanding of student performance for that particular audience, and various ways that lead to improvements in student performance. The methods you use to communicate with students, parents, and administrators may or may not be the same (Wiggins, 1992).

10. Finally, you need to decide how much support you will provide so that students achieve at the desired levels of performance. This involves how much support you provide during the assessment and how much support you provide in your classroom instruction before expecting students to take the assessments. Brown (1994) cautions against providing too much support, such as including step-by-step or recipe-like procedures, because this robs students of the opportunity to figure out the procedures themselves and also limits the information that can be obtained from the assessment. The amount of instructional support is also determined by whether your performance tasks are diagnostic, formative, or summative assessments. Naturally, there would much less instructional support for assessments that you give before beginning instruction than there would be at the end of a unit. The best way to support students is through effective instructional methods that model and actively involve them in activities similar to what they will be expected to do on the performance-based assessment tasks.

Success in implementing performance-based assessments depends on careful planning. It takes considerable preparation time for effective planning. It is best to be selective in beginning to implement performance tasks into your teaching. Begin small and build your diagnostic, formative, and summative performance-based assessments as your preparation time and materials permit.

As with all assessment tools, there are benefits and concerns to consider when using performance-based assessment. The next two sections will provide you with further information to help you decide when you may want to use performance-based assessments and when another form of assessment might be a better measure of your science teaching, the science curriculum, and your students' needs.

Benefits of Using Performance-Based Assessments

Performance-based assessments have many benefits for teachers and students in the science classroom. Advocates maintain that these assessment tools promote teacher and/or student collaboration, student motivation, active learning, critical thinking skills, and multidisciplinary understanding. Assessments and instruction are often difficult to separate in classrooms where teachers are adept at using inquiry-based teaching. Teachers who use performance-based assessments are more reflective in planning their instruction.

Studies of initiatives that use performance-based assessment indicate that when teachers examine and deliberate on authentic student work with other teachers, students, and their families, the result is often better understanding of what their students know and their students' learning styles, strengths, and needs. Performance-based assessment encourages science teachers to do the following:

- View assessment as an integral part of the teaching-learning process rather than as an end point
- Rely on human judgment when assessing learning
- Establish criteria to ensure that evaluations are not biased
- Determine the skills, attributes, and qualities that teachers want to develop in students
- Focus on conceptual ideas and problem-solving skills rather than on memorization of facts
- Design instructional tasks to provide students with opportunities to perform, create, or produce an end product
- Involve students in the evaluation of their own work (Reichel, 1994, p. 22)

Students benefit from the use of performance-based assessments in the science classroom. They engage in exploration of ideas and questions rather than in passive activities such as listening to the teacher, watching a movie, reading about a concept, or watching a demonstration. Students are less anxious because they are active and enjoy the learning process involved in the assessment task. This creates more reliable test results.

Performance-based assessment emphasizes developmentally appropriate teaching practices for both early childhood and young adolescent students. These practices include using concrete materials rather than passive tasks, stressing problem-solving processes over memorization of abstract ideas, allowing multiple approaches in solving a problem, integrating ideas from various subject areas, and engaging students in direct, purposeful experiences that promote learning and self-esteem.

Tolman, Baird, and Hardy (1994) offer these additional benefits. Performance-based assessments provide clear demonstrations of process skills in action. They rely less on reading, listening, and writing skills so that students who are not proficient in language arts are not penalized. Finally, students have more opportunity to show what they can do rather than their reading skills, writing skills, or content knowledge.

Mandated performance tests are currently used more often at school, district, and state levels. They are also being recommended at a national level. Therefore, a final advantage to using performance-based assessments is the assumption that when students become familiar with performance tasks in the regular science program, they have the potential to perform better on high-stakes tests that are developed beyond the classroom.

While there are numerous benefits to using performance-based assessments in your science classroom, there are also concerns about them. The following paragraphs address the main concerns that science teachers need to address before selecting or developing these assessment tools.

Concerns About Using Performance-Based Assessments

According to Khattri, Kane, and Reeve (1995), some of the concerns about performance-based assessments stem from the assumptions that advocates and designers have made about the ease of adopting them. These assumptions are that teachers have a clear understanding of the types of knowledge that can be assessed by this type of assessment, know how to use instructional methods that support these tests in the classroom, have expertise in a variety of teaching methods, and know what is evidence of critical thinking skills and multidisciplinary understanding. These authors maintain that teachers need to have these understandings as prior knowledge before they can successfully implement performance-based assessments.

In addition, performance-based tasks require a great deal of time to create, administer, and score. Another disadvantage for teachers and districts is the expense for supplies and materials. Also, there is the issue of the subjectivity of the scoring. Although scorers can be trained to follow precise scoring guidelines to reduce subjectivity and improve test reliability, training and practice require still more time.

At one extreme, some teachers ignore performance-based assessment tasks in favor of data they receive by observing children at work and interacting with them during regular activity times and follow-up discussions. While this may be possible with a wide array of process-rich activities and systematic observation, these observations may be biased for certain students, which in turn could affect the reliability of the results of the assessments. Also, with the increasing use of more districtwide, state, and national mandated performance-based assessments, these teachers may be placing their students at risk because they are unfamiliar with this type of test demands and procedures.

On the other hand, it is unrealistic to create and administer a performance-based assessment task for every skill or process that students need to learn in science. Enthusiastic teachers can overuse performance-based assessments. If the information that you need to assess student learning can be measured with a quicker and equally efficient assessment tool, use that one instead. Save the performance-based assessment tasks for the data that do not lend themselves well to other types of assessment.

A final concern is the fact that more and more publishing companies are selling what they call performance-based assessments. With the time and complex issues involved in designing these assessments, using commercial products may seem to be the simple answer, but they are not all of equal value. To be sure that any performance-based assessment meets your science assessment needs, Brown (1994) recommends that you use the following guidelines to examine the quality of any commercial performance-based assessment product before you purchase or use it:

1. Ask yourself what kinds of knowledge, processes, or skills this assessment requires students to demonstrate. Be sure that the performance assessment does not give such detailed directions about how to do the task that real problem solving is eliminated.

2. Determine how well the assessment reflects what you are teaching. Make sure what is being tested overlaps with the concepts and procedures being

taught, the targeted student learning, and what you want students to be able to do.

3. Examine whether the performance-based assessment can also serve as a good teaching activity. The difference between good performance-based assessments and science learning activities is that while the students carry out the tasks, you are an observer, not an instructor. Then, once the students are finished, you will score the assessment using a reliable scoring system.

4. The next issue to consider is interrater reliability of the performance assessment. Interrater reliability means that a student's score will be consistent no matter who does the scoring. You should consider purchasing or using only assessments with a high interrater reliability, which would be over .80 on a scale of 0 to 1. The assessment's distributor should have this information available for you.

5. The final area to examine is the usefulness of the scores. A good or adequate performance-based assessment provides information for both assessing students and informing your teaching of elementary or middle school science.

A commercial performance-based assessment must meet each of these guidelines before you select it for use in your science classroom. An assessment that does not meet these guidelines will not assist you in measuring your students' science understandings and process skills or in assessing your science instruction.

Suggested Activity 7.1
Performance-Based Assessments

1. In your collaborative groups, discuss what you consider to be the most important reasons to use performance-based assessments. Do the benefits outweigh the concerns?

2. Working in a group or individually, create a performance-based task to use with a science lesson that you have created. Be sure to include the 10 steps you used to design your task.

3. Examine two commercial science performance-based assessments. Evaluate them to determine whether they meet the five previously listed guidelines.

PORTFOLIO ASSESSMENT COMPONENTS

Another popular form of authentic assessment in science classrooms is the portfolio. Portfolios are sometimes defined as a collection of work. A true portfolio is much more than this. Johnson and Rose (1997) define a portfolio as a purposeful, systematic selection of a student's work over time that includes the following:

1. **Student participation in selection of contents**
   - Students must be involved in gathering data for portfolios because they are the ones who ultimately own their learning.
   - Teachers and students collaborate in deciding what goes into portfolios to demonstrate growth and accomplishments.
2. **Evidence of student self-reflection**
   - Portfolios include students' self-reflections in the form of checklists, essays, drafts, goal setting, statements of what they believe they have learned, and other ways to represent their examination of their learning.
   - Students also need to reflect on and state why they placed each item in their portfolio.
3. **Criteria for selection**
   - The criteria used for selection clarifies to everyone why items are included in the portfolio.
   - Criteria are best developed in collaboration with others, such as other teachers, administrators, students, and parents.
4. **Criteria for judging merit**
   - Before implementing a portfolio system, there must be agreement on the criteria that will be used to determine what constitutes excellence of entries, mastery of subject matter, evidence of growth, and other required contents.

Designing Portfolios for Implementation

There are several issues that you will need to deal with before you begin to implement portfolios. While there is no one "right" way to implement portfolios, the following paragraphs will help you plan the portfolio system that will work best for your science classroom. A list of these questions that you can use as a checklist as you plan for using portfolios in your science classroom is provided in Figure 7.2.

What are your purposes for the science portfolio? Portfolios can serve many purposes. You many want to use them to help you improve your science instruction, change your teaching methods, and provide real-world learning opportunities. Portfolios can be used to celebrate growth over time, to exhibit a student's best work, and to develop a sense of process, inquiry skills, and science knowledge. You can use portfolios to reflect students' risk taking and experimentation, to empower students to develop a sense of ownership of their science learning, to nurture students, and

FIGURE 7.2

Questions to Answer When Designing Science Portfolios

The following questions will help you design your portfolio system before you begin to implement it in your science classroom.

- What are your purposes for the science portfolio?
- What type(s) of portfolio(s) will you use for science?
- Who will decide what to place in the science portfolio?
- How will you involve students in self-reflection of science learning?
- What science items will you place in the portfolios?
- Who will have access to the portfolio(s)?
- What will you use as a container for the items in the portfolio?
- Where will you store these containers?
- When and how will portfolio items be accessed, added to, and deleted?
- How will the science contents in the portfolio be organized?
- How can you use peer evaluation to enhance science portfolios?
- Who will be the audience for these science portfolios?
- How will the information gathered be used?
- How will the science portfolios be shared with others?
- How will the science portfolios be assessed or graded?
- What will happen to the science portfolio at the end of the year?

to foster a positive self-concept for science learning. Portfolios are an excellent way to involve students in self-reflection and in determining and setting individual goals.

What type of portfolios will you use in your science classroom? The types of portfolios that you decide to use in your science classroom will depend on the purposes selected for collecting the data that will be placed in them. In many schools, portfolios will need to serve more than one purpose. Elementary teachers will also need to decide whether to have a separate science portfolio, to include a section for science in a portfolio for several subject areas, or to use it to demonstrate thematic instruction.

A review of the wide array of literature available about science portfolios and observations in classrooms with teachers who use them reveal the following types of portfolios to be those most commonly used in science classrooms:

- *Working Folders/Collection Folders:* These folders are temporary holding tanks that contain a student's work still in progress and a variety of assignments that reflect an integrated curriculum in all stages of development. Students store the items that they may eventually want to include in another type of portfolio in these folders. Much of this material will be discarded or taken home as students select the items that are most representative of their efforts and thinking.
- *Teacher Folio:* This type of portfolio contains teacher-collected evidence for evaluation and instruction, such as observations and anecdotal

records, criteria sheets and checklists of student' progress, assignments given as tests, and communications with parents. These are often kept in a file folder for each student. Items from this portfolio may also be selected to place into another type of portfolio.

- *Growth Portfolio:* A growth portfolio is kept to demonstrate learning over time. It is important that entries be dated to facilitate comparisons between new work and previous efforts. If items are selected from a growth portfolio to include in other types of portfolios, both earlier work and later work are included to show how students have progressed in learning science content, skills, attitudes, or processes.

- *Student Showcase Portfolio:* A showcase portfolio is a purposeful selection of a student's best work. These selections are collected over time, reflect the science curriculum, demonstrate higher-order thinking, often show evidence of cooperative learning, and contain students' self-assessments based on predetermined criteria. Materials placed in these portfolios are designed and selected so that they may be shared with other students, teachers, and parents.

- *Documentation/Permanent Portfolio:* This type of portfolio can be maintained for each content area or across content areas. Both students and teachers select particular pieces of students' work to include. The items are usually selected from one or more of the portfolio types described previously. It includes specific items that the child, parents, and teacher have jointly agreed will make up the portfolio. *Documentation* portfolios provide systematic, dated evidence that is rich in description of student learning. The *permanent* portfolio is kept in a secure place, becomes part of the student's permanent record, and is often examined by teachers in following years.

Most science teachers begin with the *working/collection folders* and one of the others to share beyond the classroom for parents' or school needs. As you become more comfortable with using portfolios in your science classroom, you will adapt these basic types of portfolios to meet your instructional and assessment needs, your students' needs, and those of your school or district.

Who will decide what to place in science portfolios? The types of portfolios you have chosen to use will help you determine who will place items in the portfolio. When you use *working/collection folders,* students have the main responsibility for deciding what to place in them. Younger students will most likely need assistance in selecting which items to place in their work folders and what to take home. Older students will make most of their own decisions about what to place in their collection folders, although teachers may still make suggestions about specific items to include.

If you decide to keep a *teacher folio,* you will be the one who decides what to place into it. You will also decide which (if any) items to select from your teacher folio to place into a *growth portfolio,* a *showcase portfolio,* or a *permanent portfolio.*

Although *growth* and *showcase portfolios* may contain only student-selected or mainly teacher-selected items, most contain a combination of these two types of selections. Both the child and teacher often select the items to include jointly. This makes the learning and assessment more relevant to students. Teachers also find that they must have diverse learning opportunities in the science classroom, or the portfolio simply becomes a collection of standardized science tests and worksheets.

In some schools, only teacher-selected items are placed in the *permanent portfolio,* but in most schools students and the teacher decide together which pieces should be included and why. In some schools, the teachers and administrators within a building or others at the district level have decided what types of science items must be placed in the *permanent portfolio* to ensure comparability of content.

Parents also have valuable input to share about what goes into a portfolio because they are most often the ones who receive the portfolios. Parents can provide you with information about what is most helpful and meaningful to them as they help their children. They will then know what to look for and praise at a parent conference or when the portfolios come home.

How will you involve your students in self-reflection? A true portfolio must demonstrate evidence of student self-reflection. *Growth, student showcase,* and *permanent* portfolios all provide opportunities for students to engage in self-reflections about their learning in science.

You can use portfolios to encourage students to take more ownership of their own science learning by engaging them in goal setting. One way to assist children in setting goals for themselves is to periodically have them review and think carefully about their work samples. This can be done weekly, monthly, or at the end of a unit. You can use science journals or log entries to have them write down what they feel good about in their work and why. Then, to lead them into goal setting, have them reflect and write a thoughtful response on what they would like to improve in science. From this response, they can set goals. You will also need to provide modeling on how you set goals or perhaps some goals that students from past classes have set. These goals can then be placed in their *working folders,* and the next time they review their work, they can search for evidence that their science goals were met and set new ones.

You will need to guide students in examining their work for improvements. One way to do this is to encourage them to pair a first draft or original effort with a final draft or an improved version whenever possible. Have them share their science selections within a group of their peers to select areas where they have grown. This will make them more aware of their progress, and it can also provide incentive for continuing to improve on the quality of their science work. You can also have them write comments on the work they have gathered over a set time period. Through practice and modeling, students will learn how to accurately assess their work and identify their best work.

Self-reflections can take place in a variety of formats, such as reflections in science journals or learning logs, checklists, essays, drafts, self-reflection sheets, or statements of what they believe they have learned. Prompts for having students begin to reflect on their science learning and to set goals are provided in Figure 7.3.

FIGURE 7.3

Prompts for Science Self-Reflections

The following prompts are examples of science self-reflections in preferences, learning strategies, strengths, areas for improvement, and goal setting that you can select from to create your own self-reflection sheets.

1. **Preferences in Science Learning:**
   Name _____
   Assignment _____
   - I like this because it shows that I can _____
   _____
   - The thing I liked best about this science lesson was _____
   _____ because _____
   - The most interesting part of our science lesson today was _____
   _____
   - I would like to learn more about _____
   - My favorite part of our science lessons this week were _____
   _____

2. **Learning Strategies in Science:**
   Name _____
   Assignment _____
   - When I don't understand something in science, I _____
   _____
   - Before I begin to work on a science project, I _____
   _____
   - When I need to study in science, _____
   _____
   - When I want to remember something I have learned in science, I _____
   _____

3. **Strengths in Science:**
   Name _____
   Assignment _____
   - I want to show this to _____
   because it shows that I can _____
   - I am AMAZING! I _____
   _____
   - This shows that I am getting better at _____
   _____
   - Today, I learned that I could _____
   _____
   - I can help others with _____
   _____

4. **Areas for Improvement in Science:**
   Name _____
   Assignment _____
   - This was hard because _____
   _____
   - I could improve this science assignment by _____
   _____
   - I need to work on _____
   _____
   - I wish I could get better at _____
   _____
   - I need help with _____
   _____

5. **Goal Setting in Science:**
   Name _____
   Assignment _____
   - The science tasks I want to work on are _____
   _____
   - I want to learn how to _____
   _____
   - I plan to get help with _____
   _____
   - I am going to take responsibility for _____
   _____
   - I plan to improve my science projects by _____
   _____

In addition to setting their own goals for science learning and reflecting on what they have learned, students also need to reflect on and state why they placed each item into their *growth, showcase,* or *permanent* portfolio. Each item the child includes in the portfolio should be labeled with a caption of what it is along with a brief reason for its inclusion. This rationale should provide the portfolio's audience with information about what evidence of learning the item documents and why it is evidence. These captions provide learners an opportunity to demonstrate what they have learned.

Whether you are a kindergarten teacher or a middle school science teacher, you will need to model how you want students to create captions for the items they will place in the portfolios that you choose to use in your classroom. For primary students, you might want to brainstorm with the class some reasons why they may wish to include an item in their portfolios and then create a checklist for them to use with the items they select for inclusion. In upper elementary and middle school classrooms, it would be helpful to show them some examples of what these captions may look like.

What will be placed in your science portfolios? What is included in a science portfolio depends on the purpose and types of portfolios you choose to use in your classroom. Students place items in working draft form or items they feel show various qualities of their work in their *working folios.* Teachers place items that they believe demonstrate students' science learning and attitudes in *teacher folios.* Teacher folios often include items that impact instruction as well. A *growth* portfolio many contain items that are not examples of best work but ones that demonstrate growth in science understanding and process skills. They may include early drafts of investigations to demonstrate development of thinking and increased sophistication in applying process skills. A *student showcase* portfolio would contain examples of the student's best work. Finally, documentation/permanent portfolios would include pieces of the student's work that provide systematic, dated evidence that describes the student's science learning. Items placed into any of these portfolios should be dated so that comparisons can be made between earlier and later entries.

Growth portfolios, *student showcase* portfolios, and *permanent* portfolios usually include the following four types of documentation: artifacts, reproductions, attestations, and productions (Collins, 1992). **Artifacts** are the actual items placed in the portfolio. They are created during an investigation or while working on a project. **Reproductions** are documents that describe the artifacts rather than the artifacts themselves. They are usually created after a project or an investigation is finished to provide documentation of the work done and include items such as computer printouts, videotapes, audiotapes, and photographs. **Attestations** are evaluations of a student's work prepared by someone other than the student, such as a teacher, a parent, or a peer. Some examples are a critique by a peer, a letter from a parent, and a report card from the teacher. **Productions** are documents that help explain the contents of a portfolio. They include such items as goal statements, personal reflections, captions, and descriptions of what the items in the portfolio represent. For more information about these types of documentation see the previous section titled "How Will You Involve Your Students in Self-Reflection?"

The actual items in an elementary or middle school science portfolio are almost limitless. They can provide evidence of achievement that may include teacher-selected data such as anecdotal records, checklists, notes from conferences or interviews, notes about informal observations, results of formal observations, practical tests, performance tasks, and traditional tests. Other items that you may want to consider as evidence of learning may be student- or teacher-selected items, such as classification systems devised by students; charts and graphs; diagrams; experiment write-ups with hypothesis, method, data, and conclusion; the student's own version of an experiment; raw data and the actual measurements made during an investigation; individual and group reports; homework assignments; lists of observations made in activities; summaries of classroom and out-of-class science activities (museum visits, planetarium visits, work in clubs, or science activities created in community youth organizations); the student's demonstrations of recognition and application of science in daily life; and written class work.

The items in a science portfolio may also include creative work such as journal entries about science ideas and/or experiences, taped discussions with peers about science concepts, written reactions to new concepts, a science autobiography, original work with revised ideas showing mastery of concepts, creative science work (music, art, poetry, video, computer disk), or answers to open-ended science questions. Portfolios can also contain students' best homework (and reasons why they feel it is their best), explanations of what students feel they learned on a test, a letter to an absent friend explaining a science concept, or any other form that children decide would show their accomplishments fairly and completely.

Who will have access to your science portfolios? Those who need to have continuous access to science portfolios are the classroom teacher and students because they are the ones who must provide continuous attention to each of the types of portfolios to prevent them from becoming too large and unwieldy. The *growth, student showcase,* and *documentation* portfolios need to become a selection of items rather than an unmonitored collection. To accomplish this goal, they must be accessible to students on a regular basis.

Administrators and other teachers usually have access to *the permanent/documentation* portfolios for a variety of purposes. Parents also have access to them at conference time or when they request it. Some districts use a review team to evaluate *permanent* portfolios. Because students are entitled to privacy under the Family Education and Rights to Privacy Act (FERPA), *documentation/permanent* portfolios need to be placed in a secured location with limited access. To ensure student privacy, schools or districts should have a policy on who has access to these portfolios and guardian release forms to allow those beyond the classroom to have access to the contents of *permanent* portfolios for specific purposes.

What will you use to contain the items, and where will you store them? The possibilities for containers to hold science portfolio items range from commercial containers designed to hold items to cardboard boxes. Some teachers use accordion-style folders, while others use computer disks to hold portfolio items. One teacher used large boot boxes that could be stacked in a corner, while another used x-ray envelopes that the students used to hold their science items. The possibilities are as varied as the teachers who use them and the amount of financial support they receive from their school districts.

You may choose to store portfolios in a number of ways. Portfolios may be stored in file cabinets, in crates or cartons stacked in a corner of the classroom, or in students' lockers. Portfolios may become overstuffed and hard to manage or store unless science material is reviewed periodically and some sent home or discarded. You may want to consider using electronic portfolios to solve storage issues. The advantage to these portfolios is that they can be easily stored on disk, which greatly reduces the amount of physical space required for storage. The disadvantages are that students may have inadequate keyboarding skills or computer access may be limited in some classrooms. You will need to decide what fits best into your classroom situation when deciding how to store your portfolio containers.

When and how will portfolio items be accessed, added to, and deleted? Students should maintain their *working folders* by keeping them up to date on a daily basis as they grow, improve, and accomplish science learning objectives. If you elect to keep a *teacher folio,* you will add items to it over a period of time. To ensure that your students have materials to place into their folders, you will need to be sure to give them assignments that lend themselves to portfolio inclusion, such as planning lessons that require written work or drawings to illustrate science concepts or demonstrate an understanding of science ideas.

How many student-selected items should be in the *permanent* portfolio? That depends on many factors, including how much time you have available to work on them. Most teachers who use portfolios urge limiting the number of items to the minimum necessary to get a complete picture. Many portfolio experts suggest that five or six carefully selected items are usually sufficient for assessing a child's progress during a grading period. These are in addition to any items the teacher chooses to include from the *teacher folio.*

You will need to provide regularly scheduled time for students to spend on selecting science work to include into portfolios. Many teachers do this every other week because portfolios need to be weeded out and added to at least on a monthly basis. You will not want to scramble at the end of a grading period to create a science portfolio that can be graded or used at a parent conference.

Children can review their portfolios as a class activity, in small groups, or individually. Peers and teachers can provide suggestions to help students decide which items they want to add to or delete from their portfolios. Some teachers find it beneficial to set up a rotating schedule to conference with two or three students a day to assess and examine every child's science portfolio at least once every 6 weeks. However, portfolio experts caution against having the students review their portfolios too often because they can become too caught up in creating the portfolio as a product rather than learning science concepts and processes. When students examine their work too often, there is little opportunity for reflection because they are too busy completing checklists or because assessing their own work becomes a chore rather than a satisfying task.

How will the contents be organized? Once the contents have been selected, the next decision is how the science portfolio should be organized for those who will examine them. The organizational format can be developed collaboratively among students, teachers, administrators, and parents or selected by any combination of these subgroups. You must keep the needs of the science portfolio's audience in mind when deciding on the format you will have your students use. What will the reader need to know to understand the contents?

While the formats chosen by individual classes may vary, many science portfolios include a table of contents, a way to introduce the portfolio, captions for individual items, a logical order of contents, self-reflections, and a closing for the portfolio. Some ways to introduce the portfolio are to have older students write a paragraph that describes the contents, to have a letter addressed to "Dear Reader" to explain the portfolio, or to have an introduction that the primary teacher has created with class input. A logical order for the contents may include using categories or sections for different types of items, sorting items by units or themes, or placing items in chronological order. Some examples of items used to close a portfolio include future science learning goals, a summary reflection about what they have learned about themselves in science, changes they have noticed in their work, growth they have made in science, and comment sheets for portfolio visitors.

How can peer assessments be used to enhance portfolios? Another item you may choose to use to enhance science portfolios is peer assessment. Two main ways that peer assessment can be used in portfolio implementation are to include peer assessment sheets as entries along with the students' self-reflections, teacher evaluations, and/or parental input and as a way to assess artifacts or completed portfolios.

You will need to model appropriate behavior such as sensitivity and respect for students in your assessments and interactions with the class before your students will be able to use peer assessments effectively. Reviewing what peer assessment is, why it should be done, and ways to do it are excellent ways to introduce this form of assessment to your class. Then you can lead students into exploring how they can help give each other feedback about their progress. This involves providing students with choices in what items will be shared with peers and who will evaluate their work. You and your class will need to decide what will be expected of those doing the assessments.

Teachers who have used peer assessments successfully provide students with demonstrations for how to assess, time for reflection, opportunities to discuss results, examples of ways to interact with one another in a positive yet constructive manner, and reminders that the processes that learners used to reach products are important. Peer assessments can be used to encourage students to help each other find out what they are doing well or need to improve in science by looking through their assessment sheets. The feedback they receive must be meaningful to them. Teachers and students often collaborate to create peer assessment checklists or rubrics.

How will the information gathered be used? The information gathered in portfolios can be used in several ways. Portfolios can be used to give students more responsibility and motivation for learning science. Students can use a portfolio to demonstrate their science learning and understandings to themselves, their parents, and their teacher. Teachers can use portfolio contents to plan for teaching, to make curriculum decisions, and to guide learning. Schools and districts can use portfolios to evaluate the quality of science curriculum, programs, and teaching practices. Portfolios can assist districts in aligning their science curriculum and assessment. Science portfolios can also be used as a large-scale assessment at the district or state level to measure curricular goals beyond the classroom and to measure student achievement across classrooms.

Who will be the audience for these portfolios? There are many possible audiences for science portfolios, depending on the type of portfolio and its purpose. Students are the audience for *student folios,* while teachers are the audience for *teacher folios. Student showcase* and *growth* portfolios may have students, teachers, parents, and/or administrators for an audience. *Documentation/permanent* portfolios may have these audiences plus community members and policymakers beyond the school district.

How will the portfolios be shared with others? Although portfolios may be examined by teams of teachers and community members to determine whether science standards are being met, the information in science portfolios is most often shared through conferencing with the teacher, peers, or parents. Teachers can use portfolio conferences to help students determine the items they want to place in various portfolios, to help students set science learning goals, and to elicit student

input into evaluating the finished portfolios. These conferences are also an excellent way to prepare students to participate in student-led conferences with their parents. During portfolio conferences, teachers often ask students how they feel they have improved in science, what they feel they have learned, what they want to work on next, what they want their parents to know about their science understandings, and how they might organize their portfolios to show what they know about science.

When students share their portfolios with their peers, they have the opportunity to assist each other in assessing the most effective parts of the portfolio and to make suggestions for changes to improve the portfolio. Students can use their peers as a practice audience before presenting their science portfolios to others. Teachers can provide students with a checklist, such as the one in Figure 7.4, to use during peer conferences. The best portfolio checklists or rubrics are created collaboratively with students as a class activity.

A **student-led conference** is held between a parent and student, although the teacher may be present to provide moral support and to answer some of the parents' questions. The student is usually responsible for controlling and organizing the portfolio conference. When students are meaningfully involved in reporting their progress in science, displaying their work, and explaining the contents of their portfolios, assessment becomes an integral part of instruction and a learning experience in its own right. The goal of this type of portfolio conference is to provide students with responsibility for their own learning and for informing their parents of progress (Austin, 1994).

FIGURE 7.4
_____

Checklist for Portfolio Peer Conferences

Student _____   Conference Date _____

Peer Assessor _____

Circle the appropriate response to answer each question about this portfolio conference.

Mechanics:

    1. Is there a table of contents?   Yes   Needs improvement

    2. Is it organized in a logical order?   Yes   Needs improvement

    3. Is there an introduction to the portfolio?   Yes   Needs improvement

    4. Are all the items labeled and explained?   Yes   Needs improvement

    5. Is there a closing to the portfolio?   Yes   Needs improvement

Selections:

    6. Are there a variety of different items?   Yes   Needs improvement

    8. Are the required items included?   Yes   Needs improvement

    9. Are there additional items included?   Yes   Needs improvement

   10. Are the items quality work?   Yes   Needs improvement

Reflections:

   11. Are self-assessments in the portfolio?   Yes   Needs improvement

   12. Do the explanations make sense?   Yes   Needs improvement

   13. Did your classmate write about things he
        or she does well in science?   Yes   Needs improvement

   14. Did your classmate write about areas to
        improve on in science?   Yes   Needs improvement

   15. Does the portfolio have science goals?   Yes   Needs improvement

Presentation:

   16. Were you introduced to the portfolio?   Yes   Needs improvement

   17. Did the presentation make sense?   Yes   Needs improvement

   18. Were you told about your classmates'
        strengths in science?   Yes   Needs improvement

   19. Were plans for improvement shared?   Yes   Needs improvement

   20. Were ways to reach goals discussed?   Yes   Needs improvement

   21. Were your questions answered?   Yes   Needs improvement

   22. Were you asked for your comments   Yes   Needs improvement

Comments:

It is important that the parents and students are informed of the rationale for having the student take the leadership role during the conference. This can be done through newsletters and/or parent meetings. Some science teachers send a letter home to parents a week before the conferences. These letters usually include a choice of several possible days and times for them to come, a brief description of what the format of the conference will be, and a sample of some of the things that the parent will be able to see at the conference. You may want to have older students create their own invitations.

The main role of the student is to initiate, lead, and explain his or her science progress through the use of the portfolio. The student takes on the role of expert in sharing the portfolio and all its contents. If a report card is part of the portfolio, it is shared near the end of the conference before the student discusses future goals for improvement in science. Often the student and parents clarify and extend goals by discussing how to work on the goals both at home and at school. Before the conference is over, the student may ask the parent to complete a parent reflection sheet, respond to the portfolio, or sign in a guest book with room for comments.

How will the portfolio be assessed or graded? Assessment of portfolios varies according to the objectives of the portfolio assignment. Generally, it is most effective to look at many portfolios before you decide on a scoring rubric. The student's selections should not be simply graded by percentage correct or progress toward an external standard. You may want to consider examining such characteristics as the depth of self-reflection, the variety or quality of the selected items, the quality of required items, and the evidence of improvement in science contained within the portfolio. You could use a scoring rubric similar to the one in Figure 7.5.

Personal comments about the science portfolio are critical, and some teachers require their students to include a blank sheet for teacher comments. The teacher's selections for a portfolio are more likely to be objective in nature, including such items as process skill assessments, inquiry assessments, content assessments, interview notes, observation notes, results of hands-on process skill activity tests, checklists, test scores, activity evaluations, science homework, and class work grades.

When assessing children through science portfolios, student-selected items should be compared to teacher-selected items to establish a more complete picture. For example, if a student's daily grades are low, the portfolio may demonstrate excellence in achieving the objectives even though the grades may not have reflected it. Grades can be derived from the combination of the student's and the teacher's selections. In addition, some schools have schoolwide evaluation guidelines for portfolio assessment.

What will happen to the portfolio at the end of the year or semester? What happens to the portfolio at the end of the year depends on the type of portfolio and how it will be used the following year. The items in a *student* or *teacher folio* that have not been selected for inclusion in another type of portfolio are usually sent home with the student or discarded. *Growth* and *student showcase* portfolios are usually sent home with the students at the end of the year or kept for the next year's teacher. If *permanent* portfolios are part of a schoolwide or district policy, they are kept in a secure place. Teachers and the students access these portfolios each succeeding year. When there

FIGURE 7.5

_____

Scoring Rubric for Grading Portfolios

Selections:

3 2 1 The student's selections demonstrate what he or she wanted to show.
3 2 1 The examples indicates the student's best work and scientific thinking.
3 2 1 The selections demonstrate progress and growth in science learning.
3 2 1 There are a variety of types of items showing science learning.
3 2 1 Required items are present and demonstrate quality work.

Self-Reflections:

3 2 1 The explanations are logical.
3 2 1 The student's self-reflections demonstrate what they were intended to show.
3 2 1 Explanations of strengths and weaknesses demonstrate an understanding of learning.
3 2 1 The student has a grasp of the quality of his or her work.
3 2 1 Self-reflections indicate that the student has learned the targeted science: concepts, skills, or processes.
3 2 1 There is evidence of an attempt to improve in weaker areas.
3 2 1 Goals are realistic, and plans for achieving them are well planned.

Mechanics:

3 2 1 A table of contents that lists all the items in the portfolio is present.
3 2 1 The portfolio is organized in a logical order.
3 2 1 There is an appropriate introduction to the portfolio provided for the reader.
3 2 1 All the items are labeled, and the student has explained why each is included and what it demonstrates about his or her science learning.
3 2 1 The student has followed the format agreed on in class.
3 2 1 There is an appropriate closing for the portfolio.

_____Total points

Excellent = 45–54 points   Satisfactory = 36–44 points

Needs improvement = 35 points and below

is no agreement about how portfolios will be used in a school from year to year, it is usually best to send your science portfolios home with the students, especially if they will not be valued by the students' teacher(s) the next year.

Now that you know what a portfolio is and have some ideas for managing them, you will need to weigh the benefits and concerns for using portfolio assessment. The next two sections will provide you with a variety of information to consider before you opt to use one or more of the types of science portfolios in your classroom.

Benefits of Portfolio Assessment

Teachers benefit from using portfolio assessment in the science classroom in several ways. All facets of a student's progress and growth in science can be examined. Through the portfolio, teachers can see a picture of the whole child, including long-term achievement and concrete examples of attitudes, interests, ideas, learning styles, skill with processes, facility in inquiry, and acquisition of content.

As a science teacher, you will need to make professional judgments about student progress or grades. Portfolios can provide the information necessary to base a judgment on and can provide understandable information about pupil achievement that can be communicated to parents and to the pupils themselves. Science portfolios can enable you to determine the amount of individual growth of each learner based on specified criteria. The information you gather about student progress will also tell you whether the goals of the science lesson or unit have been reached and where any trouble spots are. As you assess student learning, you are also conducting a self-assessment as a teacher.

At conference time, a portfolio clearly demonstrates the progress each student has made. When students are prepared well over an extended period of time to tell the story of their own success or lack of it, they seem to undergo a shift in their sense of responsibility for their science learning. Their pride in accomplishments when they have a positive story to tell can be immensely motivational, especially when they have done a good job of sharing the information. The sense of personal responsibility that they feel when anticipating what it will be like to face the music of having to tell their story of nonachievement in science can drive them to more productive work (Stiggins, 1999).

When students are involved in the assessment process in science portfolios through self-selection, self-reflection, and peer assessments, they have a role in defining the criteria that will be used to judge their work. This builds trust and confidence as students monitor improvements in their science performance. Some of the additional benefits that students can receive by actively participating in the science portfolios include the following:

- Gaining an understanding of themselves as learners in science
- Taking responsibility for knowing their own strengths and weaknesses
- Gaining an understanding of the relationship between learning and assessment
- Becoming actively involved in their education
- Thinking metacognitively while using higher-level thinking skills
- Setting their own goals that they are more likely to accomplish
- Developing better communication skills
- Becoming more capable as independent, self-directed learners
- Learning to collaborate with others
- Developing a sense of self-confidence and faith in their abilities

- Becoming willing to take risks to learn from mistakes as well as successes
- Thinking critically to develop criteria to meet science standards
- Cooperating and collaborating with others in assessment
- Valuing other students' input
- Removing much of the pressure of peer competition for grades
- Allowing students to focus on their own individual progress in science

Portfolios also allow parents to see tangible and understandable evidence of what their children are learning. Parents find portfolio conferences to be rewarding and informative. Finally, parent attendance at conferences usually increases dramatically.

Concerns About Portfolio Assessment

While there are many benefits to portfolios, there are concerns about them just as there are with all forms of science assessment. The follow paragraphs delineate the common concerns about using portfolio assessment in science.

As noted earlier, parents are often more familiar and comfortable with traditional assessment. They may still want to rely on letter grades for assessment. Some do not feel that students can adequately assess their own learning and feel that teachers should be responsible for all assessment, or they are not doing their jobs as educators.

Setting up a portfolio system often seems like an overwhelming task for many teachers because of its complexity. Some teachers jump in and try to handle too many tasks at once. Then they become frustrated and abandon the process. Sometimes teachers end up with a huge folder filled with a potpourri of children's work that they have to sift through and try to make sense out of when the term ends. This happens when clear purposes have not been set or students and teachers have not made sure that all items meet the portfolio objectives. Portfolios can become cluttered. On the other hand, too few items in the portfolio makes forming a valid judgment of achievement impossible, while having too many items results in confusion. When beginning portfolios, it is best to begin with small, manageable parts and build on it over time (Ebenezer & Conner, 1998).

Time and space are two additional issues with portfolios. Time is required to teach students how to look critically at their own work. This is not always easy to find with the curricular requirements in teaching science at all levels. Before students can effectively evaluate one another's work, teachers will need to lay the groundwork for positive handling of constructive criticism and interactions among students. When children are first asked to apply the criteria, they are often reluctant to fill out the evaluation forms because they do not want to make negative comments about their peers.

Portfolios also take up classroom space. The issue of providing a storage area for them is one that is not always easy to resolve. Portfolios take organization and preparation time. For those who do not have the time, organizational skills, or desire to design and implement them, portfolios may not be the best assessment solution.

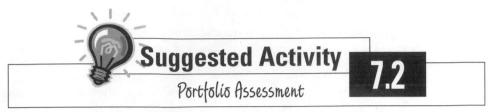

Suggested Activity **7.2**

Portfolio Assessment

1. In your collaborative group, discuss whether you would want to use portfolios in your science classroom. Be able to defend your position.
2. In your journal, provide answers for the questions for designing a science portfolio listed in Figure 7.2.

SCORING RUBRICS

Scoring rubrics are another form of authentic assessment that can be used during any portion of the instructional process. Rubrics are a clear set of guidelines for scoring student work. These guidelines are usually written in increasing order of difficulty. Each level is assigned a numeric value that moves what might have been considered subjective judgments in the past to more clearly defined and defensible numeric scores. The purpose of classroom rubrics is to help teachers clarify their goals, process instruction, and involve students in self-evaluation.

Defining Scoring Rubrics

In science, the term *rubric* refers to a scoring guide used to evaluate the quality of students' constructed responses, for example, science projects. *Scoring rubrics* are brief, written descriptions of different levels of student performance. They often use the same set of observable criteria that goes into a checklist. They evaluate criteria such as creativity, relevance to real life, impact, clarity, completeness, and organization.

Essential Features of Scoring Rubrics

According to Popham (1997), a scoring rubric has three essential features: evaluative criteria, quality definitions, and a scoring strategy. *Evaluative criteria* are used to distinguish acceptable responses from unacceptable responses. The criteria will obviously vary from rubric to rubric, depending on the science skill or concept involved. Evaluative criteria can either be given equal weight or be weighted differently. *Quality definitions* describe the way that qualitative differences in students' responses are to be judged. The rubric must provide a separate description for each qualitative level. A superior response needs to be separated from a good example or an inadequate one. A *scoring strategy* may be either holistic or analytic. Using a holistic strategy, the scorer takes all the evaluative criteria into consideration but aggregates them to make a single, overall quality judgment. Holistic rubrics measure the overall quality of an artifact, a performance, or a portfolio. An analytic strategy requires the scorer to assign criterion-by-criterion scores that may or may not ultimately be aggregated into an overall score of the item being assessed.

A scoring rubric's most important component is the set of evaluative criteria to be used when judging students' performances. The criteria should be the most instructionally relevant component of the rubric. They should guide the teacher in designing lessons because it is students' mastery of the evaluative criteria that ultimately will lead to skill or concept mastery. Teachers should also make the criteria available to students to help them appraise their own efforts.

A scoring rubric that not only helps teachers judge the quality of students' responses to a performance test but also assists teachers in helping students acquire the skill represented by that test would contain three to five evaluative criteria. Each evaluative criterion must represent a key attribute of the skill being assessed. These criteria must be teachable in the sense that teachers can help students increase their ability to use each criterion when tackling tasks that require a certain skill. The following rubric is an example of a holistic scoring rubric for the fourth-grade performance task of identifying components of common kitchen substances:

Exemplary: The student identifies all four kitchen substances—salt, sugar, flour, and alum; describes all the procedures used to identify each; provides accurate evidence for identifying each substance; lists the characteristics of each substance; and creates a chart, drawing, or diagram showing these characteristics.

Good: The student identifies all four kitchen substances—salt, sugar, flour, and alum; describes the procedures used to identify each; provides accurate evidence for identifying each substance; and either accurately lists the characteristics of each or creates a chart, drawing, or diagram showing these characteristics.

Fair Quality: The student identifies at least three of the kitchen substances, partially describes the procedures used to identify them, and provides some evidence for identifying the substances and lists some of their characteristics.

Poor Quality: The student identifies one or two of the kitchen substances and does a minimum of one of the following: partially describes the procedures used to identify the kitchen substances found, provides evidence for identifying one of the substances, or accurately lists the characteristics of one of the substances found.

Unacceptable: The student fails to correctly identify any of the kitchen substances, does not describe procedures used, provides no evidence or inaccurate evidence for identifying substances, and does not list characteristics, or the student does not attempt to complete the task.

Analytic rubrics measure artifacts, performances, or portfolios in a quantitative manner by assigning or taking away points for criteria that are present or missing. By including evaluative criteria in the scoring rubric, the teacher establishes an objective basis for judging the artifact, performance, or portfolio. Scoring rubrics also provide students with feedback or data supporting grades and evaluations. When students know the criteria on which they were judged, they can take steps to expand their knowledge and improve their skills. The following example is an analytic scoring rubric for the same performance task of identifying components of common kitchen substances:

4 points: The student

- identifies all four kitchen substances—salt, sugar, flour, and alum,
- describes all the procedures used to identify each,
- provides accurate evidence for identifying each substance, and
- shows key characteristics of each substance by listing, charting, drawing, or diagramming.

3 points: The student

- identifies all four kitchen substances—salt, sugar, flour, and alum,
- describes most of the procedures used to identify each,
- provides mostly accurate evidence for identifying each substance, and
- shows some characteristics of each through listing, charting, drawing, or diagramming.

2 points: The student

- identifies at least three of the kitchen substances,
- partially describes the procedures used to identify the three,
- provides some evidence for identifying the substances, and
- accurately lists, charts, draws, or diagrams characteristics for at least two of the substances.

1 point: The student

- identifies one or two of the kitchen substances and
- does a minimum of one of the following:
- partially describes the procedures used to identify the kitchen substances found,
- provides evidence for identifying one of the substances, or
- accurately lists, charts, draws, or diagrams the characteristics of one of the kitchen substances found.

0 points: The student

- fails to correctly identify any of the kitchen substances,
- does not describe procedures used,
- provides no evidence or inaccurate evidence for identifying substances, and/or
- provides no characteristics or inaccurate characteristics of the kitchen substances.

The criteria used in scoring rubrics depend on the teacher's goals and objectives for the science lesson. Some criteria may be mandated by state and local school districts' curriculum guidelines, while others are likely to follow national trends or curriculum frameworks such as the *National Science Education Standards* (National Research Council, 1996). Krajacik, Czerniak, and Berger (1999) suggest using criteria such as the following to assist you in designing scoring rubrics:

- *Understanding of concepts.* Have students demonstrate shallow or deep understanding in the detail in their work sample, performance, or portfolio? Are there missing links? Are explanations complete?

- *Use of higher-order thinking.* Are students demonstrating higher-order thinking? Can they formulate and answer questions, interpret or explain decisions, and discuss assumptions that underlie the sample, performance, or portfolio? Are the students able to explain relationships and formulate new problems or questions and apply information to new situations or problems?

- *Ability to answer inquiry questions.* How well are students able to answer an inquiry question? Was there a weak or strong relationship to the question? Did students specify the relationship in clear, specific terms?

- *Relatedness to the world.* How strong are the connections between the performance, work sample, or portfolio and the real world? Did students apply information to a real-life example in a strong, convincing manner?

- *Level of collaboration.* Does the performance, portfolio, or work sample demonstrate interaction with others? Is there evidence that students shared ideas and used other resources, including community resources?

- *Level of creativity.* Does the work sample, portfolio, or performance construct new ideas or connect existing ideas with new ones? Does it use ideas in novel ways or translate ideas from other subject areas?

- *Presentation.* Did students thoroughly explain the key ideas? Were their classmates engaged? Did they answer questions well? Did they use enough detail to support their conclusions?

- *Use of cognitive tools.* Did students use tools such as print media, computers, software applications, and telecommunication? What was the usage level of these types of tools?

These scoring rubrics are often used as part of everyday instruction in today's science classrooms and can be included in student portfolios along with those created by the school or district to measure benchmarks for the learning goals of your school system. Students can provide feedback into the success of the assessment and suggest changes that are needed in these rubrics. Once you are comfortable with creating rubrics, you will most likely want to have your students assist in creating them because then students will know up front the expectations for a project or other assignment.

Using these five rules for creating indicators in science scoring rubrics will help you develop scoring rubrics that will be meaningful assessment tools:

1. Indicators must be relevant to standards, benchmarks, goals, and objectives.
2. Indicators should be spelled out before the students begin the work that will be assessed with the rubric.
3. Each level in the rubric should have at least three indicators.
4. First use of the rubric should be to gather baseline data to set criteria for success.
5. Scoring rubrics should have specified levels of what will be considered as success or incomplete work.

Scoring rubrics usually have three or more levels of achievement. Many rubrics have a five-point scale. In working with teachers and students in creating rubrics, we have found it useful to begin with the third level or the one that demonstrates what a good assignment or project would look like: What must it include? What characteristics would it have? Then we move up to the fourth level: What would make this work truly outstanding? What additional features or qualities would make the work clearly superior to the good one? Next, we move down to the second level. Here the students have much of the concept or needed characteristics, but it is not quite there: What would this look like? After this we focus on the project or work that is not acceptable: What would be the characteristics of this work? It could still have some good features, but most would lack quality work. If you desire a final level, this one would show no effort, have major portions missing, or simply not be attempted.

Teachers can use scoring rubrics that they have created themselves for any area of the science curriculum. Students can use rubrics for self-assessments and to compare their results with those of their peers or the teacher. The following sections delineate the benefits and concerns about using scoring rubrics in science classrooms.

Benefits of Scoring Rubrics

A well-designed scoring rubric can assist you in scoring students' science work more accurately and fairly. It can also give students a clearer picture of what qualities their work should have. Students become aware of the characteristics of quality science work and are therefore in a better position to achieve it. Scoring rubrics often include both process and products in various contexts and can be used for any subject area at any grade level. Teachers, students, and parents can use scoring rubrics with equal ease. Not only can students help create rubrics, but they can also use them for both self-reflection and peer assessments. Rubrics are beneficial because teachers can use them to assess standards or student demonstrations and use their time effectively. Rubrics are a valuable authentic assessment tool in the science classroom because

- the criteria are explicitly stated and understandable,
- awareness of the criteria is easily obtained,
- the scorer is able to use time efficiently,

- student accountability in science is enhanced,
- they are easily modified to meet individual needs, and
- they can be adjusted to meet grade-level objectives with little difficulty.

Concerns About Using Scoring Rubrics

While scoring rubrics have many benefits, there are also concerns or cautions that apply to using them. One of the concerns is that teachers need to have time to learn how to create scoring rubrics that will match their instructional and assessment needs rather than simply adopting those that are on the market if they are to realize the potential benefits to their instructional practices. Many commercial scoring rubrics are lengthy, detailed, task specific, or excessively general. When scoring rubrics become too long and detailed, they are no longer useful for classroom instruction. In good instructional rubrics, less is more. Scoring rubrics need to focus on the concepts, skills, processes, or attitudes that you want students to learn rather than the task itself. If the evaluative criteria are so general that students and teachers can conclude only that responses are really good or really bad, the rubric serves no instructional purpose (Popham, 1997).

Before you can have students help create scoring rubrics or use them for self-reflection or peer assessment, you will need to be comfortable with the philosophy that students need to be involved in their learning and assessment. Teachers who are unwilling to share control of science learning with their students will not be able to effectively have students participate in self-reflection or peer assessment with scoring rubrics in science.

Sometimes teachers learn how to use a new assessment technique and apply it to all their teaching. Every piece of work that students produce does not necessarily need to be assessed or graded with a rubric. **Overuse of any assessment tool lessons its effectiveness.** Some science activities, assignments, or projects lend themselves better to being assessed through observations, checklists, learning logs, inventories, or other forms of assessment.

Suggested Activity 7.3
Scoring Rubrics

1. In your collaborative discussion group, discuss when you might want to use a scoring rubric in a science classroom. Discuss the merits of using either holistic or analytic scoring rubrics.

2. Working as a group or individually, use the five rules for creating a scoring rubric listed previously and design a scoring rubric to accompany a science lesson or unit. Explain why you chose the types of criteria you did and why you chose to use a holistic or analytic scoring system.

ASSESSMENTS FOR OBSERVING STUDENTS

Informal observations can help teachers make valid decisions about science curricula and instruction and determine how much progress students are making. Observations play a firm role in a teacher's minute-to-minute decision making. Teachers usually watch students' body language for evidence that any students are having difficulty with a concept or task. Students' off-task behavior might indicate problems with instructional methods. These types of observations can help you make on-the-spot curricular or instructional decisions that can refocus a science lesson.

While teachers can observe and often help students stay on track in whole-class settings, the most productive times to observe are usually in individual and small-group situations. There are many chances for monitoring or interacting with students during activity times in science lessons. Notice what your students say and do when they interact with you, a partner, or other members of a small group. What you observe gives you data for fast self-correction or for assisting individual students.

Informal teacher observations are a primary source of information about student learning and take place continuously. Most teachers develop a sense of who knows what and who is having trouble with which science concepts through observations. The key to converting informal observation into an assessment tool is to decide what student actions and behaviors you will observe to assess progress.

Classroom teachers have a large number of students to observe, and a science unit usually has many learning goals. Therefore, every teacher needs some systematic way to keep track of observations. Without a system, it is too easy to forget to observe important activities and too easy to overlook some students. Observations are often informal and are inevitably subjective to some degree because you interpret what you see. To ensure more valid data, use a variety of observation techniques, such as anecdotal records, checklists, interviews, inventories, surveys, and questionnaires, to provide varied information rather than relying on a single technique. The next portion of this chapter describes these techniques for gathering systematic observations.

Anecdotal Records

Anecdotal records are notes about student learning behaviors written during or after an observation of a student. The best notes are brief yet descriptive and capture an event with enough detail so that it can be considered again at a later time. Anecdotal records need to be dated to enable you to examine strengths, weaknesses, needs, progress, learning styles, and patterns over time. Depending on reasons for the observations, they can be taken at times that vary from whole-class to group work to conferences with individuals. In each science setting, the focus for anecdotal records must remain on individual students.

Effective anecdotal records describe a specific science event or product, report information rather than evaluating or interpreting it, and relate the material to other facts that are known about the student. Although some science teachers tend to examine students' learning by what they are not doing, anecdotal comments should begin positively with something the student can do because constructivist teaching begins with students' existing knowledge and strengths. After a positive beginning, teachers may then include student needs or deficits. These observations should be geared toward reflections about science teaching, learning, or attitudes.

Only the teacher limits the range of information that can be collected in anecdotal records. You can note points about students' learning behavior, attitudes, and choices. So much is usually happening in a science classroom that you will find it helpful to be selective in what you choose to record. You may want to simply have your note taking materials available and spontaneously record interesting or important behaviors as they are observed, or you may prefer to have planned observations that are focused on predetermined areas, criteria, or benchmarks. Focus questions such as the following may be useful: How well do students communicate their ideas during group work? How are students solving problems during science experiments? Do students respect the reactions and opinions of others? Some other suggestions include the following:

- Observing how students use various science processes
- Noticing when and how students relate information from various sources, such as trade books, student magazines, and the Internet, to what they are doing in class to determine how they are assimilating information
- Listening to conversations and discussions to find evidence of appropriate use of new technical vocabulary
- Watching students perform a science skill to reveal how well they do it and their understanding of the concepts behind it

You many want to target one or two science benchmarks to observe over a period of time and write comments on the progress made by each student. Comments can also target social behaviors, such as cooperative learning skills and leadership skills. Student responsibility demonstrated by completing work, initiating projects, or participating in discussion can also be noted. The more comments reflect the science benchmarks established by your school community, the more valuable you will find them in noting progress, learning, and patterns over time.

To begin collecting anecdotal records, examine your daily schedule for times students are engaged in independent practice or group work when you are not actively teaching science lessons. These times provide excellent opportunities for making anecdotal comments. One way to begin is to focus on only one context, while a second is to observe one or two students a day or a small group of four or five students a week. Many teachers use clipboards for jotting down their notes as they circulate through the classroom or sit with a small group. Another common approach is recording notes or observations about students on stick-on notes or index cards. Teachers usually date the notes, put the students' names on them, and place them in students' files at the end of the day or week. The simplest storage systems for anecdotal records work best. If you have access to them, handheld or palmtop computers permit you to effortlessly make observations during instruction instead of later.

Checklists

For those who are just beginning to use observation as an assessment tool, checklists are often less formidable than anecdotal records. Sometimes novices who are taking anecdotal records find that they repeatedly record the same information for certain science topics. When this happens, you will want to create a checklist for these common traits and continue recording comments on individual students for aspects of learning that are difficult to represent on a checklist or that apply only to that student. Many teachers use checklists efficiently and wisely in just such a manner.

Checklists usually contain a list of learning traits or descriptors to observe and a system for marking the occurrence or quality of the traits during observation. Main purposes for checklists include keeping observations focused, providing a way to document information that requires a minimum of writing, providing consistency across observations over time, and allowing teachers to customize assessment to match their instructional focus.

The number of specific uses for checklists may be unlimited since any learning event can have a checklist designed to facilitate its observation during or after instruction. Checklists can be used to evaluate knowledge, skills, processes, or attitudes. They can be either project specific or generic. For example, on a class list you can easily tally the frequency of students' participation in classroom discussions. Or you might maintain a checklist of important concepts and check off students who demonstrate understanding of the science concepts.

You can use a checklist to assess skills or processes by observing students during a lesson and recording which ones they are using as they are working. Checklists can also provide you with a list of affective attributes to look for in a lesson. Choose a few students to observe and mark on the checklist the science skills or processes in which they seem to be proficient or are progressing toward proficiency. See Figure 7.6 for an example of a checklist that can be used to monitor students' basic processes of observing, predicting, and communicating.

You might keep an observation sheet for each student in a three-ring binder to make a functional grade book for tracking student progress in science. Some teachers find that using a checklist attached to a clipboard as they circulate around the classroom is more helpful. They can keep the completed checklists in a file or a teacher folio to refer to at a later time.

Checklists that are developed by teachers during instructional planning are most appropriate since these will best reflect their targeted outcomes and the needs of their students. Some of the best checklists are those that provide students with the opportunity to assist in creating and monitoring the checklists. Design your checklists to reflect what you consider to be the important skills, processes, attitudes, and content in any science unit. You may want to create descriptors for the different products, worksheets, and other materials you expect your students to complete. Adding anecdotal comments to the checklists increases their usefulness in instructional planning. You can do this by creating a checklist with only a few student names per page or one that provides space for writing narrative comments

FIGURE 7.6

Checklist for Observing, Predicting, and Communicating

Student Name_____   Date _____

Indicators Observed: Frequently   Sometimes   Seldom

Observing:
1. Identifies objects
2. Uses more than one sense
3. Describes properties accurately
4. Provides qualitative observations
5. Provides quantitative data
6. Accurately describes changes in objects

Predicting:
7. Forms patterns
8. Extends patterns
9. Makes simple predictions
10. Applies predicting to appropriate situations
11. Shows sound logic in reasons for predictions
12. Suggests tests to check accuracy of predictions
13. Predicts based on supportive evidence
14. Predicts based on accurate understanding
    of cause-and-effect relationships

Communicating:
15. Describes objects accurately
16. Expresses opinions with supporting evidence
17. Verbalizes thinking
18. Explains causal relationships accurately
19. Transmits information to others accurately
20. Explains information in a way that others can
    understand

Comments:

about your observations. The following suggestions will help you create checklists to use in your science classroom:

- Limit the number of items or descriptors that you place on a checklist to keep it simple enough to use effectively.
- Select only those traits or descriptors that are most important at the time the checklist will be used.
- Review and change items on the checklist during the year to reflect changes in your instruction and students.
- Remember that checklists should always fit instructional purposes.

Interviews

One of the best ways to find out how much students have learned and how well they understand what they have learned is to ask them about it. During interviews, teachers usually ask individual students open-ended questions. The teacher takes notes about their discussion or records the student's responses on a form with a blank space provided after each question. Interviews provide information about students' perceptions about learning, specific topics, instructional practices, and their preferences. They can also be used to discover students' attitudes about themselves as learners in science. Teachers can learn what prior knowledge students have about a topic, what students are most interested in learning, the types of science activities students choose to engage in, topics they might want to learn more about, or their future learning goals.

Interviews with students can be either informal or structured. Both are authentic ways of obtaining information about children's science achievement and thinking. Informal interviews are discussions between a teacher and one or more students. Students usually find these to be less stressful than many other forms of assessment. They are often simply conversations between a teacher and a student. During the interview, the teacher asks questions relating to the lesson's science objectives and focuses on the responses. The teacher probes, asks additional questions, and attempts to discover how the child has arrived at the responses given. You can conduct informal interviews during any portion of the instructional process. At the end of an activity, an area of inquiry, or an investigation, you may want to engage the students as individuals or as a group in discussions of what they did, what they concluded, what they learned, and what their thought processes were. Discussions such as these can provide invaluable information about your students' achievement and construction of ideas and concepts.

What differentiates structured and informal interviews is that the teacher prepares the questions ahead of time as guidelines for the structured interview. For example, you might set up a structured interview to elicit the same information from each student. A list of guiding questions will keep you focused on your objectives, but you will also need to ask additional questions to clarify student answers and elicit more information to understand what the students are thinking. This interchange can also clarify children's understanding and stretch their thinking.

Open-ended questions are a great way to start either structured or informal interviews. An open-ended question gives a student a cue to explain what he or she thinks. Another effective technique for either informal or structured interviews is the "what if" question. This type of question probes students' understanding even further by forcing them to think about new variables and different situations. When using interviews as an assessment tool in the science classroom, keep in mind that you should accept all answers and value each student's thoughts and opinions. Intervene only as necessary to keep the discussion focused on the topic. Word questions carefully to promote further discussion. Begin with questions such as the following:

Tell me about . . .

What do you think about . . .

How do you feel about . . .

Can you explain why . . .

Describe how you would . . .

How did you discover . . .

How did you do . . .

How did you figure out that . . .

Maintain the discussion with further questions such as the following:

What else can you say about . . .

What do you mean by . . .

Could you give me an example of . . .

What if you were to . . .

How is this related to . . .

Is there another way to explain . . .

How could we change . . .

What question should I ask the next student about . . .

The kinds of questions that are used for the interview depend on your purpose for wanting to know the information. One of the factors to remember when constructing questions is to realize that students may not always view them in the same way you intended them or may not understand what information is appropriate for answering the questions.

The best interview questions are both reflective and nondirective. They require students to think about their answers and provide you with a glimpse of their thought processes. Nondirective questions **avoid** alerting students to the fact that they have responded incorrectly, using double questions that provide too much information, or guiding students to a specific "correct" answer. Some other common errors interfere with gathering valid information. One such error is when teachers paraphrase student responses because students will often use this version rather than their own. When a teacher uses cuing or interprets student responses, the students will often repeat the teacher's view rather than their own later in the interview. Pressuring often happens when time is short and teachers try to hurry through an interview, but students clam up and provide little useful information. The final problem is overuse of praise, which only reinforces the teacher's role and the students often attempt to give answers they think the teacher wants. Asking good probing questions while interviewing is not easy but can provide rich, meaningful science data.

Interviews can be conducted as separate entities or as part of instruction. Explaining the purpose for the questions will place students at ease and increase the chances of receiving honest responses. Teachers who are skilled at interviewing watch students carefully to see whether they understand and adjust questions accordingly. If they sense that the student is uncomfortable, they reach a stopping point and finish the interview at another time. Martin (1997) recommends that interviews become a regular component of the assessment program in elementary and middle school science education because it is only by asking children questions and listening to their responses that you will learn what students know and how they think.

Inventories, Questionnaires, and Surveys

Sometimes teachers who have little time or feel unsure of their interviewing skills find it easier to gather similar information through inventories, questionnaires, and surveys because these interviews are written rather than oral. Teachers also find it helpful to have the students or parents respond in writing to preplanned questions and then follow up on interesting or confusing responses with an oral interview.

Since these forms can be answered by an entire class at once, they are often chosen to save administration time. They can serve a variety of purposes, including the following:

- Determining prior knowledge before studying a topic
- Measuring self-reflection through surveys, inventories, or questionnaires
- Assessing students' scientific attitudes, such as curiosity, inventiveness, critical thinking, and persistence
- Listing goals on inventories

Inventories, questionnaires, and surveys are often presented in a short-answer format that uses open-ended questions. Figure 7.7 is an example of a questionnaire that provides information about students' prior knowledge, attitudes, and interests for a thematic unit covering recycling in a fifth-grade classroom.

FIGURE 7.7

Recycling Questionnaire

Name_____   Date _____

Write your answers to the questions in the spaces below. If you need more room, you may use the back of this sheet.

1. What are you interested in learning about recycling?

2. What do you know about recycling?

3. Are there different types of trash? Explain your answer.

4. What do you think happens to trash after it is removed from your home or school?

5. Do think recycling is important? Why or why not?

6. What kinds of projects do you think we should create about recycling?

7. What are some ways that we can recycle or reduce trash at school?

8. Do you recycle at home? If you do, how do you recycle? If you don't, are you interested in learning some ways you might?

A second way to construct these forms of observation is a forced-choice format where students select from a given set of responses that best matches how they feel or think. Some teachers prefer to use a Likert scale that allows them to discover the degree of students' interests in topics or for assessing science attitudes. They normally use five response categories ranging from "strongly agree" to "strongly disagree," although smiling, neutral, and frowning faces are particularly helpful response choices for early elementary children and for limited-English-proficient students. Many teachers prefer to use a combination of open-ended and forced-choice questions. By using a combination, teachers can gather more data to reach a more accurate picture of the students' science learning. Students can respond to items that you read if they have difficulty in reading.

Informal attitude inventories also provide useful information. Questions such as the following can reveal students' science attitudes:

Are you curious about nature or scientific phenomena?

Do you enjoy science as much as other subjects?

Do you complete science activities outside of class time?

Do you watch science-related shows at home on videotapes or television?

Have you read any science-related books lately?

Do you know a scientist in your neighborhood or community?

Do you like to answer questions during science class?

Have you considered a career in a science field?

Now that you are familiar with the various types of observational assessment tools and methods for constructing them, you need to consider their benefits and concerns about using them.

Benefits of Using Observational Assessment Tools

Because the nature of the various observation tools is entirely up to each teacher, they can be used to record details about virtually anything that seems significant. They allow teachers to be specific and accurate in conferences with students, parents, and administrators. They can serve as benchmarks for noting student progress. Any of these forms can be used to set instructional goals, as sources of documentation, and for sources of information for writing reports about student progress in science. Each of these assessment tools can be used to learn about students' self-reflections and attitudes.

Anecdotal records can help you form a more complete picture of individual students in a variety of science contexts. Continuous examination and evaluation of patterns in anecdotal records can help you plan for the instructional needs of individual students, small groups, or your entire class. You can also use them to help you evaluate your own science teaching.

Many teachers find that **checklists** make them feel secure. They are reassured that they are covering their science goals and objectives while observing everything they intend. If you find yourself becoming overwhelmed sorting through the wealth of observational data you collect, checklists can help you organize this information. They can also help you make sure that no one goes unnoticed. Checklists allow teachers a quick overview of a student's progress or performance in each targeted area. You can rapidly mark off evidence of mastering a skill or meeting an objective. Checklists also provide a guide for teachers for future observations.

In an **interview,** students can explain in more detail what they understand, how they are progressing, what problems they are having, and what steps might improve their science learning. You can get to know students, monitor their meaning making throughout a science unit, work on individual goals, and clarify misunderstandings. Interviews provide an opportunity for clarification of other classroom observations. The main advantage of interviews is that they are oral. Students will often provide more elaborate information orally than in writing. Teachers can clarify or further extend responses through further probing questions that are not possible with surveys, inventories, or questionnaires.

Interviews allow you to examine changes in students' learning and in your teaching over time. You can then use this information to assist you in designing appropriate strategy lessons and in making curriculum decisions that relate what students already know and are interested in learning. Questions can be used to discover what children are thinking rather than to find out if they know facts and can be used to develop higher-level thinking skills.

The main advantage in using **inventories, questionnaires, and surveys** is that they require written responses that can be filled in by a whole class at the same time or sent home for students and/or parents to fill out on their own and take much less time to administer than other observational assessments. Attitude surveys can provide useful data about students' likes, dislikes, opinions, or feelings about various science topics. When surveys are administered at various times during the year, growth and change in attitude can be documented. Through inventories you can discover what students know, what interests them most, processes they use, and how they feel about what they are learning. Questionnaires can uncover students' perceptions of the learning process, purposes for assignments, and criteria for evaluating understanding and/or learning strategies.

Concerns About Using Observational Assessment Tools

While there are many benefits to using observational assessment tools in the science classroom, there are also concerns about them. Because checklists, surveys, inventories, and questionnaires are easy to create, administer, and keep track of, teachers are sometimes tempted to overuse them. **Remember that good science assessment means using a variety of different assessment tools.** Another potential problem is that students may simply provide the responses that they think the teacher wants to hear rather than giving an honest opinion during an interview or on a survey, an inventory, or a questionnaire. These observational tools also have concerns related to each of them.

For example, if **anecdotal records** are going to be useful for instructional planning, you need to know what focus to use, and this takes practice. Many teachers have difficulty finding the time necessary for taking notes. Sometimes teachers tend to focus only on those students who have problems in science learning or who are producing exceptional work while the "average" students tend to be overlooked with few written comments. A final possible problem is that sometimes teachers will take detailed notes but not have the time to analyze them to examine their teaching practices and therefore continue with what they have been doing regardless of contradictory information found in their anecdotal records.

Some **checklists** provide limited recording space with only enough room for a check mark. This does not allow you to record comments about how or what students are doing, how they are developing and changing, or how science concepts or skills are evolving. Such checklists cannot adequately reveal individual progress. One danger is that teachers may spend most of their time focusing on the list to be checked rather than on students and may easily miss science learning that is occurring. Remain alert to significant behaviors that may not be covered on a checklist. Since checklists are set up in linear patterns, teachers can be misled into believing the skills or items are sequential and must be taught in that order. Checklists are meant to be guidelines for science assessment and not prescriptions for teaching. Most checklists present learning in a fragmented fashion, and this can lead to a view of learning that is too simplistic.

Interviews are more time consuming to administer than checklists or surveys, inventories, or questionnaires. If they do not match or inform your science instruction, they will not be worth the extra time they require. The data collected during *informal* interviews are mostly subjective in nature and cannot easily be translated into grades. While a *structured* interview provides the opportunity for students to talk and teachers to listen, the conversation does not provide as rich data about students' thinking as the *informal* interview because the questions are predetermined. Teachers need time and practice to develop good interviewing techniques and questions that provide them with rich data about their students. Even when teachers ask good interview questions, students are often used to traditional questions and respond in that manner. Building trust for honesty is not easy and takes time to achieve. Teachers can easily misinterpret students who are afraid to speak as being unfamiliar with the concept being discussed. One of the primary purposes of using an interview is to listen to students so that you can find out what they are thinking. It is not to find out if they are right or wrong. If you are interested in checking students' knowledge of facts or correct answers, then an interview is not the proper assessment tool to use.

When lengthy oral interviews are simply given to students as an **inventory, a questionnaire, or a survey,** students become overwhelmed and often give shorter or different responses than they would orally. This is especially true of those students who have difficulty with writing. While *forced-choice inventories* provide one solution to this problem, they have their own disadvantages.

- You cannot be sure that the answers students chose are the ones they would have responded on their own.

- Identifying the best response among several may not be sufficient to know what the student would choose to do when no alternatives are given in a real situation.
- Distracters could all be strategies the student might use.

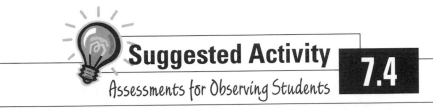

Suggested Activity 7.4
Assessments for Observing Students

1. In your collaborative groups, discuss which of the assessments for observing students your group feels would be most beneficial in their science classrooms. Be prepared to defend your choices.

2. In your journal, create a Venn diagram or a matrix that compares and contrasts the assessment tools that can be used to observe students in the science classroom.

3. Working as a group or individually, create a checklist, an interview, an inventory, a questionnaire, or a survey for a science unit.

STUDENT WORK SAMPLES

Samples of work over time are one of the best ways to show growth in science learning. The types of student work samples in a science classroom are limitless because any homework assignment or in-class task that you have students submit may double as an assessment tool on its own or be included in a portfolio.

Hein and Price (1994) provide several suggestions for interpreting student work samples in general. They recommend that you share your interpretations with some colleagues to check for assumptions and to validate your conclusions. As you begin to examine a student's work, ask yourself what you notice first about the sample; for example, is it extensive, carefully done, interesting, unusual, humorous, inaccurate, or sloppy? You may wish to search for these areas in students' work: expressions of attitudes and feelings, evidence that the desired information has been acquired by looking for vocabulary or facts, evidence of conceptual knowledge, indications that scientific processes have been carried out, or indications that skills in using equipment have been achieved. If the work is a piece of writing, pay attention to the level of detail because specificity in description and use of words can indicate knowledge of underlying concepts. Be sure to remember that these are only a few samples of a student's work and that even the best interpretations based on them may not be completely accurate in determining a specific student's feelings, learning, and thinking. You should always check your interpretations and hunches by talking with your students, observing them, and collecting additional work to examine.

Student work samples that are explored in this portion of the chapter include science journals, written reports and stories, laboratory sheets, drawings and labeled diagrams, concept maps, photographs, and videotapes. Descriptions of each along with the information about ways they can be used as assessment tools are presented. After examining these options, overall benefits and concerns of using work samples for assessment are discussed.

Science Journals, Notebooks, and Learning Logs

In many science classrooms, teachers are asking students to keep journals, notebooks, or learning logs to enhance learning and as another means of assessment. A journal offers opportunities to improve science learning because writing requires thinking. Defining concepts in writing before and after instruction enables students to assess for themselves what they have gained from their studies. Through their writing, students can examine and describe their learning processes, such as noting whether this is new learning, stating hypotheses, making predictions, organizing information, making connections that link information, brainstorming ideas, recording insights, recording observations, and listing their future learning goals in journals, learning logs, or notebooks.

Using journals allows teachers to assess students as they engage in multiple dimensions of active science learning from concept knowledge to skills or processes. Journals can serve as an effective vehicle for dialogue between you and your students because children will often write questions and thoughts in their journals that they hesitate to express publicly. Examining students' science notebooks can provide a wealth of information, including how they have kept track of changes, observations over time, a record of science activities, science experiments, recorded data, and a record of answers to questions. Learning logs often ask students to reflect on their learning, on questions they have, and on what they want to know more about on a particular topic.

The value and quality of a journal depend not only on the science activities in the classroom but also on the student's writing experience, the value you place on writing, the time you provide for writing, and how you have your students structure their journals. You may want to take 5 to 10 minutes at the beginning or end of a class period to have students respond in writing on a regular basis. You may have students write summaries of what they have learned in a lesson, give an opinion and defend it, compose interview questions, write a persuasive letter, and do much other writing. Entries written by students at different levels of development can each be assessed for clarity, logic, and completeness. Students can also evaluate their recordings by comparing them with those of other group members. Further learning occurs when they pursue reasons for conflicting data that provides an opportunity to clarify learning concepts.

Since learning logs can also be used to encourage self-monitoring and reflection, some teachers begin by asking students to reflect on three things they have learned or one thing they found to be confusing at the end of a unit or an activity. Students may then choose to share their responses with the class, a small group, a partner, or just the teacher. Another way that teachers can begin having students reflect on their own learning is to provide them with prompts or lead-in phrases, such as those presented in Figure 7.3. Once students are comfortable with responding to prompts that you provide, you can encourage them to create their own prompts.

Shepardson and Britsch (1997) recommend using science journals during investigations to provide a structure for guiding students' writing and thinking. When used this way, the science journal functions more as a tool for facilitating thinking by serving as a resource for the creation of a final product than just for checking procedural and factual knowledge. This approach involves four phases of journal activity—**preinvestigation, investigation, postinvestigation,** and **communication**—which enable teachers to assess the domains of conceptual understanding, factual and procedural knowledge, science processes, and attitudes. During *preinvestigation,* the journal entries focus on existing ideas and understandings, the purpose for the investigation, the questions to be answered, predictions, and the plan or procedures for the investigation. During the *investigation,* journal entries focus on recording observations, ideas, and thoughts based on those observations; reflecting on the connection of the observations to their prior knowledge; and creating charts or tables to organize data. *Postinvestigation* journal entries focus on answering the question(s); explaining the results; transforming the data into charts, graphs, or concept maps; revising prior knowledge based on the results; ways to improve the investigation; and proposing new questions to explore. Journal entries for *communication* focus on ways to share the investigation with others and ways to apply the findings to everyday life.

Analyzing an individual notebook entry or discussing a graph or chart provides insight into what students have accomplished at one particular point in a unit. In contrast, a journal that is analyzed as a whole can be a rich resource that provides you with information about how a student's thinking, skills, processes, and attitudes have changed over time. By analyzing the entire journal, you can determine the student's prior understandings and follow changes in those understandings throughout the science unit. Students' conceptual understandings are displayed through their use of writing to interpret or explain, while factual understanding may be expressed through labels and descriptions. You may also want to analyze the journal for specific content information that clarifies the meaning of specialized scientific vocabulary.

When assessing student journals for the use of the scientific process, you can analyze the writing and drawings for several items, such as the inquiry question, their predictions and observations, descriptions of procedures, explanations of material and equipment use, identification and control of variables, representation and organization of data, and conclusions based on evidence. Observations are essential for constructing scientific understandings, yet sometimes students struggle with making them. To assess the quality of students' observations, you can analyze journals using scoring rubrics to check for indicators such as the following: actual observations versus deductions, the level of qualitative and quantitative detail, notations of similarities and differences, comparisons between phenomena in terms of spatial position and change over time, and accurate, careful descriptions.

Science journals can also be used to assess students' attitudes toward science learning. Analyze the journals for expressions of excitement, interest, and curiosity as well as reflections on cooperation, tolerance of ambiguity, persistence, and student resourcefulness. Students reveal their feelings about science learning in their writing.

Whether you use journals, notebooks, learning logs, or a combination, dating and labeling the topic of each entry provides a framework to use when you examine the data later to compare earlier and later entries for what they can tell you about a student's growth or change in attitude toward science. When you evaluate journals, be sure to consider your reasons for giving assignments and decide whether students have met the goals. Journal and log entries are usually treated as rough drafts that are examined for content rather than as finished products that require a grade.

Written Reports and Creative Writing

Science teachers can use other types of writing to assess different areas of science. Written reports demonstrate students' research abilities, organizational skills, reporting formats, and content material understanding. A detailed lab report covers a period of time and may provide information about several aspects of a student's accomplishments in science. The amount of detail in a report can indicate whether the student actually carried out the work and demonstrate whether the student understands what occurs. The care that the student used to create any drawings that are included and to write the report shows degree of commitment to the work and how much effort was made.

Another assessment could involve using a dichotomous key or creating a vocabulary game. Essays such as problem-solution statements provide information about understanding of various processes. In another example, students may be asked to imagine themselves as a butterfly and write an essay to demonstrate their knowledge of the metamorphosis. One possibility for using descriptive writing is to identify things. For example, you may ask students to describe a dinosaur so well that without naming it their partner can tell which one it is. Assessment of these writings is straightforward. If there is a problem with conflicting answers, both partners can work to figure it out.

Creative writing also can and should be linked to concepts being studied. Writing stories can be an excellent form of final assessment, especially for younger students, by allowing them to be creative while incorporating concepts and vocabulary they have learned. If your students are writing a story about an imaginary visit to an outer planet, you might ask them to correctly use recently learning words, such as *orbit, acceleration,* and *zero gravity.* Cooperative learning groups can judge whether concepts are used correctly and consult with you as needed.

It is important to have your students assess their own writing as much as possible through clear directions and standards. You will probably want to *sample* their work from time to time, and it helps to provide some guidance for them to self-evaluate their work. Questions such as the following can be useful prompts:

How would you describe your level of participation in the science activity?

What contributions did you make to the solution of the problem?

What best describes your role in the group (leader, recorder, materials manager, maintenance crew, liaison, or bystander)?

How effectively do you manage time while completing science tasks?

What are you learning in science?

Laboratory Activities and Sheets

Laboratory activities can be easily used to assess students' psychomotor skills in science. These activities can double as learning activities and assessments of students' competency in using science processes. During laboratory activities, students are asked to manipulate equipment and materials, observe, reason, record data, and interpret results. Using these activities as assessments allows the teacher to assess students' abilities to work with basic science equipment (e.g., thermometer, balances), manipulate objects (e.g., simple laboratory equipment), collect data, record data (e.g., changes in weather), observe and classify, perform laboratory procedures, and communicate. Students can be asked to perform such tasks early in a unit and then near the end of it to document skill development, growth in using processes, or changes in attitudes.

Laboratory sheets can be used as assessments in several ways, including measuring growth in predicting, checking the ability to create graphs and charts, and assessing ability to make observations, record data, organize information, and communicate scientific information. You can design laboratory sheets that ask students to make predictions about given situations. A series of such sheets spaced throughout a science unit has the potential to document a student's increasing understanding of the material. Certain science topics lend themselves more easily to this format than others, for example, a unit on electricity. Students can be asked to collect experimental data over a number of days and use each day's data to predict their next findings. A unit on plant growth and development is an example that works well for this type of assessment.

You may want to use **structured observation sheets** that have predetermined categories to define and organize responses as well as to indicate what is considered important. Structured observation sheets can be useful for having older students communicate procedures, materials, hypotheses, and data in a particular order. These worksheets can help you find out how well your students can frame a hypothesis, isolate a single variable, define what will be constant, describe procedures (list equipment needed, describe what will be measured, and explain how it will be measured), and make a prediction. Structured worksheets are often used when students are planning experiments and recording science activities.

Once your students have been using structured laboratory sheets and tables to record their observations and experiments, you might ask them to set up their own **recording sheets** at the end of the unit. Knowing how to organize and communicate information is an important skill, and seeing how well students can do this on their own is a useful assessment. Another reason to move away from the structured forms is that they generally elicit less information from students because the limited recording space restricts writing and the predetermined categories can restrict thinking. The responses you receive will also be less characteristic of a particular student (Hein & Price, 1994).

Drawings and Labeled Diagrams

Drawings and labeled diagrams can provide much insight into students' thinking. Some students find it easier to explain themselves in this way. Drawings may be used as diagnostic, formative, or summative assessments. They are quick to administer, are simple and nonthreatening, do not exclude students with reading or writing problems, and have the potential to document change. Drawings can provide a record of what students did and what they understand as well as clear and direct feedback on their own learning. Students can record observations with a combination of drawing and writing, which can demonstrate that they actually made the observations, what their feelings are about science and the world, and whether they have used realistic or anthropomorphized depictions. When you examine students' drawings, look for the level of detail in them, whether objects are in realistic positions in relation to each other, and whether the observational drawings appear to resemble what was observed or are copied from an illustration that may be stereotypical.

Concept Maps

Concept maps are a way to represent the links or relationships between concepts in visual form that can also incorporate art in a form that is often easier for students to understand. Large posters are often used to provide enough room for students to make connections between the concepts. The better students are able to relate new information to what they know already, the easier it is for them to remember and use it.

These graphic organizers are also an excellent way to assess conceptual knowledge. When students draw a concept map, they demonstrate what they know about a topic or field of knowledge. Concept maps use a combination of the student's prior knowledge and an understanding of the work that has been completed. They can be used as pretests and posttests to measure your students' growth in learning. Concept maps can be a powerful way to assess an individual student's conceptual understanding.

Some teachers use concept maps with groups of students during discussions, interviews, and group projects. A concept map drawn on the board, projected on an overhead transparency, or shown on an LCD panel can form the basis for a class discussion about the relationship among ideas that surface while investigating an inquiry question or during a science unit. When done in groups, communication and negotiation among members help to identify student misconceptions. Science educators note that misconceptions are revealed both through incorrect concept links and through important links that are omitted. Concept maps can be used to probe students about their interpretations of investigation findings. Finally, students can collaborate on their own concept maps to illustrate the relationships among their findings.

You need to be aware that students often make different concept maps after receiving the same instruction. This happens even when they understand all the concepts in the way you intend. The students may simply view the relationships among the concepts differently. It is important for them to regularly compare their maps with partners and interact with you to more fully assess what they have learned.

Projects

Project work is another area that can be examined in the assessment process and can also be included in student portfolios or used as independent assessment tools. Some teachers find that a contract system is an efficient method of involving children in the evaluation process and of keeping track of the necessary recording. It is a good idea to view science projects as normal and regular extensions of concepts and generalizations studied by the whole class. This view offers many opportunities for students to take on projects, and they are more likely to do their own work. It also makes assessment simpler, less formal, and more frequent than when projects are reserved for science fairs.

Students' projects can reveal a great deal about their scientific attitudes as well as their concept understandings and ability to use processes. Observe behaviors such as thinking, persistence, inventiveness, and curiosity as students work and report on their projects. When you notice evidence of these scientific attitudes in students' projects, reinforce them with positive comments. Some questions you might want to ask yourself as you reflect on student projects include the following:

- Are the parts of the report logical and consistent? (thinking)
- Is there evidence that the student overcame difficulties? (persistence)
- Was the student resourceful in using materials? (inventiveness)
- Did the student ask further questions? (curiosity)

A good project usually requires self-assessment from start to finish. If guidelines are simple and your comments regarding success consistent, students will develop judgment in assessing their efforts during projects and when reporting them. Many teachers use scoring rubrics that they create from science standards and benchmarks or that they have made collaboratively with students to assess the projects created during or at the end of science units. When projects are too large to be easily stored in the classroom or in a portfolio, you can encourage students to consider using photographs or videotapes to document their projects.

Photographs

Photographs can provide an answer for including items that take too much classroom space or that do not fit in portfolios, such as three-dimensional projects, posters, or science inventions. Some teachers keep an instant or a digital camera in the classroom for just this purpose. Photographs can also be used to capture students using various strategies in the learning process that do not lend themselves well to other forms of documentation. For example, students might use photographs when they are taking risks, becoming more personally involved in learning, investigating questions or ideas, or performing experiments. Photographs can serve as excellent reminders of what students were doing, who worked in a group, and how they handled equipment.

Videotapes

Another way to document those hard to record events is through videotaping, which can provide a greater context than simply taking photographs because they are not static and can provide visual data in addition to audio records. On videotapes, students can demonstrate how they conducted an investigation, an experiment, or a performance task, or they can show how they created a project. You may wish to capture students using specific strategies on tape to analyze at a later time. You can also record performances for specific audiences, such as science projects presented to your class, other classrooms, assemblies, parents, or community members.

Benefits of Using Student Work Samples as Assessments

Student work samples provide teachers with a wider range of assessment measures to construct a more complete picture of a student's learning. These items allow teachers to focus of the process of learning as well as products. Often students select which artifacts to place in their portfolios, and student choices provide more data to assess students. Finally, providing these items as options meets the cognitive needs of a variety of learners with different learning styles and preferences for cognitive processing. Using student work samples combines instruction and assessment. They provide a teacher with an immediate view of how students are processing what is happening in the classroom and how they understand the information that has been presented.

Concerns About Using Student Work Samples as Assessments

As with any assessment tool, there are concerns about using student work samples as assessments. Before any of the items described in this portion of the chapter are used for assessment, you must take class time to teach students how to do them. For example, students cannot be expected to create a concept map to assess a science concept unless you are sure they already know how to create one.

If students are involved in selecting which items will be assessed, teachers also need to spend time discussing how to choose selections and to have the students actually select the entries they want to have assessed. If these items will be used as part of a portfolio, it is easy to include too much work and to have the portfolio simply become a scrapbook. These items can also make the portfolio more difficult to assess.

Teachers can be distracted by academic skills such as spelling, handwriting, or drawing ability rather than focusing on the science content of the sample. Students' care and positive attitudes in discussion, drawing, or writing should be recognized and encouraged, but they should not be substituted for accurate observations or scientific thinking. They must be considered as additional components.

It is tempting to overuse these strategies for both assessment and teaching. Any strategy that is used too much will lose its effectiveness because students will lose interest, and then it becomes simply busywork that does not always accurately reflect students' learning potential in science.

Suggested Activity 7.5
Student Work Samples as Assessments

1. In your collaborative group, discuss which of these types of student work samples you feel would be best to use as assessment tools. Be prepared to share your reasons for your choices with the class.

2. Working in a group or individually, create an assignment sheet that explains a science project you will use as an assessment tool for a science unit of your choice.

3. Create a chart, concept map, or other graphic that explains the benefits and concerns related to using each of the student work samples listed previously as an assessment tool.

CLASSROOM ACTIVITIES AS ASSESSMENT TOOLS

One way to link instruction and assessment in your science classroom is to use common teaching practices or activities as a part of your array of assessment tools. The main advantage of this approach is that you will be using many of these techniques as a part of your science instruction. One disadvantage includes the fact that you must add another dimension to your lessons: keeping track of student learning at the same time you are actively involved in teaching. Another is that this type of assessment cannot stand on its own because you will not be able to simply remember who has learned what without some type of recording system. You will need to combine assessment of classroom activities with one or more of the other assessment tools described in this chapter, such as checklists, anecdotal records, scoring rubrics, journals, or other assessment techniques.

Any classroom activity can be used as an assessment tool for science learning. Science teachers have found the following activities to provide additional data that can be useful in assessing both student learning and their own teaching.

Discussions

During all portions of the instructional process, discussions can provide a rich array of information about students' understanding of important science concepts, process skills and thinking patterns, and attitudes about science. Since discussions are less threatening to most students than more traditional forms of testing, they tend to result in broader student participation.

To ensure that you are using good discussion skills, **avoid** asking too many superficial questions, providing students with too little time to formulate answers to questions, and calling on the same students all the time. You will receive better answers from more students during a discussion when you use good questioning techniques, such as wait time, probing, and redirecting. **Wait time** is the amount of time you wait after asking a question before you call on a specific student and the time you wait before responding to the answer. Most experts recommend that you wait between 3 and 5 seconds. **Probing** is when you ask students to explain or elaborate further about their answers. This provides you with the opportunity to identify students' prior knowledge, to help them clarify their understanding, to form new concepts, and to identify misconceptions. **Redirecting** is when the teacher or students refer the answer to other students in the class. This strategy works best when you have already established an atmosphere where students feel comfortable enough to risk answering questions without worrying about being wrong.

KWL Group Assessment Technique

In Chapter 6, the KWL group assessment technique was demonstrated through excerpts of a teacher's unit on dinosaurs. This assessment method focuses on finding out what students know and building teaching experiences around that information. The teacher began the unit by creating a class chart listing what the students knew (K) and what they wanted to learn (W) about dinosaurs. At the end of the unit, she completed the chart by listing what the class had learned (L). This technique allows teachers to identify and correct any misconceptions the students have as the unit progresses. Throughout the unit, you will need to refer to the KWL chart to assess how students' ideas have changed, what questions have been answered, and what questions still remain as a springboard for further learning.

Brainstorming

When brainstorming is used as an introductory instructional activity, you may want to use questions that assess what students know in general rather than what they know about a specific topic. However, when the goal is to measure learning, the question should be related to what students will be investigating so that you can measure growth in that area as the unit progresses. Specific, focused questions that are based on students' prior knowledge and experiences and that are related to the topic at hand are the ones that work best. These questions allow students to draw on their own experiences and talk about the knowledge they have. Without this exchange, some students do not realize that they have relevant science information. Good questions have more than one answer, so there are no correct answers that end the discussion.

Many teachers combine brainstorming discussions with drawing or writing. One way to do this is to have students record and date their thoughts in a journal or on a worksheet before the class conversation takes place. This writing leads to more engaged class discussions because the students have already focused on the science topic and thought about what they want to say. Then at the end of a unit, the students can record their thoughts again individually and share their ideas as a class afterward.

Think-Alouds

Teachers can also engage students in discussions about their thought processes and their investigative procedures by using **think-alouds.** This is a questioning technique that you can use to informally assess students as they describe their thinking while they engage in activities, make decisions in an experiment, or work through problems. Through think-alouds, you can gather information about how students are constructing meaning and can help students clarify their own thinking.

To engage in a think-aloud, ask students to talk their way through a situation and then follow up with open-ended questions about why they do this or that. Use indirect questions so that you do not lead students to correct answers. Some typical questions for a science think aloud are the following:

- Tell me what you are thinking.
- Explain the steps you are using in your investigation.
- Explain how you are doing this.
- Tell me more about . . .
- Whys. i.e., Why did you select that response, why do you think that? etc.
- And, so . . .

Open-Ended Questions

An open-ended question is one where there is more than one correct response. The response may be an answer to a question, a procedure used to arrive at a solution to a problem, or an opinion about something. The value of this type of question is that each student can answer it differently. Open-ended questions often match good classroom questioning strategies and encourage divergent thinking. These items are particularly useful for helping teachers understand student thinking. Varieties of answers that students can give are unlimited and often reveal misconceptions. Through the use of open-ended questions, you can learn how students interpreted the question, how they made observations and inferences, how they expressed their thoughts and idea, and how they organized their knowledge. Some guidelines for writing open-ended questions include the following:

- Making sure the students can understand the question
- Letting students construct their own answer rather than leading them to one
- Posing interesting questions whenever possible
- Matching the question with the content or process being studied
- Allowing sufficient wait time for students to respond
- Encouraging many students time to answer and ask further questions before going on to another open-ended question
- Asking increasingly complex questions to get at deeper levels of understanding
- Posing meaningful thought-provoking questions to maintain interest

Evaluating open-ended assessment items can take several different forms. The completeness, clarity, accuracy of information, and the student's opinion are usually examined. Many teachers use a holistic scoring strategy that involves reading all the responses for a class and then sorting them into stacks according to those that have complete answers, those that are missing one or more components, and those that are unacceptable or ones that missed the point. Some teachers prefer to use scoring rubrics that are more analytical with points assigned to predetermined criteria.

Teaching or Reporting to Others

Some teachers ask their students to teach younger children, to give demonstrations to other classes, or to describe their science activities at a parents' night or an open house. Presentations like these are a powerful way for children to demonstrate their own learning. You should probably use the rehearsal for the public activity as the assessment because any nervousness at the actual event will not hinder an accurate assessment of the students' knowledge. When they make presentations, students have to pull together and organize what they have learned. Presentations based on group effort can require individual students to be responsible for discrete parts, providing an opportunity to assess them separately.

One fourth-grade class created a news report to show their knowledge of the rain forest that they had been studying as a 6-week thematic unit. They shared their presentation with other classrooms ranging from kindergarten to sixth grade. Then they decided to create a video of their presentation for an open house for parents. Next, the class volunteered to do a version of their presentation as the opening for a state teacher conference. There they used a combination of individual presentations and their video clip. Finally, the class did a 1-minute version of their presentation on the local public broadcasting station. Each of these presentations required the students to return to the information that they had learned about the rain forest and to rework that information into a format appropriate for each audience.

Creative Drama

Creative drama can be an effective assessment tool that allows teachers to observe the meaning students construct while science learning is taking place. When misconceptions are part of the students' acting, you can point them out and help students clarify them. Reichel (1994) recommends that you establish achievement criteria in advance to help ensure that you are fair, consistent, and unbiased in your judgment of student work with levels such as minimal achievement, moderate achievement, and excellent achievement. Some science concepts that lend themselves to drama presentations are the water cycle, a plant's life cycle, the planets in the solar system, and the rotation of the moon around the earth as the earth rotates around the sun.

The only limits are the creativity of teachers and students. For example, a sixth-grade teacher had her students go to the school playground to act out what happens to a fault line during an earthquake as part of a unit on earthquakes and volcanoes. Creative drama can take on a more complex role with students writing out and performing scripts as the fourth graders chose to do as a culminating activity when they shared their knowledge about what they had learned about the rain forest.

Suggested Activity

Classroom Activities as Assessments

7.6

1. In your collaborative group, determine which of the classroom activities listed previously would be easiest to use as an assessment tool and which would be the most difficult.

2. In your journal, describe which of the classroom activities listed previously you would consider using as an assessment tool. Provide reasons for your choices.

PAPER-AND-PENCIL TESTS

Written tests are typically found at ends of lessons, chapters, or units. These assessments can be created by teachers or commercial companies. They are designed to assess pupil understanding of science words, concepts, and generalizations; the ability to apply them; and the ability to do some critical thinking but are not recommended for measuring processes and attitudes. Cautions about the overuse of traditional testing, their benefits, and concerns about using these traditional assessments are presented in Chapter 6.

There are several different types of paper-and-pencil tests. No one type has proven more successful than any other, but matching the test format with the learning objectives to be assessed has proven to be critical. Before selecting any instrument to assess a student's achievement, you must be able to identify what it was that the student was supposed to accomplish, or objectives for lessons. Objectives become the binding thread that holds together and integrates an entire science lesson. The objectives must be examined and used as a guide in the selection of any assessment tool.

Types of Paper-and-Pencil Tests

There are six popular types of paper-and-pencil tests: multiple choice, fill-in-the-blank, true-or-false, matching, short answer, and essay. These tests involve recalling information (declarative knowledge) and identifying a correct response. Each of these can be created by teachers or be prepared by commercial companies. In some types, such as multiple choice, true-or-false, and matching, very little writing is required. The correct choice is indicated by circling, marking, drawing a line, or perhaps writing a letter or number. These three types of tests are usually considered to be objective, which means that there is one correct answer and they can be scored using a key that contains all the correct answers. The following are examples of these types of paper-and-pencil tests:

Multiple Choice. Circle the correct response for each item.

1. All matter is composed of tiny particles called
    a. elements
    b. molecules*
    c. compounds
    d. gases
2. The pressure of liquids or gases will be low if they are moving fast and will be high if they are moving slowly. This principle is called
    a. Newton's principle
    b. Galileo's principle
    c. Bernoulli's principle *
    d. Jenner's principle

True-or-False. Circle the correct response.

T*   F   1. Limestone and marble are chemically the same.
T   F*   2. The point where the earth's crust cracks and moves is called a geyser.

Matching. Draw a line to connect the word on the left with the appropriate example on the right.

a.	mammal	1.	frog
b.	amphibian	2.	dog
c.	reptile	3.	ant
d.	bird	4.	lizard
e.	insect	5.	chicken

The other paper-and-pencil tests mentioned (short answer, fill-in-the-blank, and essay) require more grading time, frequently have a variety of acceptable responses and tend to be more subjective in nature. Students must generally do more recalling and organizing of stored information in these types of tests. The simplest of these three is the *fill-in-the-blank.* Sometimes there is only one word missing, but the students must recall it without benefit of being presented with multiple choices. More often, several words are omitted, and the students must supply the missing thought. Communicating the general idea, not the exact wording, is the issue.

One variation of a fill-in-the-blank assessment that many teachers use is the *cloze procedure.* In the traditional cloze procedure, the teacher deletes every fifth word for a total of 50 blanks in a passage that is approximately 250 words in length. Correct responses are tallied, and the student receives a percentage of correct responses. Teachers can use this format to determine knowledge of the topic to be learned, to determine whether the passage is at the appropriate reading level, and to check comprehension after studying the material. In a nontraditional format for cloze, teachers control how many and which words are deleted. By controlling these features, you can assess science vocabulary knowledge, use of specific processing strategies, and real-world knowledge. The main strength of using the cloze in this manner is that you will have detailed information about the student's learning strategies (Vacca & Vacca, 1999).

For primary students, teachers often prefer to use a *maze technique* rather than a cloze to accomplish the same goals. In a maze passage, the teacher deletes every 10th word or controls how many and which words to delete, just as in either of the two versions of the cloze described in the previous paragraph; however, the students are provided with three words for selecting the appropriate answer. Then the percentage correct is tallied, just as in the cloze procedure. A maze test can yield the same data as the various types of cloze procedures.

The *short answer* and *essay* forms of evaluation expand on the fill-in-the-blank type. Generally, a question is asked or a term given, and the learner must define, describe, explain, or give examples in answering the question. This type of assessment is most appropriate for children who are toward the end of the concrete operational state of mental development or already operating at the formal level. Children at lower levels of cognitive development have not sufficiently developed the skills necessary to organize and express their thoughts through writing. Following are some examples of these types of paper-and-pencil tests:

Fill-in-the-Blank

1. Most plants have four parts: ___(root)___, ___(stems)___, ___(leaves)___, and ___(flowers)___.

2. One of the main purposes of the stem of a plant is (to carry water from the roots to the leaves).

Short Answer

1. How does a rock differ from a plant?

2. What causes food to spoil?

Essay

1. Describe and compare two ways in which a plant can reproduce.

2. How does the environment affect living things?

Paper-and-pencil tests provide an effective means of assessing learners' achievement. A variety of forms allows the teacher a choice as to which form or combination of forms would be best for assessing students knowledge or concepts. Paper-and-pencil tests should not limit learners to low-level memory responses. The recall of facts and information is certainly a necessary part of all learning, but it must not be all that is required. Higher levels of cognitive functioning should be elicited also. One way to move these tests to a higher level of thinking is to have students justify their choices to multiple choice or true-or-false tests by explaining why they selected the responses that they did and then justify their answers. Most paper-and-pencil tests are used as summative assessment to provide a basis for grading, but they can also be used effectively as diagnostic or formative assessments.

Text Publishers' Tests

Commercial tests include end-of-chapter tests, tests that accompany texts, and specific subject matter tests. Commercial tests are more obtrusive to instruction than the previous assessment tools mentioned in this chapter because they are decontextualized or created by outsiders who do not know the specific curriculum, instruction methods, activities, and student needs in your science classroom. The tasks are usually not the same as those that are used for instruction, there are often time constraints, and answers are usually right or wrong. These tests can reveal only what students do in a limited setting, administered in a short time period, and containing only the tasks that were tested.

On the other hand, commercial tests provide data that can be compared across science classrooms, schools, and districts and can provide information about students' test-taking abilities and mastery of skills. If these items are placed in a portfolio, the teacher *folio* or *permanent* portfolio is the best place to house them (Johnson & Rose, 1997).

Suggested Activity 7.7
Paper-and-Pencil Assessments

1. In your collaborative group or at your table, decide which of the paper-and-pencil assessments you might be most likely to use for which purposes.
2. Create a paper-and-pencil assessment of your choice designed to assess a science unit.

SUMMARY

The wide array of assessment tools that can be used in the science classroom were explored in this chapter. Assessment tools that were presented included performance-based tasks, portfolios, scoring rubrics, tools for observing students, student work samples, classroom activities, and paper-and-pencil tests. Each assessment tool has its own set of design and implementation considerations. Although the benefits and concerns about each of these assessment tools have been explored, you will need to select those that best fit the needs of your curriculum and students in your own science classroom.

Suggested Activity 7.8
Assessment Activities

1. All assessments can be used in one or more parts of the instructional process. As a group, categorize the assessment tools listed in the chapter into diagnostic, formative, or summative assessments. Note that assessment tools may be used as more than one type of assessment. Be prepared to justify how you sorted the various tools.
2. Which of the assessment tools described in the chapter do you feel you would be most likely to use in your science classroom? Share reasons for your choices with those in your collaborative group.
3. Which assessment tools would be most appropriate to use with special needs students? Share your thoughts with those in your group and be prepared to justify your choices.
4. Observe a teacher in a science classroom over an extended period of time and list any of the assessment tools presented in the chapter, or interview an elementary or middle school teacher to find out which assessment tools he or she uses on a regular basis.

REFERENCES

Austin, T. (1994). *Changing the view: Student-led parent conferences.* Portsmouth, NH: Heinemann.

Brown, J. H. (1994, September). Science for everyone: New ways to measure what students know and can do. *Instructor,* 58–61.

Collins, A. (1992). Portfolios for science education: Issues in purpose, structure, and authenticity. *Science Education.* 76(4), 451–463.

Ebenezer, J. V., & Conner, S. (1998). *Learning to teach science: A model for the 21st century.* Columbus, OH: Merrill.

Hein, G. E., & Price, S. (1994). *Active assessment for active science: A guide for elementary school teachers.* Portsmouth, NH: Heinemann.

Johnson, N.J. & Rose, L.M. (1997). *Portfolios: Clarifying, constructing, and enhancing.* Lancaster, PA: Techmonic Publishing Company.

Khattri, N., Kane, M. B., & Reeve, A. L. (1995, November). How performance assessments affect teaching and learning. *Educational Leadership,* 80–83.

Krajacik, J., Czerniak, C., & Berger, C. (1999). *Teaching children science: A project based approach.* Boston: McGraw-Hill College.

Martin, D. J. (1997). *Elementary science methods: A constructivist approach.* Albany, NY: Delmar Publishers.

National Research Council. (1996). *National Science Education Standards.* Washington, DC: National Academy Press.

Popham, W. J. (1997, October). What's wrong—and—what's right—with rubrics. *Educational Leadership,* 72–75.

Reichel, A. G. (1994). Performance assessment: Five practical approaches. *Science & Children,* 32 (2), 21–25.

Shepardson, D. P., & Britsch, S. J. (1997, February). Children's science journals: Tools for teaching, learning, and assessing. *Science & Children,* 13–17.

Solano-Flores, G., & Shavelson, R. J. (1997). Development of performance assessments in science: Conceptual, practical and logistical issues. *Educational Measurement: Issues and Practices,* 16(3), 16–25.

Stiggins, R. J. (1999, January). Assessment, student confidence, and school success. Paper presented at the Large Scale Assessment Conference, Salt Lake City, Utah.

Tolman, M. N., Baird, J. H., & Hardy, G. R. (1994). Let the tool fit the task. *Science & Children,* 32(2), 44–47.

Vacca, R. T., & Vacca, J. L. (1999). *Content area reading: Literacy and learning across the curriculum* (6th ed.). New York: Longman.

Wiggins, G. (1992). Creating tests worth taking. *Educational Leadership,* 48(6), 26–34.

CHAPTER 8

Inquiry-Based Teaching and Learning of Physical Science Concepts

INTRODUCTION

The *National Science Education Standards* (National Resource Council, 1996) identify specific categories of content that "students should know, understand and be able to do in natural science." This chapter will provide you with a review of the identified **physical science standards,** give you an opportunity to engage in actual inquiry-based physical science activities to help prepare you for your work with students in grades K to 8, and involve you in examining curricular resources to locate inquiry-based physical science activities for K–8 students that are related to the identified standards. Chapters 9 to 11 will continue with life science standards, earth/space science standards, and science and technology standards.

It is important for you to understand that these content standards are not meant to prescribe a science curriculum. They **do** provide teachers with an outline of what students should learn in each of the content categories. They establish a "set of outcomes for students" and are viewed by the developers as "one component of the comprehensive vision of science education presented in the *National Science Education Standards.*" This document makes clear that "the content standards must be used in the context of the standards on teaching and assessment. Using the standards with traditional teaching and assessment strategies defeats the intentions of the *National Science Education Standards.*"

As you begin to focus on the content standards, think back to all the previous chapters in this text. Each chapter has provided you with an important component of the complex vision that comprises the inquiry-based approach to teaching and learning science. Science content is not separate from the rest of the vision. It must be meshed with and become a part of the total science program. In an inquiry-based program, content is much more than knowing specific facts. It involves a true understanding of the concepts involved and the ability to apply this understanding to real-world contexts.

PHYSICAL SCIENCE CONCEPTS (K–4)

Physical science concepts include understandings about the nonliving aspects of our world. Typical topics for grades K to 8 include air, magnets, electricity, changes, energy, matter, sound, simple machines, and light. We will look first at the physical science standards for K to 4, then we will examine the standards for grades 5 to 8. The physical science standards included in the *National Science Education Standards* for K–4 students state that as a result of the activities in grades K–4, all students should develop an understanding of the following:

1. Properties of objects and materials
2. Position and motion of objects
3. Light, heat, electricity, and magnetism

Students must be provided with opportunities to interact with objects, materials, and ideas as they investigate the concepts related to these three areas. Before you begin to select, adapt, modify, or develop science experiences for students in these areas, it might be helpful to explore your own understanding of these content standards. Let's start with the first one.

Physical Science | Activity 1

Properties of Objects and Materials (K-4)

A. **How skilled are you in observing, manipulating, describing, comparing, and sorting objects and materials in the environment? To begin this activity, you are to select an item from those provided and to list at least 10 properties of that item that you can observe. Record your answers and reactions. You may work with a partner or small group in completing this activity. Remember to list only those properties that you directly observe. In other words, you must have first-hand knowledge of all properties listed. For example, if you listed "it will float" or "it will dissolve when mixed with warm water," you must have directly observed it with your selected object or material. You must not use past experience with something similar: test it out.**

✓ SELF-CHECK

1. Did you use all your senses in describing the properties of your selected object or material? Most people tend to rely on sight. If you find your observations heavily weighted toward visual descriptions, try using your other senses of hearing, touching, and smelling. You may omit tasting. Remember, even if the object or material makes no sound while stationary, that is an observation. Are there other observations that you can add using your other senses? If so, add them now.

2. Did you include a property that required you to make a *quantitative* measurement? Did you use standard tools to weigh and measure the size of your object or material? Did you include a time or temperature measurement? Are there other quantitative measurements you can make that would add meaningful information to your description of the object or material you selected? If you did not include quantitative observations using standard measuring tools, find the appropriate measurement devices and add these observations to your description of your selected item.

   (1) Have you listed properties that are *qualitative* in nature, such as large, soft, hard, or smooth? If so, you need to give a reference point. Larger than what? Your hand? The textbook? As soft as what? A cotton ball? A feather pillow? Giving a reference point for qualitative observations helps to make the description much more meaningful.

   (2) Did several of your observations result from manipulating the object or material in some way? Does it float, roll, dissolve in water, or change shape easily?

Are there other manipulations that you could make that would help describe your object or material? Try some other manipulations that you think would result in additional meaningful information about your object or material.

(3) Check over your revised list and make sure the properties listed include those that are unique to the object being described. Could someone else easily identify the object by reading your list of properties? Make sure that the final list of properties is specific enough to identify your selected object. Give your list to someone who does not know what item you selected and see if he or she can identify it by reading the property list that you made. Are there important additional properties that need to be added?

B. **What have you learned about your selected item? Did your description include size, weight, shape, color, temperature, and ability to react with other substances? These are the categories identified by the *National Science Education Standards* that are used to describe the observable properties of objects. Students should be given many opportunities to observe, manipulate, and measure objects and materials in the environment. Young children will usually create their own *qualitative* measuring tools, such as their hand or their pencil. Standard measurement tools, such as scales and balances, thermometers, meter sticks, and graduated cylinders, should be available for making *quantitative* observations. Objects made of many different kinds of materials, such as wood, paper, plastic, and metal, should be provided for students to observe and manipulate. Other objects that can be taken apart and examined should be available. Materials such as clay, sand, and various liquids should be provided. Experiences with materials such as water that can exist in different states (solid, liquid, and gas) allow students to explore other important properties. As a teacher, you must be aware of the information included in this discussion along with the criteria for making good observations presented in the self-checks. Your ability to understand and apply this information when you teach will allow your students the opportunity to be involved in quality learning experiences that lead to an understanding of the properties of objects and materials. Gaining a basic understanding of properties of objects and materials at this level (K–4) is necessary for students to be able to continue to develop the related concepts at higher levels.**

C. **Reflect on the experience that you just completed with observing, manipulating, and describing the properties of your selected item. Share your ideas and insights with others related to involving K–4 students in similar experiences. Think about how you would structure these types of experiences for the different kinds and levels of learners you will encounter. How will you design the learning experience so that it is inquiry-based? You may wish to refer to previous chapters. Share your ideas with your instructor and ask for feedback.**

D. **To continue your experience with the properties of objects and materials, select a container from those provided and separate the contents into groups. Identify and label each group according to the property you used to separate the groups. Begin by separating the contents into two groups. Then find several other ways** to separate the contents into two groups. Label each group. *After* you complete the grouping activity, read over the self-check.

✓ SELF-CHECK

1. Be sure that all objects in your container fit into one of the two groups you identified. But make sure that no *one* object could fit into both groups of one set. In other words, each object in your container must have one of the two properties you used to separate the contents into the two groups, but no one object can have both of the identified properties.

2. Look over your sets of groups to see if you have any set that would allow the inclusion of additional objects not included in the set of objects provided for you. If none of the sets of groups formed thus far would allow for any other objects to be included, then form two groups that *will* allow for the inclusion of an additional object. For example, if you have grouped objects on the basis of color, and if your groups are "red objects" and "black objects," then yellow objects will fit in neither group. By making your groups "red objects" and "nonred objects," you allow any object to fit into one of the groups. This kind of thinking helps students begin to think like a scientist and to understand other science classification schemes, such as living and nonliving. Discuss any problems you are having with others and ask your instructor for feedback.

E. **Now that you have had some practice in grouping, or classifying, objects into two sets based on identified properties, try to separate the contents of the container into three groups. Make as many sets of three as you can and label them. Use the criteria given here in the self-check to help you make good groupings.**

F. **Compare your groupings with those of your classmates. Discuss how you would use a similar activity to involve K–4 students in developing an understanding of the physical science standard related to properties of objects and materials. Why do you think it is important for students to be able to describe, group, and sort objects and materials based on observable properties? How does this relate to inquiry-based science? What real-world connections can you make for using the skills and information gained in doing this activity? How might students use grouping, sorting, and classifying skills to help them develop an understanding of a selected science concept?**

Physical Science Activity 2

Position and Motion of Objects (K–4)

A. **Work with a small group to complete this activity. Use the following materials to design and build a structure that can be used to demonstrate how marbles move: paper towel tubes or wrapping paper tubes cut in half lengthwise, tape, books,** and marbles. (If these items are not available, substitute other similar items that will allow you to observe and identify concepts related to the position and movement of objects.) Begin to investigate the movement of the marbles within your structure. Do some free exploration.

B. What kinds of information can you gather by trying a variety of things to move the marbles in and around or up and down your structure?

C. Design an investigation to answer a question about the movement of a marble within your structure. Describe the position of a moving marble at various points along the structure and in relation to other marbles. What could you do to describe its motion? Is there a way to trace and measure the movement? Try out your idea.

D. What kinds of things can you do to change the position and motion of the marble? Describe the size of the changes in relation to what you did.

E. How does the moving marble interact with other stationary marbles? How does it interact with other stationary objects? Design several investigations that will allow you to answer these questions.

F. Discuss all your observations within your group and identify important concepts related to position and motion of objects that you have observed by doing this activity. After the initial discussion and sharing of ideas, everyone in your group should read the following and include this additional information in a wrap-up discussion to answer the following question: What ideas do you have for organizing learning experiences that will help K–4 students develop an understanding of the physical science standard related to position and motion of objects? Include your instructor in your final discussion.

During the time that students are completing grades K to 4, they need many exploratory as well as structured experiences with a variety of objects to develop an understanding of the concepts related to position and motion of objects. A variety of objects can be available for students to roll or slide on flat surfaces or down ramps and observe. Ramps can be adjusted in height and width and be made of different materials so that different factors can be observed interacting with the moving objects. Students must be encouraged to verbalize and write down their descriptions of the position of objects relative to other objects or the background. Challenge students to find different ways to trace and measure an object's motion over time. For example, carbon paper or paint could be used. Have students investigate what happens when different objects are placed so that a moving object strikes a stationary one(s). Have them observe and verbalize what happens when the strength of the push or pull on the stationary object is varied.

When students have developed a good basic understanding related to position and motion of objects, they are ready to move into the part of this concept that focuses on sound and how it is produced. By building on numerous previous learning experiences in the area of position and motion of objects and participating in new experiences that target specific concepts related to sound, students are able to make connections to the concept of vibrating objects producing sound. They can observe and describe the changes in pitch when the rate of vibration is varied.

There are many good activities that teachers can use to involve K–4 students in concrete experiences that will help them construct knowledge related to the specific concepts in the area of sound. A few ideas are included here. Students can be given rubber bands to stretch and pluck. They can listen to the sound made, then change the length so that when it is plucked, it vibrates faster or slower, causing a change in the sound. Rubber bands of different widths and thickness can also be used to gather information about pitch. A drum can be used by placing bits of paper on the surface and watching them move or vibrate with the drumhead when it is struck. Vibrations from the vocal cords can be felt when fingers are placed gently on that area of the throat while talking. Stringed instruments can be provided so that students can pluck the strings, listen to the sounds, stop the vibrations, and listen again. Tuning forks are great to use to help students "see" the vibrations as well as feel and hear them. Observing and listening to the sound produced by the wires inside a piano as they are struck by the keypads is another useful learning experience related to sound. Once students learn how sound is produced, they will be ready to investigate how it travels and through which substances it travels best. Popular activities engage students in making tin-can telephones and homemade stethoscopes. "Pop-bottle music" is another activity that students enjoy and can use to learn more about pitch and tone. In this activity, students can investigate the vibrations of solids, liquids, and gases. These are just a few of the many types of activities that you can use to provide students with concrete learning experiences that lead to the development and understanding of the various concepts related to sound. You may wish to locate some of these or similar activities that have been developed for K–4 students and "try them out" with a small group. Talk to your instructor about how to structure this experience.

Physical Science Activity 3

Light, Heat, Electricity, and Magnetism (K-4)

A. **Choose one of the content areas: light, heat, electricity, or magnetism. Some suggested investigations are given here for each area. Form small groups of four or five with others who have selected the same area and choose one of the suggested investigations to complete. Locate related activities in the various resource materials available to you and use them to guide your investigation. Check with your instructor for additional directions.**

B. **Before beginning your investigation, have all group members share what they know about the selected content area. Then formulate some questions that you** would like to investigate related to that content area. Finally, design an investigation that will allow you to gather, organize, and analyze the data needed to use in reaching a conclusion. Identify and discuss the specific terms and concepts that emerge related to your investigation. You may find it helpful to do some preliminary research or background reading before beginning the actual investigation. Discuss your plan with your instructor and ask for feedback.

1. *Light Investigations (K–4)*

   a. How does light travel? Does the substance through which light travels affect what we see?

   b. What happens when light strikes or passes through other objects or materials, such as a mirror, lenses, prisms, and translucent, opaque, or transparent objects or materials?

   c. Does color affect energy absorbed from light?

2. *Heat Investigations (K–4)*

   a. How is heat produced?

   b. How do we measure heat?

   c. Can heat move from one object to another?

3. *Electricity Investigations (K–4)*

   a. How does a flashlight battery, wire, and bulb work together to produce electricity?

   b. How does a complete electrical circuit—wire(s), battery(s), and appropriate additional items—work to produce heat, sound, and magnetic effects?

4. *Magnetism Investigations (K–4)*

    a. What effects do magnets have on one another?

    b. What effects do magnets have on other materials?

B. When your group completes the selected investigation, obtain a copy of Physical Science Content Standard B (K–4) , pages 123–127, in the *National Science Education Standards*. Read and discuss this information together. Relate it to your group's investigations and share ideas of how you could design learning experiences for students that will help them develop an understanding of the concepts related to this standard. Find a way to share your information with other members of the class. Perhaps each group could design a learning experience in which other members of the class participate in manipulating materials and equipment to become directly involved in reviewing the concepts related to every other group's investigation. These concepts should be discussed with the entire class, along with a variety of effective ways to help students gain an understanding of them.

PHYSICAL SCIENCE CONCEPTS (5–8)

This section will involve you in carrying out investigations related to the identified physical science concepts in Content Standard B for grades 5 to 8 in the *National Science Education Standards.* According to the *Standards,* students are expected to "develop an understanding" of these concepts "as a result of their activities in grades 5–8." These concepts continue to build on the knowledge constructed in grades K–4. During the K–4 years, students should have had numerous experiences with a variety of objects and materials. These experiences have given them many opportunities to identify properties of various items and use these properties to sort and group the items. The *Standards* state that at the K–4 level students "learned that some properties, such as size, weight, and shape, can be assigned only to the object while other properties, such as color, texture, and hardness, describe the materials from which objects are made." At the 5–8 level, students focus on "characteristic properties of the substances from which the materials are made." The following concepts are included in the *Standards* Physical Science Content Standard B (5–8):

1. Properties and changes of properties in matter
2. Motions and forces
3. Transfer of energy

The next set of activities is designed to help you experience firsthand inquiry-based learning related to developing a better understanding of the concepts discussed previously. These activities should also provide you with personal experience that will help you design and organize effective inquiry-based learning experiences for 5–8 students.

Physical Science Activity 4

Properties and Changes of Properties in Matter (5-8)

A. **Form small groups of four or five and complete the suggested investigations to review the concepts related to this area. Locate related activities in the various resource materials available to you and use them to guide your investigation. Check with your instructor for additional directions.**

B. **Before beginning your investigation, have all group members share what they know about the area related to the selected investigation. Then formulate some questions that you would like to investigate related to that area. Finally, design an investigation that will allow you to gather, organize, and analyze the data needed to use in reaching a conclusion. Identify and discuss the specific terms and concepts that emerge related to your investigation. You may find it helpful to do some preliminary research or background reading before beginning the actual investigation. Discuss your plan with your instructor and ask for feedback.**

1. *Density, solubility, and boiling point investigations (5–8)*

   a. Do all liquids have the same density? (Try comparing a variety of liquids, such as corn syrup, colored water, vegetable oil, baby oil, liquid detergent, and rubbing alcohol, by "layering" them in a plastic cylinder. Use the same volume of each liquid.)

   b. Do solid materials, such as coins, marbles, or pieces of wood, steel, iron, aluminum, wax candles, and plastic, differ in density? Does the size or weight of the solid object change the density of it? (Use the same plastic cylinder you used with the layered liquids to test the solid materials.)

   c. Do all liquids have the same boiling point?

   d. Will sugar mix with water to form a solution? How about salt? When mixed with 50-milliliters of water, how much salt is needed before no more of the salt is dissolved? Does it take more, less, or the same amount of sugar as salt to saturate 50-milliliters of water? Does heating the water before adding the salt or sugar change the amount needed for saturation? Can the salt and sugar be removed from the water by evaporation? How do the amounts of salt and sugar *after evaporation* compare to the amounts of each used to saturate the 50-milliliter container of water? Was the dissolving of the salt and sugar in the water a physical or a chemical change? Explain. Discuss the terms that students would learn as part of this experience.

e. What conclusions can you reach regarding the properties of density, boiling point, and solubility? After your group has discussed insights and information gained from these activities, read the next paragraph and include this additional information in your discussions.

Density, boiling point, and solubility are considered "characteristic properties" of substances. They vary from substance to substance but do not change for a particular substance when the amount of the substance changes. For example, the density and boiling point of water remain the same for 5-milliliters as it does for 25- or 100-milliliters, but water differs in density and boiling point from other substances. In Physical Science Activity 4.1A, you observed that the same volume of different liquids "layered" in a specific way. This order will remain the same each time these substances are "layered" because the density of each substance remains constant. This is also true when you use larger or smaller amounts of a substance. You should have observed this when you varied the size and weight of the solid items being dropped into the layered liquids in Physical Science Activity 4.1B. These "characteristic properties" often can be used to separate mixtures into their original substances.

2. *Chemical changes in substances investigations (5–8)*

   a. Using a small amount of milk or lemon juice and a toothpick, write a "secret word" on a piece of white paper. Wait until it dries and the word cannot be seen. Then carefully hold the paper close to, but do not touch, a burning lightbulb. What happens? Can you explain it?

   b. Obtain four small identical jars and dishes. Push a wad of steel wool into the bottom of one of the jars. In another, push a few cotton balls into the bottom. Be sure that the steel wool and cotton balls are wedged in so that they will stay when each jar is turned upside down. In a third jar, tape some nails to the bottom. Tape a wooden block to the bottom of the fourth jar. Place the four dishes side by side in an area that will not be disturbed and can easily be observed during the next week. Put about 2 centimeters of water into each dish and stand the jars upside down in the dishes, one in each dish. Over the next week, examine them every day if possible. Jot down your observations, noticing such things as water level and the appearance of the items placed in the bottom of the jars. Do any changes take place? Which substances undergo a change? Are these changes reversible? How do you explain what you observe? What other items might you put into the jars to observe to gather additional information related to this area? What real-world experiences have you had related to how a particular substance has reacted with another so that a chemical change has taken place? Could you design an investigation to see if similar substances react in the same way when placed in jars as described here?

c. Discuss your observations and inferences related to the previous activities. What have your observations and inferences led you to conclude related to how substances react chemically with other substances?

d. Discuss the terms, compounds, and elements with other group members. How are the two related? How would you help students develop an understanding of these terms? How would you help students make real-world connections? Find resources that give information about these terms and relate that information to what you observed in these activities. Ask your instructor to join your discussion to give you feedback and clarification.

Physical Science | Activity 5

Motion and Forces (5–8)

A. Form small groups of four or five. Before beginning your investigations, have all group members share what they know about motion and forces. Review the concepts and information related to this area presented earlier in the activities for students in grades K–4. Identify and discuss the specific terms and concepts that emerge as your group completes the suggested investigations that follow. You may find it helpful to do some preliminary research or background reading before beginning the actual investigation. Discuss your plan with your instructor and ask for feedback.

B. Design investigations that will allow you to gather, organize, and analyze the data needed to answer the following questions:

1. *How many different ways can you make objects move?*

   a. As your group plans the investigation related to this question, talk about forces such as pushing, pulling, throwing, dropping, and rolling that act on objects to make them move. Also, talk about how the properties of an object, such as shape, affect its motion.

   b. Gather some materials that can be used to move objects such as a ramp, string, rubber band, paper clip, or straw. Consider using more than one type of object in conducting this investigation.

   c. What are some of the factors that could affect an object's movement? Look for these as you conduct the investigation.

   d. Record your findings so that you can share them with others. Include quantitative observations. Describe the forces acting on the objects that cause the object to move.

2. *How does the mass of an object affect its motion?*

   a. Set up a ramp and select test objects that are the same size and shape but have a different mass/weight. Spheres that are the same size but differ in mass/weight work well. Identical film canisters or other small cylinder-shaped containers can be used by filling one with some substance, such as sand or water, to increase the mass and leaving the other one empty.

b. Record your findings so that you can share them with others. Be sure to include quantitative observations.

c. Describe the forces acting on the objects that cause them to move.

3. *Does the surface affect the way an object moves?*

a. Select an object from those used in the first two investigations in this area. Set up a ramp and place a variety of different-textured surfaces on it one at a time to test how each affects the movement of the selected object.

b. Try several different objects and observe their movement down the ramp before selecting one to use in completing the investigation. Once you have decided on the one object to use, set up and carry out the investigation to determine how the different surfaces affect the way the objects move down the ramp.

c. Use materials such as sandpaper, carpeting, paper toweling, different fabrics, plastic, water, and cooking oil to create the different surfaces.

d. Place the selected object at the top of the ramp that has been covered with one of the materials you are testing and release it. Observe the movement down the ramp.

e. Give a quantitative description of your observations. What forces are acting on the object? How do these forces affect the speed and direction of the object's motion? What conclusions can you reach based on the data you collected?

4. *Does the height of a ramp affect the distance that an object will roll once it leaves the ramp and moves across a textured flat surface?*

a. Select an object that will roll, such as a marble, ball, toy car, or cylinder-shaped container. Construct a ramp with a smooth surface, a meter long, that will easily accommodate your test object.

b. Decide on the type of textured flat surface that the ramp will rest on at the lower end—toweling, carpet, sandpaper, or other.

c. Select three different heights to test. Set up the ramp and do some trial runs to see if the decisions you have made about the materials to use will work well. Discuss the controls to be used so that the only manipulated variable is the height of the ramp. All other possible factors that could affect the outcome—the distance the object rolls after leaving the ramp—must be controlled.

d. Conduct your investigation by following the procedure you have established, allowing only the height of the ramp to affect the distance that the selected object rolls on the flat surface after leaving the ramp.

e. Select the lowest height to be tested and make three trials. Measure and record the distance traveled on the flat-textured surface for each of the three trials. Calculate the average distance rolled in the three trials. Continue this same procedure at the other two heights to be tested.

f. Graph your results. Label with all necessary information. Compare the resulting averages of the three trials at each height being tested. Compare your group's results with others who conducted the same investigation. Discuss any conflicting results. Retest if necessary to resolve unanswered conflicts.

g. What forces acted on the selected object? How did these forces affect the speed and direction of the object? What would students learn about forces and motion from doing a similar investigation?

h. How would you design an investigation in which students tested the affect of the length of a ramp on the distance an object rolled after leaving the ramp?

Transfer of Energy (5–8)

A. Form small groups of four or five. Before beginning your investigations, have all group members share what they know about the concepts related to transfer of energy. Review the information related to this area presented earlier in Activity 3 for students in grades K to 4. Discuss the idea of energy as an identified property of many substances. Talk about the association between energy and light, sound, mechanical motion, chemical changes, heat, and electricity. Identify other areas that are associated with energy. Share ideas related to the many ways energy is transferred. Include the terms "energy source" and "energy receiver." Identify and discuss specific terms and concepts that emerge as your group completes the suggested investigations that follow. You may find it helpful to do some preliminary research or background reading before beginning the actual investigations. Discuss your plan with your instructor and ask for feedback.

B. Design investigations that will allow you to gather, organize, and analyze the data needed to answer the following questions:

1. *How does the amount of hot and cold water affect the amount of energy transferred when the cold water is put into a small beaker (100 ml) and the beaker is then placed in a larger beaker (250 ml) of hot water?*

    a. Determine three different amounts of water that will be tested. Measure the first amount of cold water to be tested and put it into the 100-milliliter beaker. Measure out the identical amount of hot water and put it into the 250-milliliter beaker.

b. Place a thermometer in each beaker to measure the starting temperature. Leave the two thermometers in place and carefully put the smaller beaker of cold water into the larger beaker of hot water. Make sure that the amounts chosen do not cause the water in the larger beaker to spill over.

c. Observe and record the temperature change in 1-minute intervals for 10 minutes.

d. How do you describe the energy transfer taking place? Identify the energy source and energy receiver.

e. Graph your results. How do your results compare with others doing this investigation? What concepts would students encounter as they participated in this activity? What conclusions can you come to related to how heat energy is transferred?

2. *Does the color of paper wrapped around a beaker affect the amount of light energy that is transferred from a light source to the air inside the covered beaker?*

a. Locate a heat lamp, two identical beakers, two thermometers, and one sheet of white and one sheet of black construction paper. Make sure that the two sheets of paper are the same size and thickness and differ only in color.

b. Wrap the sheet of white construction paper around one of the beakers and secure with tape. Wrap the black construction paper around the other beaker and secure with tape. Place the thermometers upright, one in each beaker, facing in the same direction. Place the wrapped beakers side by side, leaving about 10 centimeters of space between them. Record the temperature shown on both thermometers. (They should register the same starting temperature.)

c. Place the heat lamp about 50 centimeters away from the wrapped beakers and position it so that it shines equally on both.

d. Record the temperatures of the two thermometers every minute for the next 10 minutes. What changes in temperature do you observe? How is the light energy interacting with the two wrapped beakers? What would students learn about light energy by doing this activity? How do you explain what you observe? How would you explain it to students in grades 5 to 8?

3. *How can electrical energy be transferred?*

a. Locate a 1½-volt dry-cell battery, 1 meter of 22-gauge insulated copper wire stripped on both ends, one 3- or 4-inch iron nail, and several paper clips.

b. Hold the nail close to the paper clips. What happens? Are the paper clips attracted to the nail?

c. Place the nail about the middle of the wire and coil the wire 10 times around the nail. (The ends of the wire will extend from each end of the nail.) Hold the nail close to the paper clips again. What happens? Are the paper clips attracted to the nail now?

d. Connect one end of the wire to a terminal of the battery and hold the nail near the paper clips once more. Touch the other end of the wire to the other terminal. What happens?

    e. Disconnect one end of the wire from the battery terminal and observe what happens to the paper clips. Make the connection again and hold the nail near the paper clips. Disconnect one wire again and observe.

    f. How can you explain your observations in terms of energy transfer? Describe how electrical circuits are used to transfer energy that produces heat, light, sound, and chemical changes. How would you help students understand the concepts involved in energy transfer?

C. **Review the information and questions used in the introduction to this activity. Discuss what you have observed and insights gained related to energy transfer. Obtain a copy of Physical Science Content Standard B for grades 5–8 from the** *National Science Education Standards.* **Read pages 149 to 155 and discuss and relate this additional information to the knowledge gained in completing the activities related to this content standard. How does this information help you gain a better understanding of the concepts related to properties and changes of properties in matter, motion and forces, and transfer of energy? How would you help students develop an understanding of the concepts and principles that underlie this standard?**

D. **Ask your instructor to conduct a class discussion to deal with questions, clarifications, and additional information needed related to this content standard.**

SUMMARY

This chapter has focused on the identified physical science concepts outlined in the *National Science Education Standards.* First we looked at those for grades K–4, then at those for grades 5 to 8. At the K–4 level, students are developing an understanding of properties of objects and materials, position and motion of objects, and light, heat, electricity, and magnetism. At the 5–8 level, students build on the knowledge and experience gained at the K–4 level and expand their understanding to include properties and changes of properties in matter, motions and forces, and transfer of energy.

    The activities in this section provided you with opportunities to experience first hand involvement with objects and materials similar to those you will provide for your own students. You were involved in constructing and understanding knowledge related to each of the identified areas in order to prepare you to provide students with inquiry-based learning experiences related to these same areas. You were asked to make connections to your prior knowledge in each area before completing the suggested activities. During the activities, you were asked to identify terms and concepts that emerged that related to your observations. Additional information was provided in this text and from other resources to help you accommodate the new information. You were also involved in sharing insights and ideas with others related to how you could develop learning experiences for students that would help them develop an understanding of the identified K–4 and 5–8 physical science concepts included in this standard.

Remember that content knowledge is not separate from the other areas of learning that have been discussed in prior chapters. As mentioned at the beginning of this chapter, content is one of the components of the complex vision that makes up the inquiry-based approach to teaching and learning science. It must be meshed with and become a part of the total science program. In an inquiry-based program, content is much more than knowing specific facts. It involves a true understanding of the concepts involved and the ability to apply this understanding to real-world contexts. Students must be given opportunities to construct this knowledge by engaging in many inquiry-based learning experiences.

Check out http://www.cln.org on the Web for a variety of links that include content information, activities, themes, and lesson plans related to physical science topics. This resource will provide you with additional input as you reflect on how you will provide opportunities for your students to construct knowledge related to physical science concepts. The next two activities will give you a chance to apply what your have learned by selecting physical science activities to use with elementary and middle school students and sharing your ideas with your classmates through workshop presentations.

Physical Science | Activity 7

Collecting Physical Science Activities to Use With K–8 Students

A. You may work with a partner or small group to complete this activity. Use the science resources available to you and review and select at least six science activities (two for each of the three areas) that you could use with students in grades K to 4 to help them develop an understanding of (1) properties of objects and materials, (2) position and motion of objects, and (3) light, heat, electricity, and magnetism. Make a photocopy of the selected activities.

B. Review and select at least six science activities (two for each group) that you could use with students in grades 5 to 8 to help them develop an understanding of (1) properties and changes of properties in matter (2) motion and forces, and (3) transfer of energy. Make a photocopy of the selected activities.

C. Discuss all the selected activities with your small group. Decide if any adaptations, modifications, additions, or deletions are needed for any of the activities so that they could be more effectively used in an inquiry-based science program. Make the needed changes on the photocopy, write the level (K–4 or 5–8) and the appropriate content reference (e.g., "Properties of Objects and Materials" or "Motion and Forces") at the top of the activity, add other helpful comments, and place the selected activities in a notebook. You will be adding to your collection of activities related to the science standards as you complete the next three chapters of this text.

Physical Science Activity 8

Workshop Presentations

A. Work with a partner or small group and select one of the activities that was collected in Activity 7 to use in presenting a workshop for other members of your class. Your workshop should involve your peers in a variety of activities that include direct manipulation of materials and equipment. Most likely, an adapted or modified version of the original activity will be necessary to make it appropriate for your peers. Design your workshop so that your peers are engaged in an inquiry-based approach. Remember to begin by building on prior knowledge, allow your peers to experience the process of constructing new knowledge related to the physical science concept that is the focus of your workshop, and apply content knowledge along with knowledge about teaching and learning to develop strategies for using a similar activity with students. It is strongly recommended that your peers do not try to act like elementary or middle school students but instead be themselves as they participate in a workshop designed for preservice teachers.

B. Ask your instructor for additional guidelines and directions for completing this activity.

C. When all workshop presentations have been completed, ask your instructor to conduct a total class discussion related to inquiry-based teaching and learning of physical science concepts. Talk about any remaining areas in which you feel the need for more information or clarification. Reflect on what you have learned that will help you provide opportunities for elementary and middle school students to develop understandings of the physical science concepts that were identified by the *National Science Education Standards*.

REFERENCES

American Association for the Advancement of Science. (1993). *Benchmarks for scientific literacy.* New York: Oxford University Press.

Full Options Science Systems (FOSS). Objects and Properties Unit. Lawrence Hall of Science. Berkeley: University of California.

National Research Council. (1996). *National Science Education Standards.* Washington, DC: National Academy Press.

National Science Teachers Association. (1997). *NSTA pathways to the science standards: Guidelines for moving the vision into practice.* (Elementary School Edition). Arlington, VA: Author.

National Science Teachers Association. (1998). *NSTA pathways to the science standards: Guidelines for moving the vision into practice.* (Middle School Edition). Arlington, VA: Author.

Science Curriculum Improvement Study3 (SCIS3). Energy Sources Unit. Nashua, NH: Delta Education.

Science Curriculum Improvement Study3 (SCIS3). Material Objects Units. Nashua, NH: Delta Education.

Victor, K. (2000). *Science for the elementary and middle school.* Columbus, OH: Merrill/ Prentice Hall.

CHAPTER 9

Inquiry-Based Teaching and Learning of Life Science Concepts

INTRODUCTION

In this chapter, we will continue our review of the content standards by examining the identified **life science standards** for grades K to 4 and 5 to 8. It is important for you to be reminded again that these standards identify student outcomes and provide teachers with an outline of what students should learn, but they are *not* the science curriculum. They are, however, an important component of the total science program. Used in the context of the other standards on teaching and assessment, the life science content standards offer teachers valuable information that can be used in planning and organizing for inquiry-based science teaching and learning.

What are some topics and concepts that you associate with life science content? Do you remember a particular life science topic or theme that you really enjoyed and learned a lot about when you were in elementary or middle school? What kinds of experiences did you have that helped you learn and understand the information related to that particular topic? What experiences do you remember as being frustrating or nonhelpful?

LIFE SCIENCE CONCEPTS (K–8)

Life science topics focus on the living aspects of our world and typically include such areas as plants, seeds, animals, habitats, life cycles, heredity, ecology, and in some cases health and nutrition and the five senses. According to Life Science Content Standard C, students in grades K to 4 should develop an understanding of the following:

- The characteristics of organisms
- Life cycles of organisms
- Organisms and environments

In grades 5 to 8, students continue to develop and broaden their understandings of organisms. Life Science Content Standard C for students in grades 5 to 8 lists the following:

- Structure and function in living systems
- Reproduction and heredity
- Regulation and behavior
- Populations and ecosystems
- Diversity and adaptations of organisms

As with the physical science standards, **direct experience** is necessary for learners to develop an understanding of concepts and principles that underlie these life science standards. Teachers must provide students with many opportunities for direct experiences with a variety of living things. Young children tend to be naturally curious about the world around them. They come to school with varied experiences and intuitive ideas about plants and animals and how they grow. Some children will have experienced the birth and death of pets or farm animals. Others will have less direct contact with such things. It will be your job to provide a variety of experiences that allow students to assess their prior knowledge, construct new knowledge, clear up misconceptions, and begin to develop deeper understandings related to life science concepts.

At the K–4 level, students focus mainly on individual organisms, but at the 5–8 level they begin to look for patterns in ecosystems. Comparisons between species are made and how the different species interact with the others and with their environment. Students at this level begin to look more closely at the function of cells. They learn about reproduction and how traits are passed from one generation to the next through the genes. Behavioral responses of organisms to their environment are investigated. Concepts related to producers, consumers, decomposers, and food webs are studied.

By the time students reach fifth or sixth grade, they are able to routinely include quantitative observations and use computers for organizing and communicating findings. At the same time that cognitive abilities are developing to allow increased abstract reasoning and logical thinking, fine motor skills are improving so that more precise measurements can be made and more sophisticated equipment used.

The following activities have been designed to help you explore your own understanding of the life science concepts identified for students in grades K to 4.

LIFE SCIENCE ACTIVITIES (K-4)

Life Science   Activity 1

Characteristics of Organisms

1. Form a small group of four or five. Have one person in your group locate the container of mealworms provided and carefully remove one mealworm for each member of your small group. Place each mealworm in a small plastic or paper dish in order to observe and investigate its observable characteristics. Have another member of your group get a hand lens for each to use. Remember to treat your mealworm carefully; it is a living thing. Do not do anything that would injure it.

2. Mealworms are the larval stage of the grain beetle *(Tenebrio molitor)* and are usually found around flour mills or in grain warehouses and feed stores. They are commonly used as fishing bait. (This should give you a clue as to where to obtain a supply to use with your students.) Examine the structure of your mealworm using the hand lens. Describe its structure; then draw a picture. Share your observations and drawing with others in your group. Do all the mealworms have the same physical characteristics? How would you compare the feel and look of the mealworm with earthworms? Is the mealworm a "real worm"? To what category of animals does the mealworm belong?

3. Have each person in your group investigate one of the following questions. Make sure each person selects a different question; then share your findings with each other. Keep in mind that a mealworm has chemical reactors over its entire body and that putting a drop of irritating liquid on a mealworm is somewhat like having it poured into your mouth or nose. Irritating liquids should be dropped near, but not directly on the mealworm.

   a. How do mealworms move?

   b. Can mealworms see?

   c. Can mealworms back up?

   d. Can mealworms follow walls?

   e. How do mealworms react to a drop of water, vinegar, and alcohol that is placed near them?

   f. What other activities can you suggest for elementary children to investigate related to the characteristics of mealworms?

Life Cycles of Mealworms

1. Continue to work with your small group as you observe examples of the three stages in the life cycle of the mealworm. Ask your instructor for a small container of mealworms that has all three stages represented. Find an example of each stage of development: larva, pupa, and adult beetle. Describe each stage. On a separate sheet of paper, identify and sketch each stage.

2. Have group members identify and discuss other animal life cycles that they are familiar with, such as butterflies and frogs. Talk about the human life cycle also. Which characteristics of mealworms that you have observed so far seem to be inherited? Which do you think might be learned?

Organisms and Their Environment

1. Continue to work with your small group and observe the mealworms in the habitat constructed for them in your classroom. How do you describe their con-

structed habitat? Where do mealworms prefer to stay? How are their basic needs met in this environment? How does the constructed habitat compare to their natural habitat?

2. How are the mealworms' patterns of behavior related to their environment? What do you think would happen if the constructed habitat were changed in some way? Discuss possible changes and possible results with your group.

3. Identify other animal habitats that you are familiar with and discuss these with your group. Talk about constructed and natural habitats. Identify and discuss some animal habitats that you know of that have undergone change that impacted the animal population of that habitat.

Gathering Information About Organisms

Use the resources available to you to find out more about mealworms, their life cycle, and their natural habitat. Also, look for information related to other organisms that could be used in a classroom to help students gain an understanding of the concepts related to characteristics, life cycles, and environments of organisms. Check out http://ericir.syr.edu/virtual/lessons/Science/Biological/index.html on the Web.

Examining Standard C

1. Obtain a copy of Life Science Content Standard C (K–4), pages 127 to 129, in the *National Science Education Standards* (National Research Council, 1996). Read and discuss this information with your small group.

2. Share ideas of how you could design learning experiences for students in grades K to 4 that would help them develop an understanding of the concepts related to this standard.

3. Participate in a class discussion and share your group's ideas.

Life Science Activity 6

Collecting Life Science Activities to Use With K-4 Students

1. Use the science resources available to you and review and select at least six science activities (two for each of the three areas) that you could use with students in grades K to 4 to help them develop an understanding of (1) characteristics of organisms, (2) life cycles of organisms, and (3) organisms and their environments. Make a photocopy of the selected activities.

2. Discuss all the selected activities with your small group. Decide if any adaptations, modifications, additions, or deletions are needed for any of the activities so that they could be more effectively used in an inquiry-based science program. Make the needed changes on the photocopy, write the level (K–4) and the appropriate content reference (e.g., "Characteristics of Organisms") at the top of the activity, add other helpful comments, and place the selected life science activities (K–4) in the notebook with the physical science activities you collected.

3. Working with your small group and using one of the selected life science activities collected, design a learning experience so that students are directly involved in constructing and reflecting on the targeted life science content knowledge. Design a workshop presentation and present your group's ideas to others in your class. If possible, try out your ideas with K–4 students.

Now that we have looked at the life science concepts (K–4) that form the foundation on which later, more complex biological concepts emerge, we will examine the life science concepts from Standard C for grades 5 to 8. In grades 5 to 8, the emphasis shifts away from individual organisms to populations and communities of species. Students become involved in activities in which they investigate the following:

- Structure and function in living systems
- Reproduction and heredity
- Regulation and behavior
- Populations and ecosystems
- Diversity and adaptations of organisms

The activities included in this section have been designed to involve you in learning experiences that will help you review these concepts and become more familiar with resources and techniques to use in helping students in grades 5 to 8 gain an understanding of these concepts.

LIFE SCIENCE ACTIVITIES (5-8)

Populations and Ecosystems

1. Form a small group with others in your class. Take a walk with your group and explore the wide range of environments that exist in nature and the different organisms that thrive within each. For example, walk through a forest, near a pond, in a grassy area, on a well-traveled pathway, or in another local area that is available to you.

2. Read through the following questions to guide your observations. Keep a pencil and paper handy throughout your walk to jot down your observations and answers to these questions:

   a. What organisms exist in these areas?

   b. Is there evidence of an organism's interaction with and dependence on other organisms and/or the environment?

   c. How are the organisms that live in one area alike?

   d. How are they different?

   e. How do the characteristics of organisms from *different* environments compare?

   f. What characteristics are important for survival in a specific habitat that you observed?

   g. What do you think would happen to the organisms if the environment in which they live changed?

h. How do the organisms in an environment change the environment?

i. Why do you think some species are extinct?

j. Identify some ways organisms are dependent on their natural environments.

k. Identify some ways humans change their environments that are beneficial to themselves and other organisms.

l. In what ways have humans changed environments that have been detrimental for themselves and other organisms?

Life Science   Activity 2

Designing Life Science Learning Experiences

1. Form five small groups. Each group should select one (be sure that each selects a different one) of the following areas:

    • Structure and function in living systems
    • Reproduction and heredity
    • Regulation and behavior
    • Populations and ecosystems
    • Diversity and adaptations of organisms

2. Each group should obtain a copy of Life Science Content Standard C, grades 5 to 8, pages 155 to 158, and read the section related to the previously listed areas. Discuss the information with your group to review the fundamental concepts and principles that underlie your selected area.

3. Locate other content resources, such as textbooks or Internet sites, and retrieve additional information to share in your group. (Check out http://ericir.syr.edu/virtual/lessons/Science/Biological/index.html on the Web.)

4. Talk with your instructor and other knowledgeable people to gain a deeper understanding of your selected area.

5. Working together as a group, select several activities that could be used with students in grades 5 to 8 to help them begin to understand some of the basic concepts and principles associated with your selected area. Complete at least one or two of the selected activities as a group.

6. Have a group discussion about how helpful the selected activities would be with students in grades 5 to 8. What modifications and adaptations would make the activities more meaningful? How would you use them as a part of a planned learning experience?

7. Select one of the activities related to your group's assigned area to use in presenting a workshop for others in your class. Your workshop should involve your peers in a modified version of the original activity. Design the workshop so that your peers are engaged in an inquiry-based approach. Remember to begin by building on prior knowledge, allow your peers to experience the process of constructing new knowledge related to the life science concept that is the focus of your workshop, and apply content knowledge along with knowledge about teaching and learning to develop strategies for using a similar activity with students. It is strongly recommended that your peers do not try to act like students in grades 5 to 8, but instead be themselves as they participate in a workshop designed for preservice teachers.

8. Ask your instructor for additional guidelines and directions for completing this activity.

Life Science   Activity 3

Summarizing Discussion for Life Science Activities

1. When all workshop presentations have been completed, ask your instructor to conduct a total class discussion related to inquiry-based teaching and learning of life science concepts. Talk about any remaining areas in which you feel the need for more information or clarification. Reflect on what you have learned that will help you provide opportunities for K–8 students to develop understandings of the life science concepts that were identified by the *National Science Education Standards* for grades 5 to 8.

Collecting Life Science Activities to Use

1. Use the science resources available to you and review and select at least 15 science activities (three for each of the five areas) that you could use with students in grades 5 to 8 to help them develop an understanding of (1) structure and function in living systems, (2) reproduction and heredity, (3) regulation and behavior, (4) populations and ecosystems, and (5) diversity and adaptations of organisms. Make a photocopy of the selected activities.

2. Discuss all the selected activities with your small group. Decide if any adaptations, modifications, additions, or deletions are needed for any of the activities so that they could be more effectively used in an inquiry-based science program. Make the needed changes on the photocopy, write the level (5–8) and the appropriate content reference (e.g., "Structure and Function in Living Systems") at the top of the activity, add other helpful comments, and place the selected life science activities (5–8) in the notebook with the physical and life science activities you have already collected.

SUMMARY

In this section, you have been involved in reviewing the life science concepts listed in the *National Science Education Standards* for grades 5 to 8. The activities in this section gave you many opportunities to experience directly many of these concepts. You have collected various activities to use with students in grades 5 to 8 that will help them gain an understanding of how populations and communities of organisms live and interact with each other and with their environment. As with all science concepts, direct experience is a necessary part of learning and understanding. Teachers must plan field trips to a variety of environments so that students can be directly involved with the populations and ecosystems found there. Science journals in which students write their observations, jot down questions, make sketches, and reflect on investigations are an excellent instructional tool. Teachers can use these journals as one of the tools in determining the level of understanding that a student has related to the specific life science concepts being studied.

The last two chapters have focused on examining the content standards related to physical and life science. We will continue in the next two chapters by looking at the content standards for earth and space science and science and technology.

REFERENCES

American Association for the Advancement of Science. (1993). *Benchmarks for scientific literacy.* New York: Oxford University Press.

National Research Council. (1996). *National Science Education Standards.* Washington, DC: National Academy Press.

National Science Teachers Association. (1997). *NSTA pathways to the science standards: Guidelines for moving the vision into practice* (Elementary School Edition). Arlington, VA: Author.

National Science Teachers Association. (1998). *NSTA pathways to the science standards: Guidelines for moving the vision into practice* (Middle School Edition). Arlington, VA: Author.

Science Curriculum Improvement Study 3 (SCIS3). Life Cycles Unit. Nashua, NH: Delta Education.

Victor, K. (2000). *Science for the elementary and middle school.* Columbus, OH: Merrill/Prentice-Hall.

CHAPTER 10

Inquiry-Based Teaching and Learning of Earth and Space Science Concepts

INTRODUCTION

What do you know about the materials that make up the earth's surface? Can you remember learning about the different kinds of rocks—sedimentary, igneous, and metamorphic? Can you identify and describe each? Are all rocks made of a single substance? How important is this information? Did you ever have a rock collection?

How would you explain the phases of the moon to students? How are they different from a lunar eclipse? What kinds of activities would help students develop an understanding of the changes that take place on a daily basis in the observable shape of the moon? How comfortable are you with helping students understand weather patterns, volcanic eruptions, landslides, and earthquakes?

In this chapter, we continue our review of the content standards by examining the identified earth and space science standards for grades K to 4 and 5 to 8. As you read in the previous two chapters, these standards identify student outcomes and provide teachers with an outline of what students should learn, but they *are not* the science curriculum. They are, however, an important component of the total science program. Used in the context of the other standards on teaching and assessment, the earth and space content standards offer teachers valuable information that can be used in planning and organizing inquiry-based science teaching and learning.

Earth and space science concepts for grades K to 8 are typically grouped under headings such as (1) the earth—its surface, features, and resources (this is sometimes referred to as the geosphere); (2) water—its characteristics, different forms, movement, and location on the earth (this is also described as the hydrosphere); (3) the atmosphere—its composition and characteristics; (4) weather—kinds, causes, and seasonal changes; and (5) the solar system—sun, moon, earth, other planets, and the motion of objects in the solar system.

Children in grades K to 4 should be engaging in earth science activities that involve them in observing a variety of earth materials. The playground and nearby fields, ponds, or parks can provide different kinds of rocks, soil types, vegetation, and water for students to investigate. Frequent visits to these types of sites help students observe changes that take place over time. In addition to investigating rocks, soils, and vegetation, students at this level are developing a deeper understanding of day and night by observing objects in the sky, noticing changes, and finding patterns in the changes they observe. They also begin to learn about weather patterns and changes to the earth's surface caused by erosion, landslides, volcanic eruption, and earthquakes.

The *National Science Education Standards,* Earth and Space Science Content Standard D (National Research Council, 1996), lists the following understandings for students in grades K to 4:

- Properties of earth materials
- Objects in the sky
- Changes in earth and sky

In order to learn and understand the concepts associated with each of these areas, students in grades K to 4 must be involved in activities that emphasize making, recording, and describing observations as they explore and investigate the world around them. Children at this level have difficulty grasping the complex nature of the solar system and are able to develop only a limited understanding from the use of models to explain the changing location and relationship of the objects that they observe in the day and night sky. Most science educators feel that going beyond what students can understand based on their own observations is not appropriate at this level. Many misconceptions exist, and understanding is limited. The *Standards* suggest that the focus for earth and space science concepts at the K–4 level should be on the development of observation skills. Students should be encouraged to record their observations by making sketches or drawings and keeping journals. Measurements can be taken and recorded. Discussions should be held so that students can talk about their observations with others and offer explanations of recorded changes based on their observations.

According to Earth and Space Content Standard D, students in grades 5 to 8 should be involved in activities that develop their understanding of the following:

- Structure of the earth system
- Earth's history
- Earth in the solar system

At this level, most students are ready and able to apply the basic understanding they gained through observations in grades K to 4 to the more complex and abstract concepts related to earth and space science. Students in grades 5 to 8 **investigate the water and rock cycle and learn about the history** of the earth. The notion of systems is introduced. They begin to develop an understanding of the interactions of the earth's major components or systems—geosphere, hydrosphere, atmosphere, and biosphere—and how they are continuously changed by physical, chemical, and biological processes. Most students are now able to use models to increase their understanding of the relationships that exist among the earth, sun, moon, and other planets in the solar system.

The activities included in this chapter offer you an opportunity to review and deepen your own understanding of concepts for students in grades K to 8 related to earth and space science. You will also be given opportunities to apply what you have learned about inquiry-based teaching and learning in designing earth and space science learning experiences for students in grades K to 8. As you complete these activities, reflect on how you can use the ideas, strategies, and resources included within the activities in helping K–8 students develop an understanding of the fundamental concepts and principles that underlie each of the areas in Earth and Space Science Content Standard D.

EARTH/SPACE ACTIVITIES (K-4)

The first set of activities relates to the earth and space science concepts identified by the *Standards* for grades K to 4 and include the three major areas of properties of earth materials, objects in the sky, and changes in the earth and sky.

Earth/Space — Activity 1

Properties of Earth Materials

1. Form a small group with four or five others in your class. Get a copy of the book *Everybody Needs a Rock* by Byrd Baylor. Select someone from your group to read this book to the group. Each group member will select a rock to observe by following the 10 rules given in the book.

2. Closely examine your rock. Describe the color(s) and shape and feel of your rock. Record this information. Use a string to measure the length and distance around the rock. Lay the string on a meter stick and record the measurements. Use a metric balance scale to measure the mass/weight. Record. Describe and record other features of your rock that you observe.

3. Share your rock with the other members of your group. Put all the rocks in the middle of the table and compare your rock with all the other rocks, being careful not to get confused about which rock belongs to whom. Working as a group, make a "rock train" with the rocks, so that each rock in the train is different in one way from the rock in front of it. Identify the one property that is different as you point to the rocks in the train. Make sure that all group members agree. Make a new "train" with each rock being different in *two* ways from the one in front. Can you think of other games to play or activities to do with the rocks that would help you become more familiar with the various observable properties of rocks? Discuss your ideas with your group. Select one and try it.

4. All the rocks from your group should be placed in a paper bag. Wait 2 or 3 minutes, then one at a time, each person in the group should reach in and try to identify his or her rock using only the sense of touch. When a group member is able to identify his or her rock in this way, the rock is pulled from the bag for the other group members to see and confirm the rock's identity. The rock is then returned to the bag and the next person repeats the procedure to identify his or her rock. When each group member has had a turn, discuss the results. Was everyone able to identify his or her rock by touch? Do you think you could pick out your rock by touch if you dropped it in a paper bag with another group's rocks? Try it.

5. As a group, discuss what you know about rocks.

   Students at the K–4 level should focus on observing and describing the properties of rocks, collecting rocks, and sorting and grouping rocks according to their observable properties—color, size, mass/weight, texture, pattern (plain or striated), buoyancy, or layering. The *Standards* suggest that K–4 students should begin to notice that some rocks seem to be made up of a single substance but that most seem to be composed of several substances. It is recommended that teachers not try to explain the mineral makeup of rocks or extend the study to include the source of the rocks (sedimentary, igneous, and metamorphic) at the K–4 level. Students at this level have difficulty understanding and making meaningful connections to this kind of information. Their time is better spent constructing information based on their active observations of various study sites, which provide opportunities to observe and interact with a variety of earth materials.

Other earth materials studied at the K–4 level include soils, water, and the gases of the atmosphere. Students should begin to understand how important these earth materials are to humans. They provide the resources that we use to grow our food as well as materials used for shelter and fuel.

Earth/Space   Activity 2

Objects in the Sky

1. Form a small group with four or five others in your class. Go outside and find an open area where you can view the sky. What do you observe? Describe the properties of the things that you see in the sky. Describe the location of these different objects. Compare your observations with others in your group.

2. Discuss what you have observed in the past as you looked into the day and night sky. Make a group list of all the objects observed in the sky today and in the past.

3. What patterns have you noticed? Would you expect to see the same objects in the sky if you came back to this same location 12 hours from now? Would you expect the location of the objects to be the same each day and each night over a period of a month? What kinds of objects would you expect K–4 students to notice?

Children are fascinated by what they see in the day and night sky. Teachers in grades K to 4 must provide many opportunities for their students to directly observe and describe the various objects in the sky—clouds, rainbows, sun, moon, stars, and even birds, airplanes, and hot air balloons. They should notice the position of the sun and moon at various times during the day and evening. As they observe these location changes, they can begin to look for patterns in these changes. They should be able to reach the conclusion, based on their observations, that the sun provides us with the light and heat that are needed to support life on our planet. By third or fourth grade, students should also be able to determine that the sun and moon appear to have established patterns of movement. They are able to observe over time the location of the sun early in the day, in the middle of the day, and late in the afternoon and identify the daily location sequence. The location of the moon in the sky can also be observed over time and a pattern identified. They can draw what the moon looks like each night for a month. The drawings can be used to determine the existing pattern of changes in the lighted portion of the moon that is seen from earth. At this level, the emphasis should be on making and describing observations. Explanations and conclusions should be based on observations made by the students. Activities should include recording and verbal sharing of observations, drawings, and journal keeping. The *Standards* encourage teachers to wait until students are older (fifth grade and up) to use models of the solar system in attempting to extend students' understanding beyond their observations. Science educators are finding that most children at the K–4 level are limited in their understanding of the various concepts related to the makeup of the solar system (e.g., gravity, properties of light) necessary to construct meaningful knowledge beyond that gathered through direct observation. The many misconceptions that are a part of children's thinking at this level make it very difficult for them to effectively process information about the solar system that is presented through models and that is not based on direct observation. Time is better spent involving them in actively observing, describing, and recording properties, locations, and movements of objects in the sky. These kinds of concrete experiences will provide K–4 students with a solid base on which to build a deeper and more complex understanding of our solar system as they develop the cognitive abilities to process more abstract information.

Earth/Space   Activity 3

Changes in the Earth and Sky

Select at least one of the suggested activities and complete it with a small group. Share your results, insights, and ideas for using the activity with K–4 students with the others in your class.

1. Form a small group with four or five others in your class. Describe and discuss changes to the earth's surface that each of you has directly observed in the past related to erosion and weathering. Take a brief walk outside and try to find examples of these changes. Discuss and describe other changes that occur due to landslides, volcanic eruptions, and earthquakes. If possible, look at a poster, picture, computer site, or video that shows some of these changes. Report your group's findings and ideas for helping K–4 students learn more about changes in the earth's surface.

2. Working with a partner, find and conduct an activity that simulates erosion using a stream table or small trays of soil and a water sprinkler. Think of several different ways to test for soil loss and erosion. Predict the outcome of each test; then perform the action and compare your prediction with the actual outcome. (Try comparing the tilt of the tray with amount of soil loss. Also, compare the

effects of adding "vegetation" to leaving the soil bare.) Compare your observations with real-life photographs of changes caused by erosion. Present your findings to the whole class and suggest ideas for using a similar activity with K–4 students.

3. Work with a small group and prepare a "weather report" for the rest of the class. Take a walk outside and make observations, take measurements, and gather other pertinent information. Your report should include today's temperature, wind direction and speed, precipitation, and other information related to the weather. Present your report to the whole class and include your ideas about involving K–4 students in ongoing weather activities.

4. Form a small group and discuss what you have observed related to the change in location of the sun during various times of the day. What kind of pattern have you observed? Describe the pattern. What have you observed about the change in location of the moon in the sky? Describe the pattern. Are changes in location similar for the sun and moon? Is the moon ever visible in the daytime? Go outside and find an area where you have a clear view of the sky. If the sun is visible, describe its position using the directions of north, south, east, and west. If the moon is visible, describe its observable shape and position. (If either is not visible, recall the location in the sky you last saw it. Describe the shape of the lighted portion of the moon visible to you.) Discuss with your group how you might involve K–4 students in making observations of the sun and moon on a daily and monthly basis, with a focus on their changing location in the sky. Report your result and ideas to the whole class.

By becoming involved in activities in which they make observations over time and using these observations to reach conclusions about changes in the earth and sky, K–4 students come to a meaningful understanding of the fundamental concepts and principles related to this area. They can observe changes in the earth's surface caused by erosion and weathering on their own school grounds, in nearby parks, and perhaps around their own backyard. Other changes in the earth's surface due to landslides, volcanic eruptions, and earthquakes can be seen on television, videos, Web sites, and still pictures. These can also be simulated in various hands-on classroom activities.

K–4 students can collect weather information on a daily basis. Many teachers help students set up weather stations with various weather instruments, such as rain gauges, wind socks, anemometers, and thermometers that can be used to measure and collect needed weather information. Weather reports can be made each day and weather patterns observed. Information gathered by the students can be compared with that given by the local TV weather forecaster and found in the local paper.

The daily, monthly, and seasonal change in the location of the sun and moon relative to our earth can be observed and recorded and patterns established. The moon can be viewed over the span of several months so that the observable changes in the shape of the lighted portion that students can see can be drawn to correlate with the days of the month. By viewing and recording these changes over several months, students can recognize the cycle or phases of the moon that repeat each month.

Examining Earth and Space Content Standard D (K-4)

1. Obtain a copy of Earth and Space Science Content Standard D (K–4), pages 130 to 134, in the *National Science Education Standards* and read and discuss this information with your small group.
2. Share ideas of how you could design learning experiences for students in grades K to 4 that would help them develop an understanding of the concepts related to this standard.

Collecting Earth and Space Science Activities to Use With K-4 Students

1. Use the science resources available to you and review and select at least six science activities (two for each of the three areas) that you could use with students in grades K to 4 to help them develop an understanding of (1) properties of earth materials, (2) objects in the sky, and (3) changes in the earth and sky.
2. Make a photocopy of the selected activities.
3. Discuss all the selected activities with your small group. Decide if any adaptations, modifications, additions, or deletions are needed for any of the activities so that they could be more effectively used in an inquiry-based science program. Make the needed changes on the photocopy, write the level (K–4) and the appropriate content reference (e.g., "Properties of Earth Materials") at the top of the activity, add other helpful comments, and place the selected earth and space science activities in the notebook with the physical and life science activities that you have collected.

EARTH/SPACE ACTIVITIES (5–8)

Students in grades 5 to 8 continue to expand their understanding of earth and space science concepts by exploring the following three major areas:

- Structure of the earth system
- Earth's history
- Earth in the solar system

The activities included in this section have been designed to involve you in learning experiences that will help you review the fundamental concepts and principles associated with the previously listed areas and become more familiar with resources and techniques to use in helping students in grades 5 to 8 gain an understanding of these concepts.

Earth/Space   Activity 1

Structure of the Earth System

Select at least one of the suggested activities and complete it with a small group. Share your results, insights, and ideas for using with students in grades 5 to 8 with the others in your class.

1. Work with a small group to review the resources you have available to you—textbooks, trade books, Web sites, and other resource materials—related to the geosphere (crust, upper and lower mantle, and core of the earth). Use the information you gather and the ideas you generate to construct models or visuals that include cross sections of the earth, scale models of landforms, and maps of plate boundaries. Identify the various components represented in your model or visual and describe and explain the specific features represented.

2. Working together as a group, review the resources available to you—textbooks, trade books, Web sites, and other resources—that would help you create a chart or visual that illustrates the rock cycle. Label each stage and describe and explain the process. Include samples and/or pictures of appropriate rocks.

3. Use the resources available to you—textbooks, trade books, Web sites, and other resources—to gather information about the water cycle. Working with your group, construct a model that demonstrates the water cycle. Identify, describe, and explain each process.

4. Use the resources available to you—textbooks, trade books, Web sites, and other resources—to gather information about the influence of atmospheric movements and the oceans on the earth's weather and climate. Construct a model or

visual that shows how global patterns of atmospheric movements and the oceans influence our weather and climate. Identify the gases that make up the atmosphere and include information about the properties of the atmosphere at different elevations. Describe and explain the effect that oceans have on our climate.

5. Use the resources available to you—textbooks, trade books, Web sites, and other resources—to gather information about the biosphere and the many roles that living organisms play in the earth's system. Describe and explain how they have affected the composition of the atmosphere, been instrumental in producing some types of rocks, and contributed to the weathering of rocks. Prepare a visual presentation to use in describing and explaining how living organisms interact with the other earth systems—geosphere, hydrosphere, and atmosphere—to cause continual change in the earth's crust, oceans, atmosphere, and biosphere.

Earth/Space   **Activity 2**

Earth's History

1. Use the resources available to you—textbooks, trade books, Web sites, videos, and other resources—to gather information about the earth's history. Within your small group, discuss and describe the changes that have occurred to our earth in the past. Identify and describe the processes as well as the occasional catastrophes that were instrumental in causing the changes. Explain how fossils provide evidence of change to the earth's systems. Obtain several examples of fossils and carefully observe them. Find pictures of fossils and read the information provided with the pictures to learn more about those particular fossils.

2. Use the materials and directions provided and make a "fossil." Compare your resulting imprint with real fossils formed by nature. You should be able to see that your created fossil is very similar to the real fossil.

3. Share your findings with others in your class and participate in a whole-class discussion. Include ideas and strategies for involving 5–8 students in activities that would help them develop an understanding of the concepts and principles related to our earth's history. Explain the connection between this earth science concept and the life science concept of diversity and adaptation of organisms (Content Standard C, 5–8). Ask your instructor to provide additional information and clear up any remaining questions that you have.

Earth in the Solar System

1. Work with a small group and review information and a variety of activities from several different sources—textbooks, trade books, Web sites, inquiry-based science programs, videos, and other resources—that would be helpful to you in preparing learning experiences for students in grades 5 to 8 related to understanding the concepts and principles included in the content area "Earth in the Solar System." Specifically, look for information and activities that that could be used to help them understand our earth's place in space and its relationship with our moon, the other planets and their moons, the sun and other stars, comets, asteroids, and the other objects of our solar system. Discuss all the information and activities reviewed within your small group and with your instructor. Include in your discussion ideas for helping students gain an understanding related to the regular and predictable motion of the objects in our solar system and how these motions explain such things as the day, the year, phases of the moon, and eclipses. Discuss the role of gravity on our earth and in our solar system. Identify and explain how the sun affects our earth.

2. Select two of the activities from those reviewed by your group; make photocopies and complete them as a group. Discuss the results. Decide if any adaptations, modifications, additions, or deletions are needed for these two activities so that they could be more effectively used in an inquiry-based science program with students in grades 5 to 8. Make the needed changes on the photocopy, and write the level (5–8) and the content area (e.g., "Earth in the Solar System") at the top of the activity. Add other helpful comments and save these two activities to put with the others you will collect for the "Earth and Space Science Activities" section of your notebook.

Examining Content Standard D (5-8)

1. Obtain a copy of Earth and Space Content Standard D, pages 158 to 161, in the *National Science Education Standards*. Read and discuss this information with your small group.

2. Relate ideas and information gained from previous activities in this section to the information found in this standard.

3. Participate in a whole-class discussion related to helping 5–8 students understand the concepts and principles related to this standard.

SUMMARY

This chapter has focused on the identified earth and space science concepts outlined in the *National Science Education Standards*. In grades K to 4, students learn about properties of earth materials, objects in the sky, and changes in earth and sky. They continue at grades 5 to 8 with structure of the earth system, earth's history, and earth in the solar system. The understandings that students develop in each of the identified areas listed in this chapter are rooted in observations made as part of planned learning experiences.

The activities in this section provided you with opportunities to experience first-hand involvement with objects and materials similar to those you will provide for your own students. You were involved in constructing and understanding knowledge related to each of the identified areas in order to prepare you to provide students with inquiry-based learning experiences related to these same areas. You were asked to make connections to your prior knowledge in each area before completing the suggested activities. During the activities, you were asked to identify terms and concepts that emerged that related to your observations. Additional information was provided in this text and from other resources to help you accommodate the new information. You were also involved in sharing insights and ideas with others related to how you could develop learning experiences for students that would help them develop an understanding of the identified K–4 and 5–8 earth and space concepts included in this standard.

Remember that content knowledge is not separate for the other areas of learning that have been discussed in prior chapters. As mentioned at the beginning of this chapter, content is one of the components of the complex vision that makes the inquiry-based approach to teaching and learning science. It must be meshed with and become a part of the total science program. In an inquiry-based program, content is much more than knowing specific facts. It involves a true understanding of the concepts involved and the ability to apply this understanding to real-world contexts. Students must be given opportunities to construct this knowledge by engaging in many inquiry-based learning experiences.

Check out http://www.ericir.syr.edu/virtual/lessons/science/earth/index.html and http://www.ericir.syr.edu/virtual/lessons/science/space/index.html on the Web for lesson plans related to earth and space science topics. These resources will provide you with additional input as you reflect on how you will provide opportunities for your students to construct knowledge related to earth and space science concepts.

The culminating activities will give you the opportunity to add earth and space activities for students in grades 5–8 to your science activity notebook and to participate in presenting a workshop for your classmates using one of the selected earth and space activities.

Collecting Earth and Space Activities to Use With 5–8 Students

1. Use the science resources available to you and review and select at least six science activities (two for each of the three areas) that you could use with students in grades 5 to 8 to help them develop an understanding of the following:

    - Structure of the earth's system
    - Earth's history
    - Earth in the solar system

    Make a photocopy of the selected activities.

2. Discuss all the selected activities with your small group. Decide if any adaptations, modifications, additions, or deletions are needed for any of the activities so that they could be more effectively used in an inquiry-based science program. Make the needed changes on the photocopy, write the level (5–8) and the appropriate content reference (e.g., "Structure of the Earth System") at the top of the activity, add other helpful comments, and place the selected earth and space science activities in the notebook with the physical and life science activities that you have collected.

Workshop Presentations (K–8)

1. Work with a partner or small group and select one of the earth and space science activities that you collected for grades K to 8 to use in presenting a workshop for other members of your class. Your workshop should involve your peers in a variety of activities that include direct manipulation of materials and equipment. Most likely, an adapted or modified version of the original activity will be necessary to make it appropriate for your peers. Design your workshop so that your peers are engaged in an inquiry-based approach. This approach should include having them (1) build on their prior knowledge base, (2) construct new knowledge

related to the targeted earth and space concepts, and (3) apply content knowledge along with knowledge about teaching and learning in developing strategies for using a similar activity with K–8 students. It is strongly recommended that your peers *do not* try to act like elementary or middle school students but instead be themselves as they participate in a workshop designed for preservice teachers.

2. Ask your instructor for additional guidelines and directions for completing this activity.

3. When all workshop presentations have been completed, ask your instructor to conduct a whole-class discussion related to inquiry-based teaching and learning of earth and space science concepts. Talk about any remaining areas in which you feel the need for more information or clarification. Reflect on what you have learned that will help you provide opportunities for elementary and middle school students to develop understandings of the earth and space science concepts that were identified in Standard D.

REFERENCES

American Association for the Advancement of Science. (1993). *Benchmarks for Scientific Literacy.* New York: Oxford University Press.

Moore, G. R. (1994). Revisiting science concepts. *Science and Children, 32* (3), 31–33, 60.

National Research Council. (1996). *National Science Education Standards.* Washington, DC: National Academy Press.

National Science Teachers Association. (1997). *NSTA pathways to the science standards: Guidelines for moving the vision into practice* (Elementary School Edition). Arlington, VA: Author.

National Science Teachers Association. (1998). *NSTA pathways to the science standards: Guidelines for moving the vision into practice* (Middle School Edition). Arlington, VA: Author.

Victor, K. (2000). *Science for the elementary and middle school.* Columbus, OH: Merrill/Prentice Hall.

CHAPTER 11

Inquiry-Based Teaching and Learning of Science and Technology Concepts

INTRODUCTION

In the last three chapters, we have reviewed the content standards for the traditional areas of physical, life, earth, and space science. Together with the other standards on teaching and assessment, these content standards offer teachers valuable information that can be used in planning and organizing for inquiry-based science teaching and learning. In this chapter, we will explore Content Standard E: Science and Technology. This is an emerging area and was not traditionally included as a content area in elementary science programs before 1990. It is included here along with the traditional content areas because of the tremendous impact that technology is having and will continue to have on our lives. The children you will teach will grow up in a world that is more dependent on technology than ever before. It is important that they have a variety of educational experiences involving science and technology.

What comes to mind when you think about "science and technology"? How do you define technology? How are science and technology related? Most people think of technology as practical or applied science. Indeed, the standards speak of connecting students to the designed world. Human-made or designed objects and their relationship to inquiry-based science is the focus of this standard. Technology uses information gained by scientists as they investigate the natural world to develop products that solve human problems or meet human needs. Science and technology have a reciprocal relationship. One example of this is that scientific investigation demands sophisticated instruments, and technology provides them.

The *National Science Education Standards*, Science and Technology Content Standard E (National Research Council, 1996), lists the following abilities and understandings for students in grades K to 4:

- Abilities of technological design
- Understanding about science and technology
- Abilities to distinguish between natural objects and objects made by humans

SCIENCE AND TECHNOLOGY CONCEPTS (K–4)

Children in grades K to 4 can be introduced to science and technology content by collecting and displaying a variety of natural and human-made objects. These objects can be closely examined to determine their properties. Students can identify and use tools to improve their observations, such as hand lenses and measurement instruments. Teachers can provide containers of water and magnets for students to use in discovering the various properties of the collected objects. They can be asked to separate the objects into natural and human-made (designed). A discussion can take place related to how an object is determined to be natural or designed.

Students can continue to gain an understanding of science and technology by examining technological products that are a part of their immediate world, such as pencil sharpeners, jacket zippers, can openers, batteries, thermometers, and toys. A discussion can take place in which they determine the purpose of each of the human-made objects, the problem each solved or need each met, and how well each product does what it is supposed to do. The human-made objects can also be examined to determine if any natural materials were used to make them. A walk around the school building and grounds would allow students to identify and observe other human-made objects and examine them to determine the purpose they serve. Multimedia materials can be used to illustrate other examples of objects not found in the immediate environment. Students can add to this growing list by thinking of human-made objects in their own homes or things they have seen elsewhere. Activities such as the ones suggested here, provide young learners with a good concrete foundation for developing the abilities and understandings listed in Science and Technology Content Standard *E*.

Most museums have artifacts of household items or farm tools that can be used for students to investigate and try to determine what they were used for. You might even find a collector who would be willing to come in and share some of the older technological devices with your students. These "mystery objects" provide opportunities for students to engage in inquiry as they learn about the role of technology and its relationship to science.

As students reach grades 3 and 4, they are able to engage in simple technological problem solving. This design process involves them in science activities in which they (1) identify a simple problem related to a human need, (2) propose and design a technological solution that would meet that need, (3) implement the proposed design, (4) evaluate the effectiveness of the designed product in meeting the original purpose or need, and (5) review the process used in solving the identified problem by describing each step and offering possible alternate solutions.

In Chapter 3, you had the opportunity to design and conduct a scientific investigation using the steps of inquiry as a guide. These steps include (1) Identifying a problem or question to be answered scientifically; (2) deciding on a method or strategy to be used in answering the question; (3) constructing a hypothesis or tentative answer; (4) designing the investigation so that all possible variables are identified and controlled except the one selected to be manipulated; (5) conducting the investigation by manipulating one variable at a time to see how the outcome is affected and recording the data collected; (6) organizing, analyzing, and evaluating the data collected; (7) reaching a conclusion; and (8) sharing your results with others. Notice how closely the steps of technological problem solving parallel the steps of inquiry-based science. In both technological problem solving and scientific investigations, students at this level develop their abilities by engaging in firsthand learning experiences that have clearly defined purposes. Both types of problem solving focus on the **process** that the students are engaged in. Investigations and technological activities should be closely related to the students' immediate environment and be developmentally appropriate.

Science and Technology **Activity 1**

K–4: Designed and Human-Made Objects

1. Form a small group with four or five others in your class. Carefully observe the different objects in your classroom. Identify those that are designed or human-made and determine if any natural materials were used to make them.

2. Examine several of the identified objects and discuss what human need or problem they were designed to meet or solve. Determine how well the object does what it was designed to do.

3. Brainstorm with the other group members to identify several developmentally appropriate design tasks for students in grades 3 to 4 that would meet a human need or solve a human problem. Then select one to complete using the five steps of technological problem solving listed previously. (Some suggestions: design a better bubble-making solution, construct a bridge out of straws or toothpicks that will hold toy cars and trucks as they cross, design a holder for something, or design a better way to organize materials in the classroom.) You may use any resource material available to help you in identifying and selecting a design task to complete. Ask your instructor for guidance as you complete this activity.

4. Compare your group's project with others that were done and participate in a whole-class discussion related to the process of technological problem solving at the K–4 level.

5. Obtain a copy of Science and Technology Content Standard E (K–4), pages 135 to 138, in the *National Science Education Standards*. Read and discuss this information with your group and ask your instructor to answer any questions you have related to providing quality learning experiences for K–4 students related to science and technology.

SCIENCE AND TECHNOLOGY CONCEPTS (5–8)

Students in grades 5 to 8 continue to gain in their knowledge of the principles of design that were introduced at the K–4 level. At this level, the problems become more and more complex. Students in grades 5 to 8 are ready to begin to distinguish between scientific inquiry and technological design. Before students reach the level of cognitive reasoning associated with upper elementary and middle school learners, this distinction is not easily understood and is not really necessary for establishing a solid foundation on which to build understandings and abilities related to science and technology. However, by fifth grade, most students have developed the ability needed to understand the similarities and differences between scientific inquiry and technological design.

Content Standard E: Science and Technology (5–8) identifies the same first two abilities and understandings that were listed for grades K to 4. At the 5–8 level, all students should develop the following:

- Abilities of technological design
- Understandings about science and technology

The activities selected to help 5–8 students continue to develop these abilities and understandings at a more sophisticated level should involve them in scientific investigations that result in meeting a human need, solving a human problem, or developing a product. These kinds of activities enable the students to go beyond exploring ideas about the natural world (scientific inquiry) to designing solutions to meet human needs and wants (technological problem solving). They are able to become more aware of the connection between scientists and engineers. They can experience both roles by proposing explanations for questions about the natural world, as scientists do, and then proposing technological solutions that meet an identified human need or want, as engineers do.

As 5–8 students engage in science and technology tasks, they should become aware of the limitations of technological solutions. They must realize that technology has both benefits and risks. Often unintended consequences result. On the other hand, there have been many historic breakthroughs in science and technology. Can you think of some? What are some recent medical advancements that you are aware of? What information have we gathered about life on other planets? What made it possible to collect this data? How has your life been affected by science and technology? How do you describe the reciprocal nature of science and technology?

One of the important facets of the abilities and understandings associated with science and technology is teamwork. Teachers must provide students with many opportunities to work cooperatively as a team, with each team member having specific responsibilities. This cooperative classroom structure parallels the real-world structure of individuals working together, each providing unique contributions to solve problems and reach common goals.

5–8: Developing a Design Activity

1. Form a small group with four or five of your classmates. Discuss various strategies that could be used to organize and involve 5–8 students in a design activity that would result in the development and testing of a "container" that would prevent a raw egg from breaking when dropped from a height of 10 feet. The activity must be designed so that students can complete it entirely in the classroom within a relatively short period of time—not more than one or two class periods. Identify the physical science content/concepts that students would need to use in completing the design process successfully. You may use any resource materials that are available to you.

2. After discussing several alternative strategies, as a group decide on the one you feel would provide the best opportunity for 5–8 students to develop the abilities and understandings related to the science and technology standard. Think in terms of what would be possible from a material and time standpoint in a real classroom with real students.

3. Develop the selected design activity so that the students solve the egg-drop problem by using the five design principles or the steps of technological problem solving listed earlier in this chapter.

4. As a group, actually do the design activity that you developed for students in grades 5 to 8. Be sure your group follows the five design principles in completing the egg-drop task.

5. Compare your group's results with other groups who completed this task. Which group's technological solution seems to work best? In evaluating your own product as well as others that were produced, consider the following factors: (1) time spent to create the product, (2) cost, (3) efficiency, (4) appearance, and (5) safety. What constraints did you encounter?

6. Identify one thing that your group would propose in order to improve your container. Describe how your group would test the effectiveness of the improvement. If time permits, actually test out the proposed improvement and share the results.

7. Meet with your instructor to discuss your groups' results, ask questions, and receive feedback and more information about the content area of science and technology.

8. Obtain a copy of Science and Technology Content Standard E (5–8), pages 161 to 166, in the *National Science Education Standards*. Read and discuss this information with your group and ask your instructor to answer any questions you have related to providing quality learning experiences for 5–8 students related to science and technology.

SUMMARY

This chapter has focused on the identified science and technology concepts outlined in Content Standard E of the *National Science Education Standards*. In grades K to 4, students should be given opportunities to engage in activities in which they develop abilities of technological design, understandings about science and technology, and abilities to distinguish between natural objects and objects made by humans. They continue to develop these same abilities and understandings introduced in grades K to 4 at the 5–8 level but on a more complex and sophisticated level. At the upper elementary and middle school levels, students begin to distinguish between science as inquiry and technological problem solving. They should be given activities and tasks that combine scientific investigation (designing and conducting investigations that result in an explanation for questions about the natural world) and technological problem solving (designing and testing a proposed solution that meets a human need or want). As a result of such activities, they are able to understand the parallel processes of scientific inquiry and technological problem solving. (See the steps of each listed earlier in this chapter.) Students should be led to discover the reciprocal nature of science and technology. Technology provides scientists with tools, instruments, and techniques that allow them to explore, investigate, and analyze a variety of objects and phenomena related to understanding our world. In turn, scientists greatly affect technology by seeking and demanding better tools, instruments, and techniques as they explore, investigate, and analyze objects and phenomena.

The activities in this section provided you with opportunities to experience firsthand involvement with objects and materials similar to those you will provide for your own students. You were involved in constructing and understanding knowledge related to the targeted science and technology concepts identified in the *Standards* in order to prepare you to provide students with inquiry-based learning experiences related to these same areas. Additional information was provided in this text and from other resources to help you accommodate the new information. You were also involved in sharing insights and ideas with others related to how you could develop learning experiences for students that would help them develop abilities of technological design, understanding about science and technology, and abilities to distinguish between natural objects and objects made by humans.

Remember that content knowledge is not separate for the other areas of learning that have been discussed in prior chapters. As mentioned before, content is one of the components of the complex vision that comprises the inquiry-based approach to teaching and learning science. It must be meshed with and become a part of the total science program. In an inquiry-based program, content is much more than knowing specific facts. It involves a true understanding of the concepts involved and the ability to apply this understanding to real-world contexts. Students must be given opportunities to construct this knowledge by engaging in many inquiry-based learning experiences.

Check out http://www.sln.fi.edu/tfi/activity/act-summ.html and htpp://www.ofcn.org/cyber.serv/academy/ace/sci/cecsci/cecsci017.html on the Web for information and activities related to science and technology. These resources will provide you with additional input as you reflect on how you will provide opportunities for your students to construct knowledge related to science and technology concepts.

The next two activities will give you the opportunity to add science and technology activities for students in grades K–8 to your science activity notebook and to participate in presenting a workshop for your classmates using one of the science and technology activities.

Collecting Science and Technology Activities to Use With K-8 Students

1. Use the science resources available to you and review and select at least six science and technology activities (three for K–4 and three for 5–8) that you could use with students to help them develop the following:

   - Abilities of technological design
   - Understanding about science and technology
   - Abilities to distinguish between natural objects and objects made by humans

2. Discuss all the selected activities with your small group. Decide If any adaptations, modifications, additions, or deletions are needed for any of the activities so that they could be more effectively used in an inquiry-based science program. Make the needed changes on the photocopy, write the level (K–4 or 5–8) and the appropriate content reference (e.g., "Science and Technology: Abilities of Technological Design") at the top of the activity, add other helpful comments, and place the selected science and technology activities in the notebook with the physical, life, and earth science activities that you have collected.

Workshop Presentations (K-8)

1. Work with a partner or small group and select one of the science and technology activities that you collected for grades K to 8 to use in presenting a workshop for other members of your class. Your workshop should involve your peers in a variety of activities that include direct manipulation of materials and equipment. Most likely, an adapted or modified version of the original activity will be necessary to make it appropriate for your peers. Design your workshop so that your peers are engaged in an inquiry-based approach. Remember to begin the workshop by having your peers build on their prior

knowledge. Allow them to experience the process of constructing new knowledge related to the science and technology concept that is the focus of your workshop. Close the workshop by having your peers apply content knowledge along with knowledge about teaching and learning in developing strategies for using a similar activity with students. It is strongly recommended that your peers do not try to act like elementary or middle school students but instead be themselves as they participate in a workshop designed for preservice teachers.

2. Ask your instructor for additional guidelines and directions for completing this activity.

3. When all workshop presentations have been completed, ask your instructor to conduct a total class discussion related to inquiry-based teaching and learning of science and technology concepts. Talk about any remaining areas in which you feel the need for more information or clarification. Reflect on what you have learned that will help you provide opportunities for elementary and middle school students to develop understandings of the concepts that were identified in Science and Technology Content Standard E.

REFERENCES

American Association for the Advancement of Science. (1993). *Benchmarks for Scientific Literacy*. New York: Oxford University Press.

Cox, J. (1994, January). Rube Goldberg contraptions. *Science Scope*, 44–47.

Etchison, C. (1995, April). Tales from a technology teacher. *Science and Children*, 19–20, 30.

Mechling, K. (1991, February). Consumer cohorts. *Science Scope*, 20–23.

National Research Council. (1996). *National Science Education Standards*. Washington, DC: National Academy Press.

National Science Teachers Association. (1997). *NSTA pathways to the science standards: Guidelines for moving the vision into practice* (Elementary School Edition). Arlington, VA· Author.

National Science Teachers Association. (1998). *NSTA pathways to the science standards: Guidelines for moving the vision into practice* (Middle School Edition). Arlington, VA: Author.

CHAPTER 12

Becoming an Effective Inquiry-Based Science Teacher

Suggested Activity 12.1: Sciencing Action Plan

I. References

This chapter is designed to help you begin to reflect on the learning and understanding that have taken place as you have progressed through this textbook—reading; participating in the activities; sharing ideas, insights, and experiences with others; and listening and trying things out. It is hoped that you will be able to involve yourself in a personal assessment—looking back to where you were before beginning this text and your science methods class. In Chapter 1, you were asked to think about how you would define or describe science or sciencing. Has your definition changed? If asked now to describe an inquiry-based approach to teaching and learning science concepts, skills, processes, and attitudes, what would your description include that it did not include before? What have you learned about the nature of science? How is *science* as a noun different from *sciencing* as a verb? What does it mean when science is described as a continuous process of inquiry? How does a science activity that involves students in active construction of knowledge differ from one in which students follow a step-by-step, recipe-like procedure to see what happens? What is the relationship of process-inquiry skills to the learning and understanding of science concepts? How is the development of a scientific attitude essential to an inquiry-based science program? Discuss your responses to these questions during in-class discussions with others reading this material. Can you identify and agree on some essential components that should be a part of any inquiry-based science program?

The American Association for the Advancement of Science revealed the following core of scientific literacy goals for American students in the Project 2061 report compiled by a 26-member panel of educators and scientists in 1989:

- Being familiar with the natural world and recognizing both its diversity and its unity
- Understanding key concepts and principles of science
- Being aware of some of the important ways in which science, mathematics, and technology depend on one another
- Knowing that science, mathematics, and technology are human enterprises and knowing what that implies about their strengths and limitations
- Having a capacity for scientific ways of thinking
- Using scientific knowledge and ways of thinking for individual and social purposes

These literacy goals are meant for everyone. They are not just for the students who plan science-related careers. Rather, all students are expected to be scientifically literate by the time they graduate from high school. *Science for All Americans (SFAA)*, a slightly altered version of this national report, was also published in 1989 and served as a starting point for the long-term, multiphase reform process by providing the conceptual basis for the recommended changes. *Benchmarks for Scientific Literacy*, published in 1993, is a companion report to *SFAA*. This publication clearly specifies the science skills, knowledge, and attitudes to be attained by students by the end of grades 2, 5, 7, 8, and 12. In addition, several alternative curricular models have been developed by teachers located across the country to provide guidelines for accomplishing these ambitious goals. The last phase of the reform effort calls for using the tools and resources mentioned previously to bring about lasting changes in our educational system that will produce citizens who are scientifically literate.

Reform is slow, and students are still graduating from high school inadequately prepared to live in and contribute to an increasingly technological world. This reform must begin in the elementary schools with you, the elementary teacher. This is where the foundation is laid for later science understanding. Elementary teachers must have a solid knowledge base from which to draw, coupled with an understanding of and support for the need for active involvement, both mentally and physically, on the part of their students. Middle school teachers must continue by providing their students with many opportunities to engage in increasingly sophisticated science investigations. By the time our students reach high school, they should have had a wide variety of concrete experiences in which they constructed knowledge so that they are able to deal with and understand the abstract and hypothetical nature of science. Through out students' school science experiences (K–12), they should be involved in science activities that promote exploration, critical thinking, and doing—a sciencing or inquiry-based approach. Providing students with science experiences that promote active inquiry is necessary for achieving the challenge set forth in the reform effort. Working together, we can and will meet the national council's recommended core of scientific literacy goals.

In addition to *SFAA* and *Benchmarks*, the two products of Project 2061 that are tools for educators to use in bringing about a lasting science education reform, there are two other resources that science educators and teachers can use: the *National Science Education Standards* (1995) and National Science Teachers Association's *Pathways to the Science Standards* (1997). You should be familiar with the *Standards* by now because many of the activities in this text have involved you in examining the various standards that serve as a resource in developing science curricula that will enable our students to meet the national goal of becoming first in the world in science achievement. *Pathways: Guidelines for Moving the Vision Into Practice* is available in an elementary school edition and a middle school edition. *Pathways* represents the efforts of teachers and administrators who saw a need to provide a practical guidebook for elementary and middle school teachers to use in implementing the vision of the standards into the real world of the classroom and school. Teachers who use *Pathways* will find a wide variety of ideas, models, and suggestions for helping students meet the goals of the *Standards*. If possible, obtain a copy of *Pathways*—both the elementary and the middle school editions—and look through the various chapters to get an overall feel for the kinds of information and resources that it provides. Look also at the appendices, which include a complete list of all the *National Science Education Standards*, plus addresses for science programs and guidelines for designing school science facilities. This is a great resource book for teachers and one you might consider adding to your professional library.

In Chapter 3, you were reminded that an inquiry-based science approach must be led by an active decision-making teacher who is able to use acquired information, ideas, and skills effectively in the planning, organizing, and managing of the teaching/learning environment. Four areas were discussed: students, curricular materials, learning environment, and you, the teacher. What do you remember about these four areas as they relate to planning, organizing, and managing inquiry-based science experiences? Why is it important for teachers to consider individual learning characteristics as well as typical developmental characteristics as they plan science experiences for their students? Is it necessary for teachers to select science experiences that match with students' cognitive capacity? Why or why not?

Why is it important that curriculum be seen as the total experience students have while in school and not limited to "the textbook"? Think back to some of the curricular materials that you examined as you completed the suggested activities in Chapter 3. Several different programs and textbook series were listed and assessment criteria provided to use in determining how well each one supported students' achievement of the learning goals recommended in *Benchmarks* and *Standards*. What were the results of your assessment? Can you describe the kinds of curricular materials that you want to use with your students? How might children's literature be used to help students understand science concepts? What are some important features for teachers to consider when selecting a children's book with a science theme as a curricular resource? Name some of the other "curricular" resources discussed in Chapter 3 that teachers could use in planning, organizing, and managing the science teaching/learning environment. Discuss with others how you plan to use these resources. If you need help in remembering, look back and review the material in Chapter 3.

How will you arrange the learning environment in your classroom to encourage self-directed, responsible student behavior and support your students' efforts as they engage in inquiry-based science learning experiences? Chapter 3 discussed three areas of concern related to the learning environment: the physical learning environment, safety factors/legal guidelines, and managing time and grouping patterns. Think about some of the suggestions that were made. Which ones do you consider the most important for enhancing learning in the classroom? How important is flexibility in providing students with an optimal classroom learning environment? Describe several ways that you plan to extend the classroom beyond the four walls. What are some safety issues associated with active science investigations that you have become more aware of? How will you address these in your classroom? Why is it important to structure your science program so that students have blocks of time for "doing" science? Describe how you will use different grouping patterns (independent grouping, small groups, large groups) in your classroom science program. How will you decide on the makeup of the groups?

Rhonda Beaman, the winner of the first National Education Association Excellence in the Academy award for an article on the art of teaching, commented in an interview that "education should be a process of drawing out rather than putting in" (1999). How will you become a teacher who "draws out" rather than "puts in"? Why do you think this is an important distinction? What characteristics do you possess that will enable you to be an effective teacher? Refer to Chapter 3 and see which of the characteristics listed there you have continued to develop while completing this text and which ones you want to spend more time on. Think about ways you will do this.

A variety of research-based and experience-tested strategies, techniques, and methods that could be used to guide and facilitate active science learning was examined in Chapter 4. The *Standards* refer to a body of knowledge that skilled teachers of science exhibit as "pedagogical content knowledge." This special knowledge is comprised of understandings and abilities that integrate their knowledge of science content, curriculum, learning, teaching, and students. Teachers who exhibit this kind of knowledge are able to construct learning situations that meet the needs of individual students as well as groups. As you reflect over the information presented in Chapter 4, think about how you have expanded your pedagogical content knowledge by reading this text, actively participating in the various activities, sharing insights, asking questions, and listening and working with others. Summarize what you have learned about how learning occurs. How does learning theory influence science instruction? How have the findings of Piaget and Vygotsky impacted the strategies, techniques, and methods that teachers use to guide and facilitate active science learning? How does constructivism fit into the picture? What role does intelligence play in teaching and learning? How will you use the ideas in Gardner's multiple intelligences theory to guide and facilitate student learning in science? How does the information presented on brain research in Chapter 4 affect your thinking about the strategies to use as you teach science? How will you ensure equity in your classroom? What kinds of modifications will you make to accommodate students with disabilities? What will you do to make sure that gifted students are engaged in challenging science activities? Which specific methods and strategies presented in Chapter 12 did you find most helpful? Chapter 4 also presented you with information and guidelines for science unit designs. How does an integrative unit design help with meeting the goals set forth for science instruction in *Benchmarks* and the *Standards*?

Think about the benefits of using instructional technology in meeting the needs of students and promoting increased student performance and learning presented in Chapter 5. What were some of the practical activities for students that were suggested? How did the information and activities included in Chapter 5 help you gain insights into the effective use of instructional technology in the classroom? In what ways has instructional technology redefined the way we teach science? What does it mean when people say that technology is transforming the local classroom into a global classroom? Do you feel comfortable with this change? How will you continue to develop your skills and abilities in this area?

Chapter 6 examined the multiple roles of assessment in inquiry-based classrooms. What kinds of changes related to assessment have taken place since you were in elementary school? Describe authentic assessment and explain how it differs from traditional testing methods. How do you plan to incorporate the assessment standards for science education into your teaching and learning strategies? What is the value of ongoing assessment? How have changes in the science curriculum caused teachers to rethink science assessment? There were concerns discussed in Chapter 6 that teachers must be aware of as they begin to use authentic assessment strategies. Which of those discussed do you consider to be most bothersome to you? How will you make purposeful choices about science assessment strategies when you teach?

There were a wide variety of assessment tools presented in Chapter 7 that can be used to assess science learning. Both benefits and concerns of each were discussed. Think back over the various ones described and explain how as a teacher you would decide on which to use. What are the factors you would take into consideration in making your decision?

Chapters 8, 9, 10, and 11 all focused on content areas identified in the *Standards.* The four content areas examined included physical science, life science, earth/space science, and science and technology. Each area was summarized, concepts were identified, and activities were provided to engage you in actual construction of content knowledge as well as pedagogical knowledge. If you completed the suggested activities, you now have a collection of activities representing each of the four content areas included here and have worked with others to present your ideas for using selected activities with elementary and middle school students.

How will you use the knowledge gained in these chapters to meet the challenge set forth in the reform effort? Can you explain the relationship of content knowledge to pedagogical knowledge? Do you have a clearer understanding of the complex vision that comprises the inquiry approach to teaching and learning science? Are you willing to accept the challenge of making a real difference in the lives of the students you teach? Will your students be prepared to meet the challenge of life in the 21st century?

This is an exciting time for science teachers. We have a great opportunity before us—providing students with science experiences that will lead to their being scientifically literate. It is hoped that this text, the suggested activities, and the interaction that you have had with others have helped you gain insight into the teaching of elementary and middle school science and made you more aware of your role in achieving a scientifically literate world for tomorrow. Soon you will join other teachers who are already making strides toward moving science teaching and learning toward the vision and goals described in the various reports and publications that have resulted from Project 2061.

The final activity is designed to involve you in a personal assessment—where you are now and where you want to go from here. Learning is a lifelong process. You are encouraged to build on your present knowledge as you continue to gain further insights, refine your thinking, and build a deeper understanding of the content as well as the pedagogical knowledge related to science teaching and learning. According to the *Standards,* all teachers of science should focus on developing skills and abilities in the following:

1. Planning an inquiry-based science program that includes both short- and long-term goals
2. Guiding and facilitating students' science learning
3. Selecting and implementing ongoing assessment strategies for use with their own teaching and students' learning
4. Managing learning environments so that students have time, space, and resources needed for inquiry-based science experiences

5. Developing communities of science learners that reflect the intellectual and social environment needed for all students to develop the skills and disposition necessary for lifelong learning

6. Working with others to maintain and improve the quality of the school science program at the district, state, and national levels for all students

The final activity will involve you in preparing a personal Sciencing Action Plan in which you identify specific actions that you will take to continue your progress toward meeting the previously listed standards.

Suggested Activity
Sciencing Action Plan   12.1

1. How will you continue to prepare for the exciting challenge of providing a science program for students that will lead to their being scientifically literate? Prepare a Sciencing Action Plan for doing this. On a sheet of paper, outline and describe how you intend to continue to prepare yourself for meeting the challenge of providing elementary and middle school students with a science program that will enable them to use scientific information to make intelligent choices, discuss important issues that involve science and technology, and experience the personal fulfillment that comes from understanding and learning about the natural world.

2. Share your plan with a small group of your classmates. Ask for feedback and suggestions. Offer feedback and suggestions to others in your group as they share their plans.

3. Using the information gained from the interaction in the small-group setting, refine and finalize your plan. Turn in a copy of your written plan to your instructor. Read over the plan from time to time, making modifications and adjustments, as you continue to become the kind of science teacher who views the process of teaching and learning as one of "drawing out" instead of "putting in."

REFERENCES

National Research Council. (1996). *National Science Education Standards.* Washington DC: National Academy Press.

National Science Teachers Association. (1997). *NSTA pathways to the science standards: Guidelines for moving the vision into practice* (Elementary School Edition). Arlington, VA: Author.

National Science Teachers Association. (1997). *NSTA pathways to the science standards: Guidelines for moving the vision into practice* (Middle School Edition). Arlington, VA: Author.

Thought and Action: The NEA Higher Education Journal. 1999 (spring) (interview of Ronda Beaman).

Index

*Bold numbers indicate figure entry